WRITING WAR

THE BEST CONTEMPORARY JOURNALISM ABOUT
WARFARE AND CONFLICT FROM AROUND THE WORLD

WRITING WAR

THE BEST CONTEMPORARY JOURNALISM ABOUT WARFARE AND CONFLICT FROM AROUND THE WORLD

EDITED BY CLINT WILLIS

Thunder's Mouth Press
New York

WRITING WAR: THE BEST CONTEMPORARY JOURNALISM ABOUT WARFARE AND CONFLICT FROM AROUND THE WORLD

Published by
Thunder's Mouth Press
An Imprint of Avalon Publishing Group Incorporated
161 William Street, 16th floor
New York, NY 10038

Frontispiece photo: Holiday Inn, Sarajevo, 1993, © Patrick Durand/Corbis Sygma

Library of Congress Cataloging-in-Publication Data is available.

ISBN 1-56025-507-2

Book design: Sue Canavan

Printed in the United States of America

Distributed by Publishers Group West

For Peter Kadzis

contents

Introduction

Strictly speaking, not all of the pieces in the collection are journalism; for example, some originally appeared in books rather than newspapers or magazines. And while most of the contributors write as professional war correspondents, a few write from different perspectives—Carolyn Nordstrom as social anthropologist; Rezak Hukanovic as victim; John Sundin as surgeon.

Then again, the best of the professional reporters of war often appear in odd guises—as outraged witness (Robert Fisk), casualty (Philip Caputo), seeker (Scott Anderson), sympathizer (Robert Kaplan). They take on those roles—in addition to their paid roles as observers—by accident or because they are human: They cannot help it.

War hardens men (and women and children, who these days are its most common victims). It also reaches and inspires some of them, including some of the men and women who report on it. War outrages and disgusts and angers them; it fascinates them and horrifies them. They travel to war (or it travels to them), and if they survive (as growing numbers do not) they return with stories that provide a whiff of what war is really like.

The corporate media increasingly trivialize war, spreading ignorance and pandering to our instincts of self-indulgence, arrogance and hypocrisy. The writers represented in this collection offer up to us the stench of war as soldiers and civilians must endure it—today, and tomorrow and the day after that. These writers at their best serve the truth—an ideal sharply at odds with much recent war coverage and, ultimately, with war itself.

—Clint Willis

from Means of Escape
by Philip Caputo

Philip Caputo is a novelist and reporter. This passage from his 1991 memoir describes his experience as the victim of a sniper in Beirut.

t was always strange returning to our neighborhood. The *fighting* skirted it but never touched it. People relaxed on their terraces or around the pools, listening to gun and shellfire only two or three miles off. They watched the army's armored cars and half-tracks clanking down the Corniche as if on parade. Some expatriates, mostly bankers and businessmen, began to concoct fantasies that the factions had deliberately spared us because they did not want to drive foreign corporations and financial institutions out of the country. They know where their bread's buttered, they'll leave us alone to fight it out among themselves, and when they settle this thing, we'll be back to business. At dinners and other social gatherings I became Cassandra and Jeremiah all rolled into one, the resident prophet of doom. It's just a matter of time, I would say. This whole city, this whole country is finished.

Finally, sometime in late summer, we got a taste of it. Late one night, everybody in our building and in several buildings nearby were rocked out of their beds by an immense explosion. In our apartment, thick black smoke rolled through the windows. Jill and I ran into the boys' room, snatched them from their beds, and huddled in the hall, thinking the blast had been a shell and that others would soon follow. But it wasn't a mortar or artillery: Moslem *plastiquers*, retaliating for Christian bombings, had blown up Smith's, a Christian-owned supermarket about three blocks away. Jill and other expat wives often shopped there. Leaving her and the boys in the hall, I took the elevator to the top floor, then climbed the stairs to the roof. A huge circle of fire glowed where Smith's had been, a devil's eye in the darkened face of the neighborhood. South and eastward, near the Palestinian camps, rifles and mortars flickered and tracers made continual, solid red lines across the night sky, like speeding taillights photographed on an expressway at a slow shutter speed. Counting by thousands between the shell bursts and their sound, I calculated that the *fighting* was within two miles of us. Yes, it would come and engulf us, too; there would be no exemptions, not in a place where a supermarket was considered a legitimate military target. I had a vision, almost a premonition, alone on the roof that noisy night alight with war's fires. I was watching a preview of coming attractions. If ever the day came when the social contract went into the shredder everywhere, then the whole of the civilized world would look like Beirut. The Beast had not slouched toward Bethlehem to be reborn; Beirut was its manger.

I think that's when my hatred and contempt of the Lebanese came squalling out of its womb. It was like the hatred and contempt a veteran beat cop feels for the citizens of a high-crime neighborhood, only it was deeper. I could not find a single redeeming quality in a people destroying themselves with such unflagging energy and enthusiasm. Now and then I thought of my journey through Sinai—which seemed so long ago—with Muhammad and Suleiman and of the codes of honor and behavior that governed the bedouin. City Arabs derided the nomads as primitives, but who were the real primitives? The tribesmen of Beirut wore suits instead of nomads' robes, rode in cars instead of on camels, lived in houses instead of goatskin tents, but in times of feud or war, they might as well have been Cro-Magnons, clubbing each other on some Mesolithic plain.

I broke my pact with Nick. I started to cover the *fighting* because its pointlessness was the point. It was war distilled to its essence, which was utterly senseless killing, war purified of the purposes and morals man gives to it to make it acceptable and coherent. All wars were ultimately meaningless, with the possible exception of the war against Hitler (and a thousand years from now, how much difference would it make that our side won?). Historians, as much as journalists, had an obsession with making sense of the senseless. Through the distorting lenses of hindsight and their own biases they would study some terrible battle, which must have seemed like a complete madhouse to the men in it, and find patterns and reasons for it, then conclude that its outcome could not have been otherwise and had had enduring consequences for humankind. But what if the view of the combatants was the right one? What if there had been no pattern but, rather, a swirl of events that happened to arrange themselves into a victory for one side? What if the outcome could have been otherwise and made no lasting difference to the course of human history? Would the world I'm living in, I thought, be significantly better or worse if Napoleon had *won* at Waterloo? If Julius Caesar had been defeated by Vercingetorix? Suppose it had been Washington who'd surrendered to Cornwallis at Yorktown, what then? The United States probably would have become another Canada or Australia, which wouldn't have been a catastrophe.

War showed its naked face in Beirut. I went out to paint it as I saw it.

A Christian militiaman, under fire for hours, crouches behind a barricade during a lull. A teenage boy comes up behind him and, playing a joke, sticks his rifle in the man's back and shouts, "Bangbangbang." *Bangyerdead.* The man spins around, cuts the boy almost in half with a burst, then falls to his knees and screams; he's killed his kid brother.

A Jesuit priest, walking on crutches from a month-old leg wound, crosses a street to say Mass in his church. A sniper hits him in the head. *Bangyerdead.*

On a street of shops shelled by heavy mortars, dismembered consumers and dismembered mannequins lie all over. You can't tell from a distance which legs and arms are flesh and which are plastic. A stiffened corpse sits in the doorway of a ladies' boutique, his palm out, and a laughing Moslem militiaman drops a few coins into the rigid hand.

I saw the humor in it, too. Lebanon's self-inflicted wound was funny, viewed askance, and askance was the only way you could look over there. You had to search for eccentric angles of vision because the Beast was loose and you could not stare him straight in the eye. So I looked at it all from the side and went home and had dinner and played with my boys and kissed my wife and never felt a thing. Not too surprising, is it? I was the guy who had stepped into a man's brains and scraped them from my boots as if they were dog shit. Even the hatred and contempt had gone. The *fighting* had become a gruesome amusement, the drama of the human pageant as dark comedy.

October brought the struggle for the hotel district. Men were killing and dying for possession of the Holiday Inn. That was less than a mile from our neighborhood, and you heard no more fantasies from the bankers and businessmen. They were packing up. Two who lived in our building, officers for Continental Illinois, had to ride to their branch in armored personnel carriers, loaned courtesy of the Lebanese army. I suggested they could become heroes in a comic book, possibly a TV series called "Fighting Financiers."

The foreign desk fired a new salvo of rockets. They had gotten enough bang-bang; now they wanted stories about the war's innocent victims, heart tuggers about what it was doing to the ordinary men and women of Beirut. It was no use reminding them that ordinary men and women were the ones doing the fighting. I went in search of innocent victims. I've described what I found: I was the correspondent who saw those Moslem women dead from a mortar attack, who thought the crumbs of bread lying in the pools of blood resembled croutons in dark-red bisque, who sat by his typewriter incapable of saying a thing because he was incapable of feeling a thing except scorn. The idiots, coming out on the street because there was a ceasefire, crowding together the way they did. They were asking for it. I telexed a message to Chicago: the Lebanese were not worth anyone's tears; there were no innocent victims in Beirut, all were agents of history—the men with the guns, the women who egged them on, the kids who played with toy guns, gazing with worshipful eyes at their murderous fathers and uncles. The fighting would end when the Lebanese annihilated themselves, which, I suggested, would be an excellent final solution. My emotional temperature had reached absolute zero.

October 25 was a Sunday, a day of cloudless sky and light that seemed to be falling through a topaz filter. A recoilless cannon cracked from the hotel district, as measured as a salute. Foreign embassies were making evacuation plans and had warned their citizens to stay inside. The streets were empty, traffic lights faithfully winking red yellow green to traffic that wasn't there. Jill and I were discussing how to get ourselves and our belongings out of Lebanon when the phone rang. It was the foreign desk: Joe Alex Morris, the Los Angeles *Times's* Middle East correspondent, had filed a story about an attempt by Moslem militiamen to seize a Christian neighborhood by storm during the night. That represented a change in the war, which had been mostly static. Neither side had tried to take large pieces of territory from the other. The battle had taken place near the Rue Hamra, in the same area as my office. Did I know anything about it, and why hadn't I filed? Because the embassy had warned us to stay inside. Require six hundred words. I said it was too dangerous to go out. Of course it was dangerous, but damnit, that's your job.

I slammed the phone down and called Morris. What was this about a Moslem assault? Yes, one had taken place, but it had been thrown back. He was going to Reuters to file a retop and would be glad to give me a fill if I met him there in forty-five minutes. I got in my car, telling Jill I would be back in an hour or two, and drove to my office. It was less than three blocks from Reuters' Middle East headquarters. After checking the telex, I walked toward the building, passing the high walls of the Beirut College of Law (what law could they possibly have taught there?). I saw no one, not a sign of life anywhere. I cannot recall if I felt more apprehensive than usual, but when I look back through the temporal telescope and see myself walking down those deserted streets flooded in amber light, I feel the presence of a threat more metaphysical than physical, a sense not of danger but of evil. It is as if something invisible yet real is dogging my every step: the Beast, the everlasting Beast in man.

About a dozen of its Children were standing around the building's front entrance. They wore no armbands to distinguish which militia they belonged to. They did not have to; one look at them was enough to tell me they were Mourabitoun. I started to climb the steps. A man in his early twenties shoved his palm against my chest. Where are you going, who are you? He had shark's eyes (no spark of divinity there, no light at all) and a smile immediately recognizable as the one I'd seen in the mirror when I thought of those foolish women. It was the smile of someone incapable of perceiving another human being's pain. Flashing my card, I told him I was *sahafi*—press—and that I was going upstairs to Reuters. Another, older man told me to wait. He went inside and was gone for ten minutes or so. I waited in the middle of that pack of thugs, feeling the way I would in a cage full of pit bulls. I wished Morris were there. The older man came out and told me it was all right to go upstairs.

Reuters was usually crowded with correspondents, messengers, and telex operators, but only two Lebanese employees were there, packing up equipment. Several windows had been shot out; bullets had gouged the walls. I asked what had happened to everyone. The bureau, I was told, had moved to the Commodore Hotel. It was too dangerous to stay here. Early that morning, the building had been caught in the crossfire. Had anyone seen Mr. Morris from the Los Angeles *Times*? No. Perhaps he was at the Commodore (haunting to think of him now; five years later, during the Iranian Revolution, Joe Alex would be killed by a bullet in the heart). I tried to phone the hotel, but the lines were dead. I asked one of the Lebanese for copies of the stories about the night's action. He rummaged through a stack of papers, handed me some carbons, and told me to be quick. They were clearing out as soon as they could; fighting could break out again at any second. I made hurried notes and left, cursing Morris and the foreign desk, cursing myself for leaving my front door.

Outside, the same band of Looney Tunes lurked on the steps, their postures and sullen eyes suggesting a slum street gang looking for action. They had been joined by half a dozen men wearing the red-and-black patches of the Nasserite militia. The presence of the Nasserites wasn't the only difference. I was aware, as soon as I stepped out the door, of the change that used to come over Mahmoud the Mad when his synapses misfired. There were fifteen or sixteen Mahmouds now, and the molecules of their brains had rearranged themselves, for reasons I could never know, possibly for no reason at all, into a configuration of pure hate. The air itself felt different. There was murder in it. All the currents of evil in that city seemed to have converged at that one point, on the perfectly ordinary steps of that perfectly ordinary building. I was in Azazel's kingdom.

The same guy who'd stopped me from going in now stopped me from leaving. He wanted to see my press pass.

"I just showed it to . . ." I looked around for the older man who had let me inside, but he wasn't there. "You just saw it."

He turned his palm up and fluttered his fingers, like a cop demanding a driver's license. I pulled out the card. He drew a straight razor and started to slowly cut it down the middle. I have to explain that each militia issued its own press passes, and even God could not help the correspondent who accidentally showed a Christian pass to a Moslem faction. The one that could get you into any area, and, more important, out, was the laminated pass issued by the Ministry of Information. It could be the only thing between you and a bullet in the back of the head, which was why I snatched the card from the gunman's hand. With his predatory smile, he pressed the flat of the razor under my ear.

"Sahafi Amerikai!" he said, then spat at my shoe. "Maybe I cut your throat?"

I was not too scared because I was fairly sure he would do no such thing. Most of the militiamen were absolute cowards. They would plant a bomb, they would back-shoot you, but they weren't up to intimate killing. He was no exception to the rule. He jerked the razor back and slashed the air in a demented mimic of a musketeer flourishing a foil.

I turned to the left and started toward my office. The man grabbed my shoulder from behind and spun me around.

"Go that way."

He pointed down a side street that led past the Law School campus and toward the Rue Hamra.

"My car's that way," I said, gesturing in the other direction. He waved his rifle at the side street.

"That way."

The Rue Hamra, Beirut's main shopping and banking street, was one of the few thoroughfares still under the control of the dwindling Lebanese army. It was only a hundred yards away. If I could get there, I would be safe, or safer than I was now. I started walking, reigning in an urge to run. Running would only excite the Beast. I hadn't gone fifty feet when a sniper fired at me, the bullet chipping the top of the Law School wall. I knew it was a sniper because the gunshot came from a long way off. He would get me with the next one. I turned and headed back, but the man with the razor raised his Kalashnikov and fired a burst in the air. I turned, again making for the Rue Hamra at a fast walk. A second burst of automatic fire came from behind, the bullets chopping into the pavement and the wall. I broke into a dead run, tossing a fast glance over my shoulder. The guy was running after me, firing from the hip. That helped save me; even when well aimed, an assault rifle on full automatic is inaccurate. Still, it throws out a lot of lead. One round got me, a grazing shot that burned across my back; then something clubbed me in the head, like a well-thrown hook to the temple. I slumped to the sidewalk and blacked out. It's strange how the perceptions attain an incredible clarity in such moments, how time slows down. The blackout could not have lasted more than a second, yet I formed the clear thought that I had taken a round in the head, that in the next second blackness would be all I would see because *bangyerdead*. In the next instant I realized that a fragment from the wall had struck me and that I was a long way from dead.

I heard the clang of a rifle bolt striking an empty chamber. The gunman had run out of ammunition, yet he was still firing. My eyes saw again, and the nightmare continued. A second gunman was running up the street, firing wildly while the first knelt to load a fresh magazine. My mind took clear photographs of both: the first one, with a narrow face and a shock of thick black hair and that chill grin as he raised his rifle to shoot again, the second one middle-aged and fat, with a five o'clock shadow on his jowls. I screamed: "You filthy sons of bitches! Filthy cocksuckers!"

I was up and running again, at the ultimate extremity now, on the edge of the last yawning black maw. I could hear every round fired and tasted blood in my mouth—the blood trickling from my head. Blood oozed down my back, down my left arm, down my left calf. Running zigzag, the way they trained us in the marines, I looked back and saw both men, only forty, fifty feet away, kneeling to steady their aim, and then the guns bucking, muzzles and gunmen's faces blurred by the pale haze of the smokeless powder. I was knocked down. I rolled and was on my feet and running again, enough adrenaline in me to outrun a deer. Down again, up again, hobbling instead of running, still zigzagging. A fragment or ricochet had hit my right foot. Then I felt a terrific impact in my left ankle, like a blast from a compressed air hose. I was flying, lifted off my feet by the round that had hit me solid, fair and square. No fragment or ricochet that time. I landed on my belly and, not stopping to check how badly I'd been hit, scuttled on my elbows like a crab.

I was on the Rue Hamra. I had made it! Still, I was sure the gunmen would round the corner and finish me off. They never came, too scared, I figured, of being shot themselves by the army or by Christian snipers. Two blocks ahead, in front of the BANQUE CENTRALE DU LIBAN, a squad of soldiers manned a sandbagged barricade. Behind them an armored car threw offbeat shimmers in the afternoon sun. I could see the big metal letters on the front of the building as if I were looking at them. BANQUE CENTRALE DU LIBAN. If I could get there, I would be all right. I knelt on my right knee and tried to stand, but my left leg folded like a pipe cleaner. I low-crawled again, and I do believe I was crawling as fast as I normally walked, yet the barricade never got any closer. I raised my hand and shouted for help, but my mouth was full of cotton and brass wool, my voice did not carry. BANQUE CENTRALE DU LIBAN. The soldiers were guarding the bank. Very Lebanese! Guard the money, to hell with everything and everyone else. I was growing weaker and rolled onto my back to see where I'd been hit the worst. Maybe I could tear my shirt to make a tourniquet.

I had taken a bullet though the left ankle. A hole the size of a man's fingernail pierced the outside of my boot; the hole in the other side was as big as a silver dollar, the leather shredded and black with blood. I clawed at my shirt—a red inkblot stained its left sleeve—and ripped a shred and tied it around my left calf. It wasn't tight enough. I pulled, and the strip tore in half. The hell with it. Get to the soldiers. BANQUE CENTRALE DU LIBAN. I yelled for help again. One of the soldiers saw me— he waved his rifle for me to come on. They were too scared to come out from behind the barricade. I had closed the distance to half a block when I knew I wasn't going to make it. I felt the same desertion of strength and will as a marathoner when he hits the wall at twenty miles.

"Help! Help me, goddamnit! I'm hit!"

"You are injured?"

I turned my head and saw a thin, frightened-looking man pressed against the wall of a cul-de-sac on the other side of the street.

"What the hell does it look like?"

"Please, come here. You will be safe."

"Give me a hand."

He didn't move. He wasn't going to risk a sniper or a random round. What the hell, if I made it I might live; if I didn't, a bullet in the head would be better than bleeding to death. I slithered across the street. When I got to the sidewalk, the man knelt down and extended his hand, like someone on a dock reaching out to an exhausted swimmer. I clutched it. He pulled me into the cul-de-sac, then got his hands under my arm and dragged me to the front steps of an apartment building. He looked at me, fear and confusion on his face. I had begun to feel cold; small tremors went rippling through me.

"Mister, is there anything I can bring you?"

"I'm going into shock. Put my feet up on the steps. Get a blanket."

He nodded. I had never been wounded but had seen enough people who were; the pain would come any minute now and it would be awful.

"Whiskey, too, if you have it. And a cigarette."

He elevated my legs and left, returning shortly with a blanket, a package of Marlboros, and a bottle of Remy Martin cognac.

"I had no whiskey. I hope this will do."

I said it would do very nicely, thanks. He went inside again. I tipped the bottle to my lips and drank about a fourth of it in one swallow. I had to get good and numb. Long ago, in a valley in Vietnam, I had heard the wounded from another company screaming because their corpsman had run out of morphine.

I lay drinking and smoking and wondering what to do next when my rescuer returned with a short, bald, slightly paunchy man in his early or midfifties. Strange, the details memory retains, the ones it erases. It has erased the short man's name, I'm ashamed to say, but kept what he was wearing: a pale-beige shirt worn outside his trousers, which were dark brown, and a pair of polished loafers. He was carrying what I mistook for a briefcase.

"How do you do?" he said, and I answered that I was doing as well as could be expected under the circumstances, that is, I was still breathing.

"I am Doctor Khouri. I live here in this building."

"A medical doctor, you mean."

"Yes, I am a vascular surgeon. I'll have a look at you."

I could not believe my luck and was not about to question what I'd done to deserve it.

Dr. Khouri opened the bag, took a scissors, and snipped off my shirt; then, with a larger scissors, he cut through my boots and pulled them off. I shut my eyes, but heard the blood splash when he turned the boots over. Opening my eyes again, I saw him removing my drenched socks. I did not feel a thing. My right foot was numb; so was my left leg from the knee down.

He took my blood pressure and knit his eyebrows.

"Just how bad am I?" I asked as he drenched my wounds in antiseptic and fashioned hasty dressings.

"You're going to live."

"Am I going to lose anything?"

"I don't think so. You're very lucky. It looks to me like that bullet in your left ankle just missed your Achilles tendon. No, I don't think you'll lose a thing if I can operate right away and stop any infection. We'll have to get you to the hospital."

The soldiers guarding the BANQUE CENTRALE DU LIBAN were summoned somehow or other. They pulled up in the armored car and carried me inside its iron guts, where I lay on a stretcher, Dr. Khouri crouched beneath the driver-gunner's feet. I thought I was being taken to the American University Hospital, which was in a fairly safe area near our apartment. But the good luck that had brought me to Khouri's doorstep was mixed with the bad: he practiced at Trad, a maternity hospital that had become a battlefield emergency station because it was in a Christian quarter in the eye of the storm.

I was on a gurney, rolling down a corridor with wooden floors and a high, dim ceiling, the lights above swaying from the shocks of shell-fire. A male nurse cut off my jeans, a female nurse shoved plasma and antibiotic tubes into my veins. They rolled me down a ramp, toward double doors above which, in Arabic and French, were the words: SURGERY. Beside me was a nurses' station, with a telephone. I asked Dr. Khouri if I could phone my wife. Very well, he said, but I probably could not get through; most of the circuits were down. He was right. I tried three times and got only static. I dialed Proffitt's number, and it was weird, weird, to hear Martie, his wife, answer "Hello?" in the most normal voice. I attempted a similar tone and asked for Nick.

"One sec," she said.

"Hey, el-tee, what's goin' on?"

"Gotta make this fast. I've been shot. Looney Tunes did it. Nothing mortal, okay? Worst one's are in my left ankle and right foot. I'm in Trad, going into surgery."

"Jesus Christ, this just isn't your lucky town, is it?"

"Tell Jill. Don't alarm her. I'm all right. Nobody should try to see me. Trad's in the middle of the shit storm. Tell Jill I want her to get herself and the lads out of this country right away."

"She's not going to want to go with you wounded in a hospital."

"Then coldcock her and carry her out over your shoulder if you have to. I want her and the lads out of here."

"You got it."

"And telex the *Tribune*. Maybe they can send somebody over to help out."

"Okay. Got time to tell me what happened?"

"No."

Above, the operating-room lamp swung to and fro. From outside came the unnerving snarl and crash of rocket-propelled grenades, a kind of BRRRRRRRRRRRROOOW . . . WHOMP! Dr. Khouri and four or five assistants were gowned and masked. Instruments shone on a table. A little more of my luck ran out: the upper reading of my blood pressure had dipped to ninety, the lower hovered around sixty.

"I cannot risk putting you under a general anesthetic, Mister Caputo."

I looked at him.

"We have been cut off here for days, and you can see how many injured we have here. We have no block we can give you, just some local, and we are low on that, too."

I kept looking at him.

"I must take out the bullet fragments and debride the wounds. There is a lot of debris inside your ankle and your other foot. Leather from your shoes, cloth from your socks. Dirt. There has been damage to the metatarsals in your right foot, and I'm afraid the joint in your left between your ankle and heel has been destroyed."

I nodded and looked at him.

"The lower extremities are very sensitive," he went on. "A great complex nerve system . . ."

"What are you trying to say?"

"The local will help a little, but I am afraid you are going to feel most of this. I ask you, if you can, not to move too much."

He filled a syringe or two with the local. I felt the needle's prick. A female nurse cradled my head between her hands while two men held me down by the shoulders. Dr. Khouri called for a probe. I watched the lamp, swinging back and forth, and tried to concentrate on its motion. Maybe I can hypnotize myself, I thought, and then it was as if someone had shoved a 220-volt wire into the hole in my ankle. My whole body jerked and went rigid, the way I'd seen people do in dramatizations of electroshock therapy.

"Oh my God, my God, my God . . ."

"Yes, yes, my God," Dr. Khouri said soothingly.

Again the jolt of pain that gave new meaning to the word. I almost leapt off the table. The female nurse practically crushed my cheekbones to keep my head down, the two men leaned their weight on me.

Sweat poured out of me. It seemed important that I not scream or cry out, so I clamped my teeth as the probes dug into the wound, scraped bone, pricked nerves, scalding bolts of pain shooting all through me. Someone pried my jaws open and shoved a hard rubber bar between my teeth.

The body produces its own anesthetics when the artificial kind are not available. I blacked out. The last thing I recall was seeing the overhead lamp, swinging back and forth like a glowing pendulum.

And the next thing I remember was lying in a dark room, bandages on my head and arm and across my back (I had only superficial wounds there, a birdshot peppering of lead and concrete). Stained dressings encased my left leg to the knee, more wound around my right foot. Two other casualties were in with me, constantly talking to me in Arabic. Even if I had been able to understand, I could not have responded for the pain. I am in the business of describing things, but I don't have the vocabulary for that agony. I want to say that both legs, up to their thighs, felt as if they were being sprayed by a blowtorch or stabbed by countless scalding ice picks, but neither even comes close to what it felt like. It was the nearest thing to hell I was likely to suffer on earth—that's the best I can do.

I was thinking, *I'm not going to be able to endure this, I'm going to die from it,* when one of the male nurses came in, an Iraqi with a handsomely trimmed black mustache. He held a syringe.

"Do you have much pain, Mister Caputo?"

"Is that morphine?"

"Meperidine. Synthetic morphine."

"*Please.*"

He shot me up, and within five or six minutes, I experienced the nearest thing to heaven I was likely to know on earth. The fighting was still going on, but I didn't hear it as I rose up out of myself. The blowtorch continued to hum, the ice picks kept jabbing, but I never felt them. *Oh, thank you, thank you, thank you. Thank you, Jesus!* My soul, my consciousness, give it whatever name you like, floated to the ceiling to look down on my wracked body with mixed pity and contempt. You wretched bag of bones, you miserable suffering assembly of mortal flesh and tender nerves, ah, I am so glad to be free of you, even for this little while.

The spiritual *I* levitated for a couple of hours, gradually losing altitude as the drug wore off, then slipped back into the physical *I*. The *I-I* spent another hour or two in hell, until that mustached angel returned with his needle and administered the blessed sacrament once again. And so, all night, I commuted between paradise and perdition, never making an intermediate stop. The Meperidine Express. I was sold on the stuff, I was a stone junkie before morning, whispering to the angel that great rewards would be his if he shot me up every two hours instead of four.

"I am sorry, Mister Caputo. This is highly addictive, and anyway we do not have enough."

The sky paled. I had survived my first night as a casualty of war. I began to wonder how much longer that would continue when an RPG hit a truck opposite the hospital. The window shattered. Black smoke stinking of burning gasoline poured into the room. Nurses and aides ran in and wheeled our beds into the corridor. I wasn't frightened because I was on the heaven-bound leg of my four-hourly journey.

Dr. Khouri returned me to hell a short while later. The dressings came off my feet, the hasty sutures were opened. He wanted to do another debridement. When that was done, the day-shift angel appeared and I was on the wing again.

That was how it went for the next four days. During that time, I found out later, I had become the topic of much speculation among my colleagues in the press corps. Why had the gunmen shot me? How had I managed to survive fifty or sixty bullets fired at close range? They were just doing their jobs, trying to make sense of the senseless.

I did not try, not at first. I was in too much pain, too terrified by the fighting around the hospital, and too happy for each moment of life to trouble myself with metaphysics. I would not have even if I had not been in peril and pain, having concluded that trying to make sense of the senseless was the most senseless thing anyone could do in Beirut. Certainly my narrow escape never struck me as part of God's wondrous design. God had abandoned the Beast's new Bethlehem, even though everyone there claimed to be fighting for Him. As to the gunmen's motives, I was satisfied that they had none. Beirut was quantum physics applied to human behavior and events. People just did things, and things just happened. I had been shot and had survived because events had arranged themselves that way. They could have as easily arranged themselves the other way. *Don't mean nothin', don't mean a thing.*

Later, during the ten months I spent recovering, I asked the Big Questions. Why had I been shot? Why had I survived? For a while, because I finished *A Rumor of War* during my convalescence, I thought I had been temporarily crippled so the book could live. Maybe so. But

I had read somewhere that an estimated *half a billion* human beings have died or been injured in all the wars of this ghastly century. To think I'd become a casualty merely to complete a book smacked of the worst egocentricity.

As the weeks passed I came *almost* full circle to my original impression. What happened to me *was* senseless. In and of itself, it was as meaningless as a rock—if I wanted it to be. It was my choice to impart or not impart significance. Recalling how I'd laughed at those unfortunate Moslem women, I saw myself as a man who had become disconnected from human suffering. Scorning and blaming victims for their victimization, I was not too far from the altered moral state of the gunmen who'd shot me. Through my own suffering, I was plugged back into the current of human anguish that circuits this planet without end. I had been wounded to learn pain, and I had been made to know pain to learn pity once again.

Yet that old Vietnam mantra kept echoing in the back of my mind: *Don't mean nothin', don't mean a thing.*

The *fighting* went on day and night. Trad hospital remained cut off from the outside world. I heard nothing about Jill and the boys and was in continual anxiety, wondering if they had evacuated. Supplies ran low. The Angel of the Blessed Needle extended his visitations from every four, to every six, and, finally, to every eight hours. The anguish would have been unbearable, I would have begun to feel very sorry for myself if I had not heard the moans and screams of the freshly wounded, coming in with no letup. On one of those days, an exhausted Dr. Khouri, his surgeon's smock like a butcher's apron, told me I would need skin grafts to close the wounds in my ankle. He could not perform the operation under the circumstances and was trying to find somebody to evacuate me to the American University Hospital. The day before, he had managed to get through to the U.S. Embassy and explain the situation. He had not heard from them since; maybe the circuits were down again.

When, at last, the lull came, I was visited by John Andrews, NBC's radio correspondent. I was so glad to see a face from the outside I would have hugged and kissed Andrews if I'd had the strength for it. He told me someone from the *Tribune*—couldn't recall who—was in Beirut and, with Proffitt's help, had put my family on a flight to Athens. They had even worked the miracle of loading all our belongings on a 747 cargo plane that was flying out with the household effects of embassy staffers. I felt an immense relief. My wife and kids were safe; for the moment, nothing else mattered.

"How the hell did you get here?" I asked Andrews.

"Got in the car and drove. Had to park several blocks away. Too dicey to drive, even with the cease-fire. Yon know what cease-fires are like here."

I certainly did, but, I said, I would appreciate it if he passed on to the embassy that reaching Trad was not impossible. The Angel of the Blessed Needle appeared, not, unfortunately, with his syringe but with a message that a call from the United States was waiting for me. He wheeled me to an orderly station.

It was Mike McGuire, recently promoted to foreign editor. His voice was so clear he sounded as if he were around the corner. The *Tribune* took care of its own. On his end, Mike was doing all he could to get me evacuated; he was constantly on the phone with the State department; arrangements were being made to have me treated by a specialist in traumatic foot injuries at Northwestern University Hospital in Chicago. Jim Yuenger was the man who had gotten my family out. He was still in Beirut, pressuring the embassy to rescue me from Trad. Yuenger had been on assignment in Morocco when he'd heard the news.

"He volunteered," McGuire said. "I'll never forget his telex: 'I willingly volunteer. I will move hellfire and high water. I'm going to get Caputo, goddamnit.' That's the kind of gutsy guy you've got looking after you. He knew he was flying into a real hell while other Americans were headed for safety in the other direction. That might embarrass you, but I can't call it a week until I get it off my chest."

More than embarrass me, it made me feel small and unworthy and stupid. I was putting a lot of people through a lot of grief, risk, and trouble.

That night, the *fighting* resumed and crashed on through the night into a dawn that reeked of burning rubber and cordite. The Beast's breath. I lay in the corridor, waiting for the Angel. A different sort of angel appeared, in the form of a tall, broad-shouldered American wearing a flak jacket over his sport coat. A Colt .38 was jammed into his waistband. He carried a second flak jacket. Two Lebanese security police walked beside him, and Dr. Khouri brought up the rear.

"Here is our famous patient," the doctor said.

"Caputo?" asked the tall man, holding out his hand. "Colonel Braun, U.S. Marines. I'm getting you out of here."

Orderlies rolled me off my bed into a wheelchair, extending the footrest so the blood did not rush into my feet, which caused extraordinary pain. To be sure I did not feel any, the Angel gave me, well, a parting shot. The colonel wrapped the spare flak jacket around my chest.

"Did the embassy send you?" I asked as the security cops wheeled me down the corridor.

"Yes and no," answered Colonel Braun, who was the security director for U.S. embassies in the Middle East. "I went to the ambassador myself, asked to borrow his driver and limo. It's bulletproof, armor-plated, and we'll need it. Lebanese security types were coming for you this morning, but their APC took a rocket. Had to turn back."

"Anybody killed? I don't want somebody getting killed on my account."

"I don't either." He gave me a faint grin. "Marines don't leave their wounded on the battlefield. Yon oughta know that, Lieutenant."

We came to the stairs. The policemen lifted me into a fireman's carry. An orderly folded the wheelchair while two more, flinching at the gunfire outside, swung the emergency entrance doors open.

I looked at Dr. Khouri and tried to think of the right thing to say. He gestured to say that he needed no thanks.

"I am a doctor, after all."

"And then some," I said.

Colonel Braun made sure my flak jacket was snapped.

"Let's go."

Bouncing in the cradle of the policemen's crossed arms, I saw only two things: the big black Chrysler limousine and a squad of *kataeb*, spraying rooftops with machine guns from behind a barricade on the other side of the street. I was tossed in the backseat—it wasn't the time for gentle handling—Colonel Braun jumping into the front, the policemen crowding in beside me. The driver (he and the ambassador would later be assassinated by Moslem gunmen) put the pedal to the floor, and we were gone in a squeal of tires. I shut my eyes, cringing against the blast of the RPG I was sure would hit us. The gunfire cracked and rumbled in diminuendo, the driver slowed down. In less than half an hour, I lay on another gurney, rolling down a quiet air-conditioned hall in the American University Hospital. I wanted to chalk up one more escape, though I had not escaped anything; I had been let go.

from Pity the Nation
by Robert Fisk

PLO fighters left Lebanon after Israel invaded the country in 1982. Many Palestinian civilians remained in Lebanese refugee camps, where they became easy prey for the local Christian militia. Some observers accused Israeli forces of standing by while the refugees were slaughtered.

"Pregnant women will give birth to terrorists; the children when they grow up will be terrorists."

> Phalangist involved in the Sabra and Chatila massacre, when questioned by an Israeli tank crew, west Beirut
> *17 September 1982*

"We know, it's not to our liking, and don't interfere."

> Message from an Israeli army battalion commander to his men, on learning that Palestinians were being massacred
> *17 September 1982*

It was the flies that told us. There were millions of them, their hum almost as eloquent as the smell. Big as bluebottles, they covered us, unaware at first of the difference between the living and the dead. If we stood still, writing in our notebooks, they would settle like an army—legions of them—on the white surface of our notebooks, hands, arms, faces, always congregating around our eyes and mouths, moving from body to body, from the many dead to the few living, from corpse to reporter, their small green bodies panting with excitement as they found new flesh upon which to settle and feast.

If we did not move quickly enough, they bit us. Mostly they stayed around our heads in a grey cloud, waiting for us to assume the generous stillness of the dead. They were obliging, these flies, forming our only physical link with the victims who lay around us, reminding us that there is life in death. Someone benefits. The flies were impartial. It mattered not the slightest that the bodies here had been the victims of mass murder. The flies would have performed in just this way for the unburied dead of any community. Doubtless it was like this on hot afternoons during the Great Plague.

At first, we did not use the word massacre. We said very little because the flies would move unerringly for our mouths. We held handkerchiefs over our mouths for this reason, then we clasped the material to our noses as well because the flies moved over our faces. If the smell of the dead in Sidon was nauseating, the stench in Chatila made us retch. Through the thickest of handkerchiefs, we smelled them. After some minutes, *we* began to smell of the dead.

They were everywhere, in the road, in laneways, in back yards and broken rooms, beneath crumpled masonry and across the top of garbage tips. The murderers—the Christian militiamen whom Israel had let into the camps to 'flush out terrorists'—had only just left. In some cases, the blood was still wet on the ground. When we had seen a hundred bodies, we stopped counting. Down every alleyway, there were corpses—women, young men, babies and grandparents—lying together in lazy and terrible profusion where they had been knifed or machine-gunned to death. Each corridor through the rubble produced more bodies. The patients at a Palestinian hospital had disappeared after gunmen ordered the doctors to leave. Everywhere, we found signs of hastily dug mass graves. Perhaps a thousand people were butchered; probably half that number again.

Even while we were there, amid the evidence of such savagery, we could see the Israelis watching us. From the top of the tower block to the west—the second building on the Avenue Camille Chamoun—we could see them staring at us through field-glasses, scanning back and forth across the streets of corpses, the lenses of the binoculars sometimes flashing in the sun as their gaze ranged through the camp. Loren Jenkins cursed a lot. I thought it was probably his way of controlling his feelings of nausea amid this terrible smell. All of us wanted to vomit. We were *breathing* death, inhaling the very putrescence of the bloated corpses around us. Jenkins immediately realised that the Israeli defence minister would have to bear some responsibility for this horror. '*Sharon!*' he shouted. 'That fucker Sharon! This is Deir Yassin all over again.'

What we found inside the Palestinian Chatila camp at ten o'clock on the morning of 18 September 1982 did not quite beggar description, although it would have been easier to re-tell in the cold prose of a medical examination. There had been massacres before in Lebanon, but rarely on this scale and never overlooked by a regular, supposedly disciplined army. In the panic and hatred of battle, tens of thousands had been killed in this country. But these people, hundreds of them, had been shot down unarmed. This was a mass killing, an incident—how easily we used the word 'incident' in Lebanon—that was also an atrocity. It went beyond even what the Israelis would have in other circumstances called a *terrorist* atrocity. It was a war crime.

Jenkins and Tveit and I were so overwhelmed by what we found in Chatila that at first we were unable to register our own shock. Bill Foley of AP had come with us. All he could say as he walked round was 'Jesus Christ!' over and over again. We might have accepted evidence of a few murders; even dozens of bodies, killed in the heat of combat. But there were women lying in houses with their skirts torn up to their waists and their legs wide apart, children with their throats cut, rows of young men shot in the back after being lined up at an execution wall. There were babies—blackened babies because they had been slaughtered more than 24 hours earlier and their small bodies were already in a state of decomposition—tossed into rubbish heaps along-side discarded US army ration tins, Israeli army medical equipment and empty bottles of whisky.

Where were the murderers? Or, to use the Israelis' vocabulary, where were the 'terrorists'? When we drove down to Chatila, we had seen the Israelis on the top of the apartments in the Avenue Camille Chamoun but they made no attempt to stop us. In fact, we had first driven to the Bourj al-Barajneh camp because someone told us that there was a mas-sacre there. All we saw was a Lebanese soldier chasing a car thief down a street. It was only when we were driving back past the entrance to Chatila that Jenkins decided to stop the car. 'I don't like this,' he said. 'Where is everyone? What the fuck is that smell?'

Just inside the southern entrance to the camp, there used to be a number of single-storey concrete-walled houses. I had conducted many interviews inside these hovels in the late 1970s. When we walked across the muddy entrance of Chatila, we found that these buildings had all been dynamited to the ground. There were cartridge cases across the main road. I saw several Israeli flare canisters, still attached to their tiny parachutes. Clouds of flies moved across the rubble, raiding parties with a nose for victory.

Down a laneway to our right, no more than 50 yards from the entrance, there lay a pile of corpses. There were more than a dozen of them, young men whose arms and legs had been wrapped around each other in the agony of death. All had been shot at point-blank range through the cheek, the bullet tearing away a line of flesh up to the ear and entering the brain. Some had vivid crimson or black scars down the left side of their throats. One had been castrated, his trousers torn open and a settlement of flies throbbing over his torn intestines.

The eyes of these young men were all open. The youngest was only 12 or 13 years old. They were dressed in jeans and coloured shirts, the material absurdly tight over their flesh now that their bodies had begun to bloat in the heat. They had not been robbed.

On one blackened wrist, a Swiss watch recorded the correct time, the second hand still ticking round uselessly, expending the last energies of its dead owner.

On the other side of the main road, up a track through the debris, we found the bodies of five women and several children. The women were middle-aged and their corpses lay draped over a pile of rubble. One lay on her back, her dress torn open and the head of a little girl emerging from behind her. The girl had short, dark curly hair, her eyes were staring at us and there was a frown on her face. She was dead.

Another child lay on the roadway like a discarded doll, her white dress stained with mud and dust. She could have been no more than three years old. The back of her head had been blown away by a bullet fired into her brain. One of the women also held a tiny baby to her body. The bullet that had passed through her breast had killed the baby too. Someone had slit open the woman's stomach, cutting sideways and then upwards, perhaps trying to kill her unborn child. Her eyes were wide open, her dark face frozen in horror.

Tveit tried to record all this on tape, speaking slowly and unemotionally in Norwegian. 'I have come to another body, that of a woman and her baby. They are dead. There are three other women. They are dead . . .' From time to time, he would snap the 'pause' button and lean over to be sick, retching over the muck on the road. Foley and Jenkins and I explored one narrow avenue and heard the sound of a tracked vehicle. 'They're still here,' Jenkins said and looked hard at me. They were still there. The murderers were still there, in the camp. Foley's first concern was that the Christian militiamen might take his film, the only evidence—so far as he knew—of what had happened. He ran off down the laneway.

Jenkins and I had darker fears. If the murderers were still in the camp, it was the witnesses rather than the photographic evidence that they would wish to destroy. We saw a brown metal gate ajar; we pushed it open and ran into the yard, closing it quickly behind us. We heard the vehicle approaching down a neighbouring road, its tracks clanking against pieces of concrete. Jenkins and I looked at each other in fear and then knew that we were not alone. We *felt* the presence of another human. She lay just beside us, a young, pretty woman lying on her back.

She lay there as if she was sunbathing in the heat, and the blood running from her back was still wet. The murderers had just left. She just lay there, feet together, arms outspread, as if she had seen her saviour. Her face was peaceful, eyes closed, a beautiful woman whose head was now granted a strange halo. For a clothes line hung above her and there were children's trousers and some socks pegged to the line. Other clothes lay scattered on the ground. She must have been hanging out her family's clothes when the murderers came. As she fell, the clothes pegs in her hand sprayed over the yard and formed a small wooden circle round her head.

Only the insignificant hole in her breast and the growing stain across the yard told of her death. Even the flies had not yet found her. I thought Jenkins was praying but he was just cursing again and muttering 'Dear God' in between the curses. I felt so sorry for this woman. Perhaps it was easier to feel pity for someone so young, so innocent, someone whose body had not yet begun to rot. I kept looking at her face, the neat way she lay beneath the clothes line, almost expecting her to open her eyes.

She must have hidden in her home when she heard the shooting in the camp. She must have escaped the attention of the Israeli-backed gunmen until that very morning, She had walked into her yard, heard no shooting, assumed the trouble was over and gone about her daily chores. She could not have known what had happened. Then the yard door must have opened, as quickly as we had just opened it, and the murderers would have walked in and killed her. Just like that. They had left and we had arrived, perhaps only a minute or two later.

We stayed in the yard for several more minutes. Jenkins and I were very frightened. Like Tveit, who had temporarily disappeared, he was a survivor. I felt safe with Jenkins. The militiamen—the murderers of this girl—had raped and knifed the women in Chatila and shot the men but I rather suspected they would hesitate to kill Jenkins, an

American who would try to talk them down. 'Let's get out of here,' he said, and we left. He peered into the street first, I followed, closing the door very slowly because I did not want to disturb the sleeping, dead woman with her halo of clothes pegs.

Foley was back in the street near the entrance to the camp. The tracked vehicle had gone, although I could still hear it moving on the main road outside, moving up towards the Israelis who were still watching us. Jenkins heard Tveit calling from behind a pile of bodies and I lost sight of him. We kept losing sight of each other behind piles of corpses. At one moment I would be talking to Jenkins, at the next I would turn to find that I was addressing a young man, bent backwards over the pillar of a house, his arms hanging behind his head.

I could hear Jenkins and Tveit perhaps a hundred yards away, on the other side of a high barricade covered with earth and sand that had been newly erected by a bulldozer. It was perhaps 12 feet high and I climbed with difficulty up one side of it, my feet slipping in the muck. Near the top, I lost my balance and for support grabbed a hunk of dark red stone that protruded from the earth. But it was no stone. It was clammy and hot and it stuck to my hand and when I looked down I saw that I was holding a human elbow that protruded, a triangle of flesh and bone, from the earth.

I let go of it in horror, wiping the dead flesh on my trousers, and staggered the last few feet to the top of the barricade. But the smell was appalling and at my feet a face was looking at me with half its mouth missing. A bullet or a knife had torn it away and what was left of the mouth was a nest of flies. I tried not to look at it. I could see, in the distance, Jenkins and Tveit standing by some more corpses in front of a wall but I could not shout to them for help because I knew I would be sick if I opened my mouth.

I walked on the top of the barricade, looking desperately for a place from which to jump all the way to the ground on the other side. But each time I took a step, the earth moved up towards me. The whole embankment of muck shifted and vibrated with my weight in a dreadful, springy way and, when I looked down again, I saw that the sand was only a light covering over more limbs and faces. A large stone turned out to be a stomach. I could see a man's head, a woman's naked breast, the feet of a child. I was walking on dozens of corpses which were moving beneath my feet.

The bodies had been buried by someone in panic. They had been bulldozed to the side of the laneway. Indeed, when I looked up, I could see a bulldozer—its driver's seat empty—standing guiltily just down the road.

I tried hard but vainly not to tread on the faces beneath me. We all of us felt a traditional respect for the dead, even here, now. I kept telling myself that these monstrous cadavers were not enemies, that these dead people would approve of my being here, would want Tveit and Jenkins and me to see all this and that therefore I should not be frightened. But I had never seen so many corpses before.

I jumped to the ground and ran towards Jenkins and Tveit. I think I was whimpering in a silly way because Jenkins looked around, surprised. But the moment I opened my mouth to speak, flies entered it. I spat them out. Tveit was being sick. He had been staring at what might have been sacks in front of a low stone wall. They formed a line, young men and boys, lying prostrate. They had been executed, shot in the back against the wall and they lay, at once pathetic and terrible, where they had fallen.

This wall and its huddle of corpses were reminiscent of something we had all seen before. Only afterwards did we realise how similar it was to those old photographs of executions in occupied Europe during the Second World War. There may have been 12 or 20 bodies there. Some lay beneath others. When I leaned down to look at them closely, I noticed the same dark scar on the left side of their throats. The murderers must have marked their prisoners for execution in this way. Cut a throat with a knife and it meant the man was doomed, a 'terrorist' to be executed at once.

As we stood there, we heard a shout in Arabic from across the ruins. 'They are coming back,' a man was screaming. So we ran in fear towards the road. I think, in retrospect, that it was probably anger that stopped us leaving, for we now waited near the entrance to the camp to glimpse the faces of the men who were responsible for all this. They must have been sent in here with Israeli permission. They must have been armed by the Israelis. Their handiwork had clearly been watched—closely observed—by the Israelis, by those same Israelis who were still watching us through their field-glasses.

Another armoured vehicle could be heard moving behind a wall to the west—perhaps it was Phalangist, perhaps Israeli—but no one appeared. So we walked on. It was always the same. Inside the ruins of the Chatila hovels, families had retreated to their bedrooms when the militiamen came through the front door and there they lay, slumped over the beds, pushed beneath chairs, hurled over cooking pots. Many of the women here had been raped, their clothes lying across the floor, their naked bodies thrown on top of their husbands or brothers, all now dark with death.

There was another laneway deeper inside the camp where another bulldozer had left its tracks in the mud. We followed these tracks until we came to a hundred square yards of newly ploughed earth. Flies carpeted the ground and there again was that familiar, fine, sweet terrible smell. We looked at this place, all of us suspecting what was indeed the truth, that this was a hastily dug mass grave. We noticed that our shoes began to sink into the soft earth, that it had a liquid, almost watery quality to it, and we stepped back in terror towards the track.

A Norwegian diplomat—one of Ane-Karina Arveson's colleagues—had driven down the road outside a few hours earlier and had seen a bulldozer with a dozen corpses in its scoop, arms and legs swaying from the vehicle's iron bucket. Who had dug this earth over with such efficiency? Who drove the bulldozer? There was only one certainty: that the Israelis knew the answer, that they had watched it happen, that their allies—Phalangists or Haddad militiamen—had been sent into Chatila and had committed this act of mass murder. Here was the gravest act of terrorism—the largest in scale and time carried out by individuals who could see and touch the innocent people they were murdering—in the recent history of the Middle East.

There were, remarkably, survivors. Three small children called to us from a roof to say they had hidden while the massacre took place. Some weeping women shouted at us that their men had been killed. All said Haddad's men and the Phalange were responsible and gave accurate descriptions of the different cedar tree badges of the two militias.

There were more bodies on the main road. 'That was my neighbour, Mr Nouri,' a woman shouted at me. 'He was ninety.' And there in a pile of garbage on the pavement beside her lay a very old man with a thin grey beard, a small woollen hat still on his head. Another old man lay by his front door in his pyjamas, slaughtered as he ran for safety a few hours earlier. Incredibly, there were dead horses, three of them, big white stallions which had been machine-gunned to death beside a hovel, one of them with its hoof on a wall, trying to leap to safety as the militiamen shot it.

There had been fighting inside the camp. The road near the Sabra mosque was slippery with cartridge cases and ammunition clips and some of the equipment was of the Soviet type used by the Palestinians. The few men here who still possessed weapons had tried to defend their families. Their stories would never be known. When did they realize that their people were being massacred? How could they fight with so few weapons? In the middle of the road outside the mosque, there lay a perfectly carved scale-model toy wooden Kalashnikov rifle, its barrel snapped in two.

We walked back and forth in the camp, on each journey finding more bodies, stuffed into ditches, thrown over walls, lined up and shot. We began to recognise the corpses that we had seen before. Up there is the woman with the little girl looking over her shoulder, there is Mr Nouri again, lying in the rubbish beside the road. On one occasion, I intentionally glanced at the woman with the child because I had half expected her to have moved, to have assumed a different position. The dead were becoming real to us.

Further north, in the Sabra section of the camp, women came up to us, crying with fear and appealing for help. Their men—sons, husbands, fathers—had been taken from their homes at the time of the massacre. A few had already been found at the execution walls but others were still missing. A Reuters correspondent had seen men being held under guard by Israeli troops in the ruins of the sports stadium. There were more journalists now, Lebanese newspaper photographers and diplomats. We found two Swiss delegates from the International Red Cross and told them where we had found mass graves. Swedish radio's correspondent was in the camp.

We found hundreds of the missing men in the stadium, just as the Reuters man had said. They were Lebanese for the most part— Lebanese as well as Palestinians lived in Sabra—and they were being taken away for 'interrogation' by militiamen. The whole western side of the ruined sports stadium was guarded by uniformed Israeli troops together with plain-clothes Shin Bet intelligence operatives, big, heavy-set men wearing Ray-Bans with Uzi machine-guns in their hands. There were also militiamen there, three of whom I saw leading a frightened man away from the stadium. The Israelis let them do this. They had agreed to this procedure. The Israelis themselves explained to us that this was a search for 'terrorists'. Terrorists.

The very word 'terrorists' now sounded obscene. It had become a murderous word, a word that had helped to bring about this atrocity. Jenkins and I saw hundreds of prisoners, squatting on their heels or lying in the dust beneath the stadium wall. I walked across to them, ignoring the Israelis who obviously thought that Jenkins and I were Shin Bet. I walked right into one of the underground stadium rooms which was being used as a cell. 'Help us,' one man said. An Israeli soldier appeared. Press, I said. 'Get out of here, these men are terrorists.'

But they were not. A few yards away, the Reuters correspondent found his own telex operator—a Lebanese man whose home was on Corniche Mazraa—sitting in one of the cells. We found an Israeli officer. He was a *Tat Aluf,* a colonel. We told him we had found the Reuters telex operator. He had to be released. After much pleading, the man was given to us. The British Reuters reporter led him away, an arm around his shoulders.

I walked into another of the 'cells'. 'They take us away, one by one, for interrogation,' one of the prisoners said. 'They are Haddad men. Usually they bring the people back after interrogation but not always. Sometimes the people do not return.' Another Israeli colonel appeared, pointed at me and ordered me to leave. I wanted to go on talking. The prisoners were silent. Why could they not talk? 'They can talk if they want,' the Israeli colonel said. 'But they have nothing to say.'

The nearest bodies lay only 500 yards away. The stench of the corpses filled the air where these Israeli soldiers and Shin Bet men were standing. But they were still talking about 'terrorists'. It was surreal, grotesque. Jenkins found an officer whom he recognised. 'These people are being held here for questioning—they are terrorist suspects,' the Israeli was saying. It was irrelevant. Excuse me, excuse me for one moment, I asked, but what has been happening here? There are bodies everywhere, just over there—I pointed to the side of the stadium— there are piles of them. 'I don't know about that.' But you can *smell* them. 'I'm sorry, I have no information.'

I turned to the soldier. He was a tall man with short dark hair and a tanned complexion, well-built, slightly plump. Look I said, forgive me for saying it like this, but there are scenes in there that look like something out of Treblinka. It was the first comparison I could think of to what I had just witnessed. I had not said 'Treblinka' because Jews were murdered there. Treblinka was an extermination camp. The Israeli looked at me without emotion.

I was trying to make him understand the enormity of what had happened, that this was not just a small excess but a massacre perpetrated by Israel's allies under Israel's eyes. I was trying to make him understand. Could he not *smell* the air? I asked him that. The Israeli should have argued with me. He could at least have pointed out—correctly— that there was no comparison in scale between what had happened in Chatila and what happened in Treblinka. But he did not. He had to pretend that he did not know what was in Chatila.

Jenkins was angry. 'Why don't you tell us what happened? There's been mass murder here. What happened? Tell us. Did you let the Christian militia in here yesterday?'

'I wasn't here yesterday. I only arrived this morning.'

Jenkins' eyes narrowed and he stepped back in fury. 'You're lying,' he said. 'You *were* here yesterday. I saw you. You stopped my fucking car when I wanted to go to Chatila. I spoke to you yesterday. You *were* here. You're lying.' The Israeli obviously remembered Jenkins. He held up his hand. 'I thought you were asking me something different. I don't remember. I have no idea what's been happening here.'

Along the main road, there was a line of Merkava tanks, their crews sitting on the turrets, smoking, watching the men being led from the stadium in ones and twos, some being set free, others being led away by Shin Bet men or by Lebanese men in drab khaki overalls.

We walked back towards the camp. A Palestinian woman walked up to me, smiling in a harsh, cruel way. 'Got some good pictures, have you?' she asked. 'Got some good things to write? Is everything all right for you? It's a nice day, isn't it?' I thought she was going to curse me but she just kept up her controlled sarcasm. 'You press people take good pictures. I hope everything is fine for you. Have a nice day here.'

Jenkins left to telex his office. Tveit drove to the Commodore Hotel to use the telephone. I walked back through the camp with my hand-kerchief over my face, past Mr Nouri and the other old man, to the left of the execution wall, below the barricade of corpses, the empty bull-dozer, the dead horses, the woman with the child looking over her shoulder. Only when I was approaching the exit to Chatila, the track that led onto the main road between the Kuwaiti Embassy and Fakhani, did I realise that I was the only living soul in this part of the camp.

There was a roaring of engines from the road and above the breeze-block wall, beyond the trees, I could see an Israeli tank column. The disembodied voice of an Israeli officer came floating through the trees from a tannoy on an armoured personnel carrier. 'Stay off the streets,' he ordered. 'We are only looking for terrorists. Stay off the streets. We will shoot.'

This was more than grotesque. The Israelis were instructing the dead to stay off the streets. It was farcical, absurd, monstrous. I walked to the gate, my handkerchief still across my mouth and nose. The tank column was followed by two lines of Israeli infantry. They walked behind the camp wall and then, when they reached the entrance to Chatila, they sprinted across the opening, rifles at the ready, taking position at the other side, covering each other from the ghostly 'terrorists' inside.

I walked out into the street. 'Hey, you—get out of here.' A junior Israeli officer walked up to me. Press, I said. 'You are not permitted here. Get out of here.' I refused. I had simply seen too much. 'I'm ordering you to leave at once.' I just shook my head. I felt sick. My clothes stank. I smelled of dead people. But after what I had just seen, I was beyond obeying such instructions. And I was mesmerised by these soldiers. They were still running across the entrance to the camp to avoid the phantom 'terrorists'.

The officer walked up to me and glared in my face. There's no one there, I said. 'I've given you an order to leave here. Do as you're told,' the soldier shouted. You don't understand, I said. Everyone here is dead. They're all dead in there. There's no one there—only dead people. Three Israeli soldiers stood beside the officer, looking at me as if I was mad. I looked at the officer because I suspected he might himself be a little insane. No I won't leave.

One of the three soldiers put his hand on my arm. 'There are terrorists in the camp and you will be killed.' That's not true, I said. Everyone there is dead. Can't you *smell* them? The soldier looked at me in disbelief. Really, I said, women and children have been murdered in there. There are dead babies. The officer waved his hand at me dismissively. 'You'll be killed,' he said, and walked away.

I began to feel like one of those characters in a mystery film who call the police to report a murder only to be accused of fabricating the story. Perhaps if I walked back into Chatila now, the bodies would be gone, the streets cleaned up, the hovels reconstructed, their dead owners cooking lunch or sleeping off the hot early afternoon in those back bedrooms. I went across to one of the lines of infantry that were approaching the entrance to the camp and walked along beside a tall, friendly-looking soldier.

What is going on? 'I don't know. I'm not allowed to talk to you.' No, seriously, what is going on? The man smiled. I could tell he wanted to be friendly. His uniform was dirty and he held his Galil assault rifle in his hands with ease, a professional soldier who was tired and needed friends. Everyone was dead in the camp, I said. Women, children, all murdered. 'Why?' he asked. I was wondering if he knew. 'The Christians were there,' he said. Why? 'I don't know. It was nothing to do with me. I wasn't there.' We had come to the camp gate. He crouched down.

Even this likeable, friendly man was now ready to go into action against the ghosts. I walked into the entrance of Chatila, standing upright in the centre of the road. How obsessed were these young men? To my astonishment, they too began to crouch at one side of the entrance and then to run to the other side, a distance of perhaps 30 feet, bent double, scuttling past my feet with their rifles pointed into the camp. I thought they were mad. They, of course, thought I was mad. They believed—they were possessed of an absolute certainty and conviction—that 'terrorists' were in Chatila.

How could I explain to them that the terrorists had left, that the terrorists had worn Israeli uniforms, that the terrorists had been sent into Chatila by Israeli officers, that the victims of the terrorists were not Israelis but Palestinians and Lebanese? I tried. I walked alongside these soldiers and told them I was a journalist and asked their names. After some minutes, they grew used to my presence. So I met Moshe, Raphael, Benny, all carrying their heavy rifles down the road past Chatila, all fearful of terrorists. Terrorists, terrorists, terrorists. The word came up in every sentence, like a punctuation mark. It was as if no statement, no belief could be expressed without the presence of terrorists.

'There are terrorists everywhere,' Benny said. 'Be very careful.' Benny came from Ashqelon. He was married and he wanted to go home. He had only come to Lebanon to get rid of terrorists. When the terrorists had left Beirut, he would go home. But hadn't the PLO *left* Beirut? Had he not seen the evacuation or read about it in the papers? 'They didn't leave,' he said. 'Lots of them are still here. That is why we are here.'

But everyone in this area of Chatila was dead. 'I don't know about that. But there are terrorists everywhere here. This is a very dangerous place. Haven't you heard the shooting?' I explained that the Lebanese militias had been shooting at the Israelis only because the Israelis had invaded west Beirut, that some Palestinians had tried to defend themselves against the militias inside Chatila.

It was pointless. The columns of infantry marched all the way through the southern suburbs of Beirut to Galerie Semaan—opposite their own siege front line—and eventually, in the ruins of the line, someone, some 'terrorist' who chose to oppose this occupation army, opened fire with a rifle. From the sound of the shot, I suspected it came from a narrow street off Boulevard Ariss, but the Israelis were sure it came from a ruined building.

They threw themselves into the muck beside the road and I jumped into a ditch beside an Israeli major. An armoured personnel carrier drove up the road and its crew opened fire at the ruins with a Vulcan gun, a weapon which fired a continuous stream of metal at its target and blew pieces of the building into the air like confetti. The Israeli major and I lay huddled in our ditch for 15 minutes. He asked about Chatila, very innocently, and I told him what I had seen.

Then he said: 'I tell you this. The Haddad men were supposed to go in with us. We had to shoot two of them yesterday. We killed one and wounded another. Two more we took away. They were doing a bad thing. That is all I will tell you.'

Was this at Chatila, I asked? Had he been there himself? He would say no more. In the days to come, I would discover that the major's story was only partly true. Then his radio operator, who had been lying beside us in the mud, crawled up next to me. He was a young man. He pointed to his chest. 'We Israelis don't do that sort of thing,' he said. 'It was the Christians.'

So they *did* know what had happened in Chatila.

Did *we*? Even now, after all the warnings we had heard, after all the clues, after ignoring all our journalistic instincts—after seeing the very evidence of Chatila with our own eyes—we as reporters could still not comprehend exactly what had happened. When I returned to the AP office, I found that all telex, computer line and telephone communciations were down. Steve Hindy of AP's Cairo staff was running the bureau in Tatro's absence on holiday. Hindy was arguing with Labelle and Foley about what they had seen.

'Are you sure it was a massacre?'

Foley was waving pictures in front of him. 'Look at them Steve, look at them. You haven't been there yet.'

'But how many dead are there?'

'What the fuck does it matter? It was a massacre.'

'Yes, but was it? People have been killed in Lebanon like this before.'

I sat in the corner of the room, listening to this. I smelled bad and I was tired. It was a Saturday. *The Times* would not be published until the Sunday night. I could go home if I wanted but the conversation was part of the same tragedy I had seen that morning. When does a killing become an outrage? When does an atrocity become a massacre? Or, put another way, how many killings make a massacre? Thirty? A hundred? Three hundred? When is a massacre not a massacre? When the figures are too low? Or when the massacre is carried out by Israel's friends rather than Israel's enemies?

That, I suspected, was what this argument was about. If Syrian troops had crossed into Israel, surrounded a kibbutz and allowed their Palestinian allies to slaughter the Jewish inhabitants, no Western news agency would waste its time afterwards arguing about whether or not it should be called a massacre.

But in Beirut, the victims were Palestinians. The guilty were certainly Christian militiamen—from which particular unit we were still unsure—but the Israelis were also guilty. If the Israelis had not taken part in the killings, they had certainly sent the militia into the camp. They had trained them, given them uniforms, handed them US army rations and Israeli medical equipment. Then they had watched the murderers in the camps, they had given them military assistance— the Israeli air force had dropped all those flares to help the men who were murdering the inhabitants of Sabra and Chatila—and they had established military liaison with the murderers in the camps.

All this we knew by late Saturday afternoon, but Hindy still debated whether this had been a massacre.

'Go and look for yourself,' Foley kept shouting. He held up picture after picture of corpses, the bodies locked in each other's arms. 'Look at this.' A picture of a baby with its brains missing. 'Look at this.' A woman with a bullet through her breast. 'And this, and this . . .' Foley was intense, passionate, like a man trying to sell dirty pictures to an unwilling customer at the seaside. 'For Christ's sake, Steve, it was a massacre, a *massacre*!'

I went home. I felt ill, sick because of the smell of my clothes, and I showered for more than an hour but could not shake off the stench. Four hours after I had gone to bed, I woke up sweating and nauseated, convinced that the corpses of Chatila were piled on the sheets and blankets round me, that I was actually lying between the bodies, that they were all in the room, even old Mr Nouri. I could *smell* them still, in my own home. In the morning, my cleaning lady Ayesha refused to wash my clothes. 'Please burn them, Mr Robert. They are not good.' By the following day, Chatila had become infamous. It was peopled with reporters and camera crews and diplomats. For the first time since the massacre, the living outnumbered the dead. And as the bodies lay in the heat, they expanded, contorted into shapes beyond imagination, bloated so much that belts and the straps of wristwatches cut brutally into the decaying flesh. They bubbled, cooked in the sun noisily and emitted trails of black, oily liquid that ran from the execution walls.

from # Zinky Boys
by Svetlana Alexievich

The Soviet Union's 1979 invasion of Afghanistan led to ten

years of slaughter and contributed to the fall of the Soviet

empire. The soldiers inflicted and endured horrible suf-

fering. Some 50,000 of them went home in sealed zinc

coffins, as the government did its best to hide the war from

its citizens. Byelorussian journalist Svetlana Alexievich inter-

viewed veterans and their families for her 1991 book.

1st Lieutenant i/c Mortar Platoon

I have the same dream every night. It's like watching a film over and over again. Everyone's running and firing, including me. I fall down and wake up and I'm on a hospital bed. I start to get up to go and have a smoke in the corridor. Then I realise my legs have gone and I'm back in the real world . . .

I don't want to hear any talk about a 'political mistake', OK? Give me my legs back if it was really a mistake.

Have you taken unfinished letters from soldiers' pockets . . . 'Dear Mama . . .', 'My Darling . . .'? Have you seen soldiers shot to pieces by old blunderbusses and modern Chinese machine-guns at the same time?

We were sent to Afghanistan to obey orders. In the army you obey orders first and then, if you like, discuss their merits—when it's all over. 'Go!' means exactly that. If you refuse you get thrown out of the party. You took the military oath, didn't you? And back home, when you ask the local party committee for something you need, they tell you, 'It wasn't us that sent you!' Well, who did send us?

I had a friend out there. When I went into action he always said goodbye to me and hugged me when I came back alive. I'll never find a friend like that here at home.

I hardly ever go out now. I'm ashamed . . .

Have you ever tried our Soviet-manufactured prostheses? I've heard that abroad people with artificial limbs go skiing, play tennis and dance. Why don't the authorities use foreign currency to buy decent arms and legs instead of wasting it on French cosmetics, subsidised Cuban sugar or Moroccan oranges?

I'm twenty-two, with my whole life in front of me. I need to find a wife. I had a girlfriend. 'I hate you,' I told her, to make her leave me. She pitied me, when what I wanted was her love.

> 'I dreamt of home, of nights I lay
> Listening to the rowans sigh.
> "Cuckoo, cuckoo, tell me pray
> How many years before I die. . . ?" '

That was my favourite song. I used to go into the forest, and ask the cuckoo, and count his calls, but now—sometimes I don't want to go on living one day longer.

I still long to see that landscape again, that biblical desert. We all have that yearning, it's like standing at the edge of a precipice, or high over water, and looking down until your head spins.

Now the war's over they're trying to forget all about us, or else hide us out of sight. They treated the veterans of the war with Finland the same way.[*] Thousands of books have been published about World

---

[*] The 'Winter War' of 1939–40, about which the Soviet public was, until very recently, permitted to know almost nothing.

War II but not one about the Finnish war. Our people are too easy on their rulers—and I'll have accepted it myself in ten years or so.

Did I kill anybody in Afghanistan? Yes. You didn't send us over there to be angels—so how can you expect us to come back as angels?

It took me six days by train to get to Moscow from Khabarovsk. We crossed the whole of Russia via the Siberian rivers and Lake Baikal. The railway attendant in charge of the tea-urn ran out of tea on the very first day; the water-boiler broke down the day after that. My family met me in Moscow, there were tears all round, but duty came first.

I got off the plane and saw the kind of blue sky that in our country you find only over rivers. There was a lot of noise and shouting—but all of it from our own people. There were new recruits being met, old friends seen off, and packages from home picked up. Everyone looked tanned and cheerful. Hard to believe that somewhere out there it was 30° Celsius below freezing and armour-plating was cracking from cold. I saw my first Afghan through the barbed wire of the clearing-compound. I remember having no particular feelings (apart from a mild curiosity) towards this 'foreigner'.

I was posted to Bagram to take command of the road-engineers' platoon in a sapper battalion.

We lived a regular routine of getting up early and reporting for work. We had a mine-sweeper tank, a sniper unit, a mine-detecting dog, and two APCs to provide protection. We covered the first few miles in the armoured vehicles, just as long as the tracks of previous vehicles were clearly visible on the road. Dust covered everything like a fine powdery snow. If a bird landed on it you could see the traces. If a tank had passed that way the day before, though, special care was needed, because the caterpillar tracks could be concealing a mine. After planting the device the mujahedin would recreate the tracks with their fingers and clear their own footprints using a bag or an unrolled turban.

The road wound past two abandoned villages of smouldering mud huts—perfect cover for enemy snipers, so we needed to be extra-vigilant. Once we were past the villages we'd get out of the vehicles. This was the procedure: the dog ran zigzagging in front of us, followed by the sappers with their probing rods poking the soil as they went. All you had going for you was God, your sixth sense, experience and flair. You might notice a broken branch, or a bit of rusty iron, or a rock, which hadn't been there the day before. The muj would leave little markers like that to avoid getting blown up themselves.

That bit of iron, now, was it there by chance or was there a battery under the sand, connected to a bomb or a crate of TNT? A man's weight won't trigger an anti-tank mine—it needs a 250–300 kilo load to set it off.

After my first explosion I was the only man left sitting on our tank. All the others got blown off. My place was by the barrel so I was protected from the full force of the blast by the gun turret. I quickly checked my arms, legs and head were all where they should be. We picked ourselves up and carried on.

We set off another blast a little further on. The lightly armed trailer-tractor was blown up and split in two by a powerful *fougasse*, or land-mine, which left a crater three metres long and as deep as a tall man. The tractor was transporting mines, about 200 mortars—they were thrown into the branches and on to the side of the road like a giant fan. We lost all five soldiers and the lieutenant on the tractor. I'd spent the past few evenings with them, talking and smoking and now they were literally blown to pieces. We went and collected them up, including a dust-covered head, so completely squashed it looked as though there wasn't any bone.

We filled five crates and divided them so that there would be something of each man to be sent home.

The dogs were a tremendous asset. They're just like people, some gifted with intuition, others not. A sentry might doze, but a dog— never. I was very fond of one called Toby. He'd snuggle up to us but bark at our Afghan National Army allies! Admittedly, their khaki was a bit greener, and ours rather yellowish, but still, how could he tell the difference? He could sense a mine at several paces. He'd stop dead with his tail sticking up straight, as if to say: KEEP OFF!

No two mine-traps are the same, but the worst are the homemade devices which never repeat themselves exactly. They might be hidden in a rusty tea-kettle, or a tape-recorder, watch, or can. Units who went out without sappers were known as 'suicide squads'. Mines were everywhere, on mountain paths, on the roads and in houses. It was always the sappers who went in first.

We were checking out a trench one day. There'd already been one explosion and we'd spent two days raking it through. I jumped down into it and—BANG!

I didn't pass out—I looked up at the sky, which seemed to be on fire. A sapper's first reaction after a blast is to look upwards to check that his eyes are intact. I kept a tourniquet on my gun-butt which they used to bandage me above the knees. But I knew that limbs are always amputated three to five centimetres above the wound.

'Where are you tying it?' I shouted at the medic.

'You've lost them both up to the knee, sir.'

The field hospital was fifteen kilometres away and it took them 1 1/2 hours to get me there. There my wounds were sterilised and I was given novocaine to kill the pain. My legs were amputated the same day; I lost consciousness only when I heard the saw, it sounded like a circular saw. The following day they operated on my eyes. The flame from the blast had seared my face—the surgeons practically darned my eyes and gave me twenty-two stitches. Only two or three a day could be removed—otherwise the eyeball would have fallen to bits. They'd shine a torch into my eyes, left and right, to find out whether I reacted to light and whether the retina was intact.

I'll never forget the red beam of that torch.

I'd like to write a book about the way an officer can be reduced to a housebound wreck, earning his bread assembling lamp-sockets and wall-plugs, about a hundred a day, or putting the metal bits on the ends of shoelaces. What colour shoelaces? Red, black, or white, he never knows, because he can't see; he's been officially declared totally blind. He ties string-bags, and glues little boxes—the sort of work he used to think only lunatics did. Thirty bags a day and I've reached my daily target, my 'norm'.

Sappers were the least likely of all to come back intact, or even alive, particularly the specialised mine-clearing units. They were all either dead or wounded. Out of habit, we never shook hands before going into action. The day of that last explosion our new CO shook my hand, out of sheer friendliness—no one had warned him. And I got blown up . . . Was it just superstition? Who knows? There was another belief: if you'd volunteered for Afghanistan you'd end up dead, but if you were just posted there you might get home alive.

That was five years ago. I still have this dream. I'm in a long mine-field. I've drawn up a plan, based on the number of mines and the number of rows, and markers to find them by. But I've lost the plan. (In fact we often did lose them, or else the marker was a tree which had been destroyed, or a pile of stones which had been blown up. Nobody wanted to go and check, and risk getting blown up by our own mines.) In my dream I see children running near the mine-field, they don't know there are mines there. I want to shout: 'Stop! Mines!' I want to warn the children. I want to warn the children . . . I'm running . . . I have both my legs back, and I can see, my eyes can see again . . . But that's only at night, only in my dream. Then I wake up.

Private, Intelligence Corps
We arrived at the Samarkand conscript reception-centre. There were two tents: in one we had to get out of our civvies (those of us with any sense had already sold our jackets and sweater and bought a bottle of wine with the proceeds); in the other we were issued with well-used uniforms, including shirts dating from 1945, *kirzachi* and foot-bindings.[*] Show those *kirzachi* to an African, who's lived with heat all his life, and he'd faint! Yes, even in Third World African countries soldiers are issued with lightweight boots, trousers and caps, but we were expected to do heavy building work—and sing as we worked!—in 40 degrees Celsius while our feet were literally cooking.

---

[*]*Kirzachi:* heavy, multi-layered waterproof boots of substitute leather. Foot-bindings are used in the Soviet Army instead of socks.

The first week we worked in a refrigeration plant, loading and unloading bottles of lemonade. Then we were sent to work on officers' homes—I did all the bricklaying for one of them. We spent a fortnight putting a roof on a pigsty. For every three slates we used we exchanged two others for vodka; the timber we sold by length, at a rouble a metre.

In that Samarkand training-camp we had just two periods on the firing-range: the first time, we were issued with nine rounds, the second, we got to throw a grenade each. Then we were lined up on the parade-ground and read the Order of the Day: we were being sent to the DRA 'in the execution of our international duty'. Anybody who doesn't wish to go—two paces forward—march! Three boys stepped out, but the CO kicked them back again. 'I was just testing your battle-readiness,' he said. We were issued with two days' dry rations and a leather belt—and off we went, all of us.

The flight seemed long, and we were subdued. I looked out of the window and saw those beautiful mountains. I'd never seen mountains before—I'm from Pskov, which is all meadows and forest. We landed at Shindanta: I still remember the date: 19 December 1980.

They looked me up and down: 'Six foot four, eh? Reconnaissance can do with boys like you.'

From Shindanta we drove to Gerat. We were put to work building again. We built a firing-range from scratch, digging the earth and clearing it of rocks. I built a slate roof and did some carpentry. Some of the boys never got to fire a weapon before their first taste of action.

We were hungry every minute of the day. There were two 20-gallon drums in the kitchen, one for the first course, a watery cabbage-soup without a scrap of meat, and one for the second course, a gooey paste of dried potato mash or pearl barley, also without meat. Oh, and canned mackerel, one tin between four of us. The label said: 'Year of manufacture: 1956. Consume within 18 months.' In my year and a half in Afghanistan I stopped being hungry only once, when I was wounded. You were looking for ways to get or steal food the whole time. We climbed into the Afghans' orchards and gardens, even though they shot at us and laid mines to blow us up with. We were desperate for apples, pears, fruit of any kind. I asked my parents to send me citric acid, which they did. We dissolved it in water and drank it. It was nice and sour and burnt your stomach.

We sang the Soviet national anthem before we went into action for the first time. I was a speed-cyclist before the army, and built up such big muscles that people were scared of me and left me alone. I'd never even *seen* a fight, or a knife used in anger, or blood. Suddenly there we were, going into battle in an APC. We'd driven from Shindanta to Gerat by bus, and been out of barracks once, in a truck. Now, riding on top of this armoured carrier, weapon in hand, sleeves rolled up to the elbow, well, it was a completely new and strange feeling. A sense of power and strength, and a certainty that no one and nothing could hurt us.

The villages seemed so low, the irrigation canals looked tiny, the trees few and far between. In half an hour we were so confident we felt like tourists. It all seemed so exotic—the birds, the trees, the flowers. I saw those thornbushes for the first time in my life. We forgot all about war.

We crossed a canal by a mud bridge which I was amazed could take all those tons of metal. Suddenly—BANG! The leading APC had caught a direct hit from a grenade-launcher. Pals of mine were being carried away, their heads blown off like cardboard targets, hands hanging down lifelessly. My mind couldn't take in this new and terrible world.

Command: 'Deploy mortars!'—with their 120 shells a minute. We fired every one of them into the village where the attack had come from, which meant several into every single house. After it was all over we collected up our boys in bits and pieces, even scraping them from the sides of the APC. We spread out a tarpaulin, their common grave, to try and sort out which leg or fragment of skull belonged to whom. We weren't issued with identification tags because of the 'danger' of them falling into enemy hands. This was an undeclared war, you see— we were fighting a war which wasn't happening.

We were very quiet on the way home from this new world. We had something to eat and cleaned our weapons.

'Want a joint?' one of the older guys asked me.

'No thanks.'

I didn't want to start on all that in case I didn't have the willpower to give it up. After a while, though, we all smoked—it was the only way to keep going. They should have let us have a quarter of a pint of vodka a day, like in World War II, but this was a 'dry' country. Somehow or other you had to unwind, to blot it all out. We'd put it in the rice or porridge. Your pupils got as big as saucers, you could see like a cat in the dark and you felt as light as a bat.

Recce men kill at close quarters rather than in set-piece battles and silently, with a stiletto or bayonet, almost never a gun. I soon got used to it.

My first? You mean the first guy I killed close up? We'd approached a village, I looked through the night-vision binoculars and saw a little lantern, and a rifle, and this guy digging something up. I handed my gun to my mate and got up close enough to jump him to the ground. I stuffed his turban in his mouth to stop him shouting out. The only knife I had on me was a pen-knife used to cut bread and open cans with, an ordinary little knife. As he lay there on the ground I grabbed him by the beard, pulled it up and slit his throat. The skin of his neck went taut, which made it a lot easier. There was a lot of blood.

I was usually put in charge of our night raids. We'd crouch behind a tree, knives at the ready, watching as they went past, with a scout in front. It was our job to kill him. We took turns to do it. If it was my turn I'd let him get a little bit past me and then jump him from behind. The main thing is to grab the throat with your left hand and throttle him to keep him quiet as you stick the knife into him with your right. Right through, under his liver. I used a knife I picked up from one of them, a Japanese job with a blade over a foot long which cut like it was going through butter. There'd be a quick twitch and he'd be dead without a squeak.

You soon got used to it. It was less a psychological problem than the technical challenge of actually finding the upper vertebrae, heart or liver. We learnt karate, immobilisation techniques and how to kill with our bare hands.

Only once something snapped inside me and I was struck by the horror of what we were doing. We were combing through a village. You fling open the door and throw in a grenade in case there's a machine-gun waiting for you. Why take a risk if a grenade can sort it out for you? I threw the grenade, went in and saw women, two little boys and a baby in some kind of box making do for a cot.

You have to find some kind of justification to stop yourself going mad. Suppose it's true that the souls of the dead look down on us from above?

I got back home and tried to be good, but sometimes I have a desire to cut the odd throat. I came home blind. A bullet went in one temple, came out the other and destroyed both retinas. I can only distinguish light and dark but that doesn't stop me recognising the people whose throats I'd like to cut: the ones who won't pay for gravestones for our lads, the ones who won't give us flats ('It wasn't us who sent you to Afghanistan'), the ones who try and wash their hands of us. What happened to me is still boiling inside. Do I want to have my past taken away from me? No! It's what I live by.

I learnt to walk without my eyes. I get around the city, using the metro and the pedestrian crossings, on my own. I do the cooking—in fact my wife admits I cook better than she does. I've never seen my wife but I know what she looks like, the colour of her hair, the shape of her nose and her lips. I feel everything with my hands and body, which see everything. I know what my son looks like. I used to change his nappies, did his washing, and now I carry him around on my shoulders.

Sometimes I think we don't need our eyes—after all, you close them anyhow when the most important things are going on, and when you're feeling really good. A painter needs his eyes because that's the way he earns his living, but I've learnt to live without them. I *sense* my world now, and words mean more to me than they do to you sighted people.

A lot of people seem to think I'm a man with a great future behind me. 'You've had it, boy!' Like Yuri Gagarin after that first space flight. But they're wrong: the most important part of my life is still to come. I'm convinced of it.

Your body is no more important than a bicycle, say, and I should know—I was a professional cyclist. Your body's an instrument, a machine to work with, that's all. I realise now I can find happiness and freedom without my eyes. Look how many sighted people can't see. I was more blind when I had my sight.

I'd like to cleanse myself of everything that's happened, of all the dirt they shoved us into. It's only our mothers who can understand and protect us now.

You don't know how terrified I get at night, jumping a man with my knife, over and over again. And yet it's only in my dreams I can be a child again, a child who isn't afraid of blood because he doesn't know what it means and thinks it's just red water. Children are natural experimenters, they want to take everything to bits to find out how it's made. But blood frightens me, even in my dreams.

A Mother

I rush to the cemetery as though I'm meeting someone here—and I am, I'm going to meet my son. I spent the first few nights here on my own and never felt a moment's fear. I know all the birds' little habits, and how the grass moves in the wind. In spring I wait for his flowers to grow up, out of the earth, towards me. I planted snowdrops, so that I'd have an early hello from my son to look forward to. They come to me from down there, from him . . .

I sit with him until nightfall. Sometimes I give a sort of scream, which I don't hear until the birds fly up around me. A storm of crows swirls and flaps over my head until I fall silent. I've come here every day for four years, morning or evening, except when I had my heart attack and couldn't come for eleven days. I wasn't allowed to get up, but eventually I did anyway. I managed to get to the toilet on my own, which meant I could escape to my son, even if I collapsed on his grave. I ran away in my hospital nightie.

Before that I had a dream in which Valera said to me, 'Don't come to the cemetery tomorrow, Mama. It isn't necessary.'

But I raced here and found the grave as silent as if he weren't here.

He'd gone, I felt in my heart. The crows sat quietly on the gravestone and railing instead of flying away from me as they usually did. I got up from the bench and they flew up in front of me, agitated, stopping me from going to the grave. What was going on? What were they trying to warn me about? They settled down and flew up to the trees; only then did I feel myself drawn to the graveside once again. A sense of deep peace descended and the turbulence left my soul. His spirit had returned. 'Thank you, my little birds, for telling me not to go away. I waited until he came back.'

I feel ill at ease and alone when I'm with other people. I don't belong any more. People talk to me and pester me with this and that. I feel better here with my son. If I'm not at work I'm usually here. To me it's not a grave but his home.

I worked out where his head is; I sit nearby and tell him everything about my everyday life. We share our memories. I look at his photograph. If I stare at it deep and long he either smiles at me or frowns a little bit crossly. We're still together, you see. If I buy a new dress it's only for me to come and see him in and for him to see me in. He used to kneel in front of me and now I kneel in front of him.

I always open this little gate in the railing here and get down on my knees. 'Good morning, my dear . . . Good evening, dear . . .' I say. I'm always with him.

I wanted to adopt a little boy from the children's home, someone like Valera, but my heart isn't strong enough.

I force myself to keep busy; it's like pushing myself into a dark tunnel. I'd go mad if I let myself sit in the kitchen and gaze out of the window. Only my own suffering can save me from madness. I haven't been to the cinema once in these four years. I sold the colour television and spent the money on the gravestone. I haven't switched the radio on. When my son was killed everything changed, my face, my eyes, even my hands.

I fell madly in love with my husband and just leapt into marriage! He was a pilot, tall and handsome in his leather jacket and flying boots. Was this beautiful bear of a man really my husband? The other girls sighed with envy! I was so tiny next to him, and I got so cross that our great shoe industry couldn't produce a smart pair of high-heels to fit me! I used to long for him to get a cough or cold so I could have him at home and look after him all day.

I desperately wanted a son, a son like him, with the same eyes, the same ears and the same nose. And heaven must have heard my prayer— the baby was the spitting image of his father. I couldn't believe I had two such wonderful men, I just couldn't believe it. I loved my home, even the washing and ironing. I was so in love with everything that I wouldn't step on a spider or a ladybird or a fly, but carry them gently to the window and let them fly away. I wanted everything to live and love as joyfully as I did. When I came home from work I'd ring the bell and turn the light on in the hall so that Valera could see my happiness.

'Lerunka!' I'd call. (That was my name for him when he was a boy.) 'I'm home! I've miiiissed youououou!' Out of breath from running back from work or the shops.

I loved my son to distraction, just as I do now. I was brought photographs of the funeral but I wouldn't take them, I couldn't believe it. I was like a faithful dog, dying on his master's grave. I always was a loyal friend.

One time I remember, when I was still breast-feeding him, my breasts were bursting with milk, but I'd arranged to meet a friend of mine to give her a book she wanted. I waited for an hour and a half in the snow but she never came. Something must have happened, I thought, you don't just promise to come and simply not turn up. I ran to her home and found her asleep. She couldn't understand why I burst into tears. I loved her, too—I gave her my favourite dress, the light blue. That's the way I am.

I was very shy when I was young and never believed anyone could love me, and if a boy said I was beautiful I didn't believe that either. But when I did finally launch myself into life I brimmed over with excitement and enthusiasm. After Yuri Gagarin made that first flight into space Lerunka and I were shouting and jumping for sheer joy in the street. I was ready to love and embrace everyone on earth at that moment . . .

I loved my son to distraction. And he loved me back the same way. His grave draws me as though I hear him calling.

'Have you got a girlfriend?' his army pals asked him

'Yes,' he said, and showed them my old student card with a photo of me in long, long curls.

He loved waltzing. He asked me to dance the first waltz at his graduation ball. I didn't even know he could dance—he'd had lessons without telling me. We went round and round and round . . .

I used to sit by the window in the evening, knitting and waiting for him. I'd hear steps . . . no, not him. Then more steps, yes, 'mine' this time, my son was home. I never guessed wrong, not once. We'd sit down in the kitchen and chat until four in the morning. What did we talk about? About everything people do talk about when they're happy, serious matters and nonsense too. We'd laugh and he'd sing and play the piano for me.

I'd look at the clock.

'Time for bed, Valera.'

'Let's sit here a bit longer, mother of mine,' he'd say. That's what he called me, 'mother of mine', or 'golden mother of mine'.

'Well, mother of mine, your son has got in to the Smolensk Military Academy. Are you pleased?' he told me one day.

He'd sit at the piano and sing:

'My fellow officers—my lords!
I shan't be the first or the last
To perish on enemy swords.'

My father was a professional officer who was killed in the siege of Leningrad, and my grandfather was an officer, too, so in his height, strength and bearing my son was born to be a soldier. He'd have made a wonderful hussar, playing bridge in his white gloves. 'My old soldier'— I used to call him. If only I'd had the tiniest hint from heaven . . .

Everyone copied him, me included. I'd sit at the piano just like him, sometimes I even caught myself walking like him, especially after his death. I so desperately wanted him to live on inside me.

'Well, mother of mine, your son will soon be off!'

'Where to?' He said nothing. I started to cry. 'Where are you being sent, my darling?'

'What do you mean "where"? We know very well where. Now then, golden mother of mine, to work! Into the kitchen—the guests'll soon be here!'

I guessed immediately: 'Afghanistan?'

'Correct,' he said, and his look warned me to go no further. An iron curtain fell between us.

His friend Kolka Romanov rushed in soon after. Kolka, who could never keep anything to himself, told me that they'd applied to be posted to Afghanistan even though they were only in their third year.

The first toast: 'Nothing venture, nothing gain!'

All evening Valera sang my favourite song:

'My fellow officers—my lords!
I shan't be the first or the last
To perish on enemy swords.'

There were four weeks left. Every morning I'd go to his room and sit and watch him while he slept. Even asleep he was beautiful.

I had a dream, a warning as clear as a knock at the door. I was in a long black dress, holding on to a black cross carried by an angel. I began to lose my grip and looked down to see whether I would fall into the sea or on to dry land, and saw a sunlit crater.

I waited for him to come home on leave. For a long time he didn't write, then one day the phone rang at work.

'I'm back, mother of mine! Don't be late home! I've made some soup.'

'My darling boy!' I shouted. 'You're not phoning from Tashkent, are you? You're home? Your favourite bortsch is in the fridge!'

'Oh no! I saw the saucepan but didn't lift the lid.'

'What soup have you made, then?'

'It's called "idiot's delight"! Come home now and I'll meet you at the bus stop!'

He'd gone grey. He wouldn't admit that he was home on hospital leave. 'I just wanted to see that golden mother of mine for a couple of days,' he insisted. My daughter told me later how she'd seen him rolling on the carpet, sobbing with pain. He had malaria, hepatitis and other things, too, but he ordered his sister not to say a word to me.

I started going to his room in the morning again, to watch him sleeping.

Once he opened his eyes: 'What's up, mother of mine?'

'Go back to sleep, darling, it's still early.'

'I had a nightmare.'

'Just turn over, go back to sleep, and you'll have a good dream. And if you never tell your bad ones they won't come true.'

When his leave was over we went with him as far as Moscow. They were lovely sunny days with the marigolds in bloom.

'What's it like out there, Valera?'

'Afghanistan, mother of mine, is something we should definitely not be doing.' He looked at me and at no one else as he said it. He wiped the sweat from his brow and embraced me. 'I don't want to go back to that hell, I really don't,' he said, and moved away. He looked round one last time. 'That's all, Mama.'

He had never, ever called me 'Mama', always 'mother of mine'. As I say, it was a beautiful sunny day and the marigolds were in bloom. The girl at the airport desk was watching us and started crying.

On the 7th of July I woke up dry-eyed. I stared sightlessly at the ceiling. He'd woken me, he'd come to say goodbye. It was eight o'clock and I had to go to work. I wandered round the flat, I couldn't find my white dress for some reason. I felt dizzy and couldn't see a thing. It wasn't until lunchtime that I calmed down.

On the 7th of July . . . Seven cigarettes and seven matches in my pocket, seven pictures taken on the film in my camera. He'd written seven letters to me, and seven to his fiancée. The book on my bedside table, open at page seven, was Kobo Abe's *Containers of Death* . . .

He had three or four seconds to save his life as his APC was crashing into a ravine: 'Out you jump, boys! I'll go last'. He could never have put himself first.

'From Major S. R. Sinelnikov: In execution of my military duty I am obliged to inform you that 1st Lieutenant Valery Gennadevich Volovich was killed today at 10.45 a.m. . . .'

The whole town knew. His photograph in the Officers' Club was already hung with black crepe, and the aeroplane would soon be landing with his coffin. But no one told me, no one dared . . . At work everyone around me seemed to be in tears and gave me various excuses when I asked what was wrong. My friend looked in at me through my door. Then our doctor came in.

It was like suddenly waking from a deep sleep. 'Are you mad, all of you? Boys like him don't get killed!' I protested. I started hitting the table with my hand, then ran to the window and beat the glass. They gave me an injection. 'Are you mad, all of you? Have you gone crazy?'

Another injection. Neither of them had any effect. Apparently I shouted, 'I want to see him. Take me to my son!'

'Take her, take her, or she won't survive the shock.'

It was a long coffin, with VOLOVICH painted in yellow on the rough wood. I tried to lift the coffin to take it home with me. My bladder ruptured.

I wanted a good dry plot in the cemetery. Fifty roubles? I'll pay the 50 roubles. Just make sure it's a nice dry plot. I knew it was a swindle but I couldn't object. I spent the first few nights here with him. I was taken home but came back again. It was harvest-time and I remember the whole town, and the cemetery too, smelt of hay.

In the morning a soldier came up to me. 'Good morning, mother.' Yes, he called me 'mother'. 'Your son was my commanding officer. I would like to tell you about him.'

'Come home, with me, son.'

He sat in Valera's chair, opened his mouth and changed his mind. 'I can't, mother.'

When I come to the grave I always bow to him, and I bow to him again when I leave. I'm only home if people are coming. I feel fine here with my son. Ice and snow don't bother me. I write letters here. I go home when it's dark. I like the street-lights and the car headlights. I'm not frightened of man or beast. I feel strong.

'I don't want to go back to that hell.' I can't get those words of his out of my mind. Who is to answer for all this? Should anyone be made to? I'm going to do my best to live as long as possible. There's nothing more vulnerable about a person than his grave. It's his name. I shall protect my son for ever . . .

His comrades come to visit him. One of them went on his knees. 'Valera, I'm covered in blood. I killed with my bare hands. Is it better to be alive or dead? I don't know any more . . .'

I want to know who is to answer for all this. Why do they keep silent? Why don't they name names and take them to court?

> 'My fellow officers—my lords!
> I shan't be the first or the last
> To perish on enemy swords'

I went to church to speak to the priest. 'My son has been killed. He was unique and I loved him. What should I do now? Tell me our old Russian traditions. We've forgotten them and now I need to know.'

'Was he baptised?'

'I so much wish I could say he was, Father, but I cannot. I was a young officer's wife. We were stationed in Kamchatka, surrounded by snow all year round—our home was a snow dugout. Here the snow is white, but there it's blue and green and mother-of-pearl. Endless empty space where every sound travels for miles. Do you understand me, Father?'

'It is not good that he wasn't baptised, mother Victoria. Our prayers will not reach him.'

'Then I'll baptise him now!' I burst out. 'With my love and my pain. Yes, I'll baptise him in pain.'

He took my shaking hand.

'You must not upset yourself, mother Victoria. How often do you go to your son?'

'Every day. Why not? If he were alive we'd see each other every day.'

'Mother Victoria, you must not disturb him after five o'clock in the afternoon. They go to their rest at that time.'

'But I'm at work until five, and after that I have a part-time job. I had to borrow 2,500 roubles for a new gravestone and I've got to pay it back.'

'Listen to me, mother Victoria. You must go to him every day at noon, for the midday service. Then he will hear your prayers.'

Send me the worst imaginable pain and torture, only let my prayers reach my dearest love. I greet every little flower, every tiny stem growing from his grave: 'Are you from there? Are you from him? Are you from my son?'

from Soldiers of God
by Robert D. Kaplan

*Robert Kaplan's 1990 book describes the brutality of the
Soviet invasion of Afghanistan and the courage of the
Afghan guerillas who opposed it.*

A mputations were the most common form of surgery in
Afghanistan in the 1980s. A West German doctor, Frank
Paulin, traveled around Nangarhar province in April 1985,
cutting off the limbs of mine victims with a survival knife.
"Sometimes I'd use a saw, basically anything I could get my hands on,"
he recollected. The only anesthetic that Paulin had available for his
patients was ordinary barbiturates. Some of the patients died, but the
ones who survived wouldn't have had a chance without him. Radio
Moscow accused Paulin by name of being a "CIA spy." While being
hunted by Soviet troops, he contracted cholera and had to be carried
on the back of a mule over a fourteen-thousand-foot mountain pass to
safety in Pakistan. Paulin had only one fear: that he too would step on
a mine.

An Afghan who stepped on a mine frequently died of shock and loss of blood a few feet from the explosion. More often, he was carried by a relative or friend to a primitive medical outpost run by someone like Paulin. If the victim was really lucky, he made it to a Red Cross hospital in Quetta or Peshawar over the border in Pakistan—antiseptic sanctuaries of Western medicine where emergency surgery was conducted around the clock.

I remember a Scottish surgeon at one of these hospitals who had just come off a long shift and needed to talk and get a little drunk. In the bar at Peshawar's American Club, he sat at a table with me and two other journalists and recited from memory several stanzas of Rudyard Kipling's poem "The Ballad of East and West" in a deliberately loud and passionate voice, as if to demonstrate that he didn't give a damn what people thought of him:

"Kamal is out with twenty men to raise the Border-side,
And he has lifted the Colonel's mare that is the Colonel's
     pride.
He has lifted her out of the stable-door between the dawn
     and the day,
And turned the calkins upon her feet, and ridden her far
     away."

At the table there was an embarrassed silence. Then the surgeon talked about what was really on his mind. "The philosophy of war is truly sinister," he said in a hushed tone. "Now, you take the Russians. Most of the mines they've laid are designed to maim, not kill, because a dead body causes no inconvenience. It only removes the one dead person from the field. But somebody who is wounded and in pain requires the full-time assistance of several people all down the line who could otherwise be fighting. And if you want to depopulate an area, then you want many of the casualties to be small children. The most stubborn peasants will give up and flee when their children are mutilated."

These were old facts that left everyone at the table numb. In

Peshawar the journalists and relief workers all knew these things. But the surgeon had discovered them on his own in the lonely, pulsing stillness of the operating theater, where he was in constant physical contact with the evidence. When he recited Kipling's poetry it showed all over his face.

"The future battlefield is to be liberally sown with mines," wrote the British military historian John Keegan in his prophetic work *The Face of Battle.* Never before in history have mines played such an important role in a war as in Afghanistan. Nobody knows precisely how many were sown by Soviet troops and airmen in the ten years between their invasion and their withdrawal. The figures offered are biblical. The British Broadcasting Corporation, on June 8, 1988, simply stated "millions." The Afghan resistance claimed five million. The U.S. government's first estimate was three million. Later, on August 15, 1988, State Department spokesman Charles Redmon said the figure was more likely "between 10 and 30 million." That would be 2 mines for every Afghan who survived the war; between 40 and 120 mines per square mile of Afghan territory. Tens of thousands of civilians, if not more — many of them small children—have already been disabled by mine detonations in Afghanistan. Even though the Russian phase of the war has ended, mines threaten to kill and maim thousands more, some of whom haven't been born yet.

"The widespread sowing of millions of land mines has added an ominous new dimension to the rehabilitation effort," Undersecretary of State Michael H. Armacost told the Senate Foreign Relations Committee on June 23, 1988. According to both American and United Nations officials, mines will cripple Afghanistan's economic life for years to come, inhibiting the tilling of fields, access to pasture areas, and collection of firewood.

No group of people knew as much about mines in Afghanistan as news photographers and television cameramen. Getting close-ups of the war meant traveling with the mujahidin, the "holy warriors of Islam." And the muj—as journalists called them—walked through minefields. "It's like walking a tightrope," said Tony O'Brien, a freelance photographer who would later be captured and then released by Afghan regime forces. "You're in a group, yet you're totally alone. Still, there's this absolutely incredible bond with the person ahead of you and behind you. You forget the heat, the thirst, the diarrhea. Then you're out of the minefield and instantaneously you're hot and thirsty again. The minute I start thinking about it I start worrying and I get totally freaked."

For several days I rode in a Toyota Land Cruiser through the mine-strewn desert outside the southern Afghan city of Kandahar. The trails were marked with the rusted carcasses of trucks that told you it was almost better not to survive such an explosion. My driver kept safely to previous tread marks. But when another vehicle approached from the opposite direction we had to make room for each other, and I became so afraid that I held my breath just to keep from whimpering. At night, or in the frequent dust storms when we lost the track, the fear went on for hours at a stretch, leaving me physically sick.

Joe Gaal, a Canadian photographer for the Associated Press, had been around so many minefields and had collected enough fragments of different mines that he had developed a sapper's tactile intuition about them, which was apparent in the movements of his hands and fingers whenever we discussed the matter. An intense, gutsy fellow, Gaal had an encyclopedic knowledge of Soviet mines. His terror had turned into an obsession.

The mine that could really put him in a cold sweat was what the mujahidin called a "jumping" mine, a Russian version of the "Bouncing Betty," used by the Americans in Vietnam. It is activated by a trip wire that causes a projectile to shoot up from underground a few feet ahead. The mine is designed to go off several seconds later and explode at waist level, just as you pass over it. "It blows off your genitals and peppers your guts with shrapnel," Gaal explained.

The Bouncing Betty was one of several different antipersonnel mines the Soviets employed, mines that had to be dug into the ground by special units and were meant to kill or maim anyone within a radius of twenty feet. But the vast majority of mines in Afghanistan were dropped from the air. The most common of these was the "butterfly" mine. The butterfly was *the* mine of Afghanistan, so much so that it had become part of the country's landscape, like the white flags above the graves of martyred mujahidin. Soviet helicopter gunships would fly in at one or two thousand feet and litter the ground with mines. The butterfly's winged shape caused it to go into a spin, slowing its descent. The detonator pin was set on impact with the ground. Green was the most common color, but the Soviets had a light brown version for desert areas and a gray one for riverbeds. Some mujahidin, not knowing this, thought the mines actually changed color.

Only eight inches long and blending in with the ground, the butterfly mine was hard to spot, especially if you were fatigued from hours of walking, which was most of the time. Except for the light aluminum detonator it was all plastic, so it was difficult to detect with mine-sweeping equipment. The mine was often mistaken for a toy by Afghan children, who paid with the loss of a limb or an eye. Its explosive power was about equal to that of the smallest hand grenade: sufficient to maim, not to kill. Contrary to Soviet claims, the mine has no self-destruct mechanism, and will be mutilating Afghans for a long time to come.

Butterfly mines, along with aerial bombardment, were the centerpiece of Moscow's strategy of depopulation. Depopulation had come after pacification had failed and before the Communist-inspired bombing campaign in Pakistani cities. During the heyday of depopulation, in the early and mid-1980s, the Soviets dropped plastic mines disguised as wrist-watches and ball-point pens over Afghan villages in the heavily populated Panjshir Valley northeast of Kabul.

There were even reports of mines disguised as dolls. The New York-based Afghanistan Relief Committee ran an advertisement in a number of American magazines featuring a photograph of a doll with its left arm blown off and a caption that read, "The toy that's making a lasting impression on thousands of Afghan children." The larger version of these ads contained a line in small type advising the reader that the doll in the photograph was not a real Soviet bomb, but a replica constructed on the basis of refugee accounts. In fact, no photographs of such dolls exist, even though one would have been worth thousands of dollars to a news photographer. Peter Jouvenal, a British television cameraman who made over forty trips inside Afghanistan with the mujahidin and saw every other kind of Soviet mine, suspected that the story of the dolls was apocryphal. "The Soviets were guilty of so much in Afghanistan. Why exaggerate?" he remarked.

Right up to the time of their withdrawal, the Soviets kept introducing new kinds of mines. When journalists entered the garrison town of Barikot, in Kunar province near the Pakistan border, after the Soviets had evacuated it in April 1988, they discovered mines stuck on stakes in the bushes. They dubbed them Noriega mines, on account of their pineapple texture. These were sonic mines, fitted with diaphragms that picked up the lightest footstep and sprayed shrapnel thirty feet in all directions.

In Barikot, the Soviets also booby-trapped grain bags in some of the places they evacuated, using a grenade with its detonator pin pulled, hooked up to a trip wire concealed in the sack. Several mujahidin and a dozen refugees were wounded when they opened the bags.

The overwhelming majority of hospital patients in Peshawar and Quetta were mine victims. After Red Cross doctors operated on them, the wounded were dispatched to clinics run by the various mujahidin political parties to recover. These clinics lived on donations from the refugees themselves and usually received little or no aid from either international relief organizations or the Pakistani government. Pakistani landlords owned the clinics and charged as much rent as they could. In the heat of summer, when temperatures rarely dipped below ninety degrees in daytime, there were no fans or air conditioners for the patients, who were accustomed to the bracing mountain climate of Afghanistan. The clinics were short of nearly everything, including food.

Of the twenty patients I saw at a clinic in Quetta one day in July 1988, sixteen were missing at least one limb. Many of the mine accidents had

occurred only two or three weeks earlier. But there were no signs of ill-
ness or general physical weakness on the victims' faces, even though
most of them not only had lost large quantities of blood and eaten
little in the intervening period, but also had to endure days of travel on
a mule or in a lolloping four-wheel-drive vehicle before getting to a
proper medical facility.

Many people have the idea that once a limb is amputated the pain
stops. That's not true. Pain from damaged nerve tissue lasts for
months, usually longer if a clean amputation is not done soon after
the accident, which was always the case in Afghanistan, where
painkillers were not always available. Add this to weeks of drugged discomfort, for patients were all but drowned in antibiotics in order to
prevent tetanus and other infections caused by mine fragments.

Yet, despite the pain and a missing arm or foot, the patients in these
wards looked healthy and normal. There was a vibrancy in their faces,
a trace of humor even, and a total absence of embarrassment. "I have
given my foot to Allah," said a twenty-seven-year-old man who also
had only one eye and a burned, deformed hand. "Now I will continue
my *jihad* [holy war] in another way." This man had a wife and three
children. At first, I dismissed what he said as bravado meant to impress
a foreigner. I found it impossible to believe that he really felt this emotion, that he truly accepted what had happened to him. His eyes, however, evinced neither the rage of a fanatic, which would have accounted
for his defiance, nor the shocked and sorrowful look of someone who
was really depressed. If anything registered on his face when I spoke to
him, it was bewilderment. He didn't seem to understand why I
thought he should be unhappy. He had lost an eye, a foot, and part of
a hand—and that was that.

The Afghan mujahidin came equipped with psychological armor
that was not easy to pierce or fathom. They had the courage and strength
of zealots, but their eyes were a mystery. Their eyes were not the bot-
tomless black wells of hatred and cunning that a visitor grows accustomed to seeing in Iran and elsewhere in the Moslem world. There was
a reassuring clarity about them. Sometimes, while I was talking and

sipping cups of green tea with the mujahidin, their eyes would appear so instantly recognizable to me that I thought they could have been those of my childhood friends. How could people with such familiar, nonthreatening eyes walk so readily through minefields?

from A Complicated War
by William Finnegan

Mozambique's long and destructive Civil War featured a group known as Renamo—armed bandits funded in part by neighboring South Africa. William Finnegan traveled in Mozambique during the late '80s to investigate the violence there.

Everyone knew that the highways out of Maputo were not safe to travel. Reports of Renamo ambushes had been almost daily fare for years. Of course, ambushes can happen only where there is traffic, and the fact was that the highways around Maputo were full of traffic. People had to get from town to country, and so they took their chances. Most of the traffic was in convoys with military escorts, but going by convoy was no guarantee against attack. Convoys were regularly ambushed. In October 1987, at least 278 people were killed in one attack on the national highway fifty miles north of Maputo. In such circumstances one's conception of what is safe collapses into a basic equation: if we got through, it was a safe trip, whether the bus behind us was attacked or not.

In September 1988, I rode up the highway from Maputo to Man-hiça, a rural district where Renamo was very active (the highway massacre the previous October had occurred in Manhiça), with Lina Magaia, an official in the Ministry of Agriculture. Lina drove the route every week, and she did not like to travel in convoys. "If something happens, you cannot get away," she said. "All the cars and trucks start to run into each other." So we set off unaccompanied in her van, a new, charcoal-gray, four-wheel-drive Mitsubishi Pajero, our only armament an automatic pistol on the seat between us. It was an overcast day. My plan was to spend a few days in Manhiça, where Lina worked as a sort of all-purpose rural-extension officer.

The soldiers at the checkpoints all knew Lina. They called her Mama Magaia and tried to bum cigarettes from her. Those we passed on the highway waved. At one checkpoint, she talked for several minutes with a commander. They spoke Shangaan, which left me out, but they were obviously discussing the road ahead. Lina gave the commander a pack of cigarettes. We saw a couple of convoys heading for the city but no traffic going our way. The land we were passing through was deserted. It looked like farmland reverting to scrub. We came to a large, spooky cleared stretch, in an area called Pateque. I had been told in Maputo by a local journalist that Pateque was one of the most dangerous stretches of road in the country—he said he would not travel it for anything—but Lina said his information was outdated. "This was the worst part of the road," she said. "So I went to President Samora—this was in 1985—and I asked if there wasn't something he could do to improve the security here. His solution was to bulldoze the forest away from the road, to improve the visibility. You see, now you have time to take some action *before* you are ambushed." It was true: there were no trees within several hundred yards of the road, and few places for attackers to hide. All the bulldozing had revealed a number of burned, bullet-riddled farmhouses. Lina pointed out a group of empty huts and said, "Those were used to house miners traveling between South Africa and their homes. Then the bandits used them as hiding places before their attacks."

Beyond Pateque, at a place called Maluana, the forest came back to the edge of the road. Lina said, "Now I cannot talk. I must pay attention." I began to notice burned, overturned vehicles along the shoulder of the road. Lina started driving at a very high speed—seventy-five miles an hour or more. We screamed around curves and didn't slow down even when we came to an army checkpoint. The soldiers hurried out of the way, seeming to understand. After several miles, we came to a group of inhabited houses, a place called Esperança, and Lina finally slowed down. She reached into my bag, pulled out a fifth of Scotch I had brought, and, with my permission, took two slugs from the bottle. She sighed. "Now we can relax," she said.

I felt fairly safe with Lina. She had been working in Manhiça since 1982 and knew the area well. In fact, she had been going there, she told me, since she was a child. Her mother was from Manhiça, and Lina had used to visit her grandmother there. She had watched the war come to Manhiça, and in 1986 she had moved her four children back to Maputo. Now she usually saw them and her husband only on week-ends. But she had not considered abandoning her work in Manhiça, she said.

Lina was, at forty-three, a formidable woman. She came from a prominent southern clan, the Mabjaia—the Portuguese had had trouble pronouncing the name; hence the modern form, Magaia. Her uncle was Mozambique's ambassador to Swaziland; her brother was the editor of *Tempo* magazine. Lina's father, a teacher, had become *assimilado* when she was eleven, thereby enabling her to go to a state school in Maputo. She had studied economics in Lisbon on a scholar-ship until the 1974 coup and then had left to join Frelimo in Tanzania. There she received nine months of military training and rose to the rank of sergeant. The war ended before she saw combat, and she left the army in 1977, but there was still, I thought, plenty of military dash to her manner. She handled a pistol as if she had been born with one in her hand. On the day we drove to Manhiça, she was dressed entirely in black—sweatpants, sweatshirt, boots, beret. She was big—tall, and a good 200 pounds—with a big, husky voice and an enormous laugh. She had a mobile, expressive face and a quick tongue—not, all in all, the deferential bearing found among most African women in southern

Mozambique. Lina also had a quick pen. Her weekly column for *Notí-cias*, the Maputo daily paper, was popular for its attacks on incompetent officials.

We reached Manhiça in the afternoon and found a large convoy, perhaps a hundred vehicles, getting ready to leave for Maputo. The people in the cars and trucks all smiled when they saw us arriving safely from the south. Manhiça is a pretty town, spread out on a green plateau above the Incomati River. The cement town probably has 2,000 residents, the cane town many times that. The main commercial street, which is the national highway, is flanked by old-fashioned pillared sidewalks. Two small hotel restaurants compete for the carriage trade. We turned off the highway and followed a dirt road out through the cane town, where little children started rushing at the car, all shouting excitedly, "Lina Magaia! Lina Magaia!" Lina pointed to a row of burned houses. "The bandits attacked here two weeks ago today," she said. "They burned forty-seven houses, and they wrecked the office of our farm, Ribangue, which is just coming up here. But the attack was a victory for our militia. They killed four bandits and captured a bazooka and a Mauser."

We arrived at Ribangue, a dilapidated farm headquarters at the edge of the plateau (the fields were down in the flood-plain), and were met by Domingos Jasse, a solid-looking, mild-mannered man with a glass eye, whom Lina introduced as the head of defense for the farm. (She later told me that Jasse had lost his eye in the *luta armada*. He had been living in Malawi when the war started, had gone to Tanzania to join Frelimo, and had fought for ten years as a guerrilla in his home province of Niassa.) Jasse showed me the damage to the farm's office—burned files, a burned desk—and gave me a blow-by-blow account of the attack two weeks before. The farm's militia, consisting of eighty-seven people with only five automatic weapons, had received word that an attack was coming and had moved out into the fields. The *bandidos*, they knew, were after the food, seeds, tools, bicycles, and other goods stored in the farm's magazine. When they entered the office and started smashing it up, the militia ambushed them. Two militiamen were injured when a fleeing *bandido* threw a grenade, but otherwise it had been a rout. The *bandidos* had left one body behind, and it had been handed over to the man's family, who lived nearby, but the militia now knew they had killed three more, because a young woman whom the *bandidos* had kidnapped—they had kidnapped eleven people from the adjoining cane town during the raid—had returned and told them so. She also said that the *bandidos* had had a kidnapped peasant carry one of their wounded, and had killed the peasant when the wounded man died. The *bandidos* had beaten up the young woman, and they had given her a message for the people at Ribangue: they would be coming back for their bazooka and their Mauser and to place flowers on the grave of their fallen comrade. Jasse showed me the bazooka and the Mauser, now stored with the other valuables in the farm's magazine. The *bandidos* would have to fight very hard to get these back, he said quietly.

Lina said she only wished that the newspapers covered militia victories the way they covered highway massacres, and then she showed me around the farm. There were pigsties, a henhouse, a duck farm, a large shed full of rabbits, and 600 acres of corn, beans, cabbage, bananas, and other crops. The fields were divided into small family plots, which suggested a cooperative farm, but Lina denied that Ribangue was a cooperative. It was "a project," she said. Whatever it was, she was clearly in charge of it. She upbraided workers who had not fed the chickens, went over salary sheets, and scolded the salary clerk for not paying out raises that had been set. When I asked if she received a salary herself, she said she did, but added that she did not get paid if the farm did not make a profit. Though the fields at Ribangue seemed to be flourishing, Lina said they could be far more productive. The main problems were irrigation and drainage. They badly needed a backhoe to reopen drainage ditches that had been neglected since independence. Lina wondered if I would ask Melissa Wells to help her get a backhoe. We met a man in rags in a beanfield. He grinned when he saw Lina and handed us two ears of roasted corn, which we chewed as we went bumping around the muddy roads of Ribangue.

I was supposed to stay with Lina in Manhiça, but she already had three houseguests, North Korean technicians working on an irrigation project, and they panicked when they heard that an American was coming. They were afraid, Lina said, that if their embassy heard that they had stayed in the same house as an American—or were even seen speaking to one—they would be in big trouble. They could be sent back to Korea and could lose their jobs. I had passed the North Korean Embassy in Maputo a few times and had been impressed by the tone of a display in the front yard—it was all photographs of the recent visit of the Great Leader, Comrade Kim Il Sung, to Ulan Bator, Mongolia, with captions, in English, pointing out the "rapturous" crowds waving "fervently" while wishing long life with "infinite respect" to an old, dour-looking fellow in a gray suit. So I was sympathetic, and happy to stay in a house around the corner from Lina's. (But Manhiça is a small town, and on my third day there the inevitable happened: I ran into the Koreans on the street. Without thinking, I waved. They blanched and turned away, and we all just pretended that it hadn't happened.) It was a small, bare, three-bedroom cement house that, from the outside, might have been in a postwar working-class neighborhood in Fresno. The whole street had that look, in fact. Two young men who worked at Ribangue also stayed in the house.

I was thoroughly confused by everything I had heard about the war in Manhiça, so that evening Lina brought over a huge map of the Manhiça district and we spread it out on the floor. The map, which had been drawn in 1969, was outdated but terrifically detailed, showing every house and hut in the district. Renamo had first come to Manhiça in force in 1984, Lina said, crossing from South Africa into the sparsely inhabited western parts of the district. She showed me wild swamplands, far from any road, where the bandits had established their first big encampments, and the routes they had used to move into more populated areas, and where they had first started preying on the national highway. The map clearly showed why the stretch of highway at Pateque had become so dangerous: there were many miles of heavy forest cover on either side of it, with no roads and no villages. A second major group of bandits, Lina said, had come to Manhiça from the north, after a Frelimo offensive in Gaza in 1985. They had moved down the left bank of the Incomati, preying on the villages in the valley and in the sandy, forested hills between the river and the coast. (The name *Incomati* is the Portuguese version of Nkomati. The famous Accord was signed where the river, which rises in Swaziland and then flows northward into South Africa, crosses the border into Mozambique; ironically, the first Renamo force to enter Manhiça was probably sent out of South Africa in accordance with the then-new "nonaggression" pact.) The Incomati River describes a long, lazy loop inside Mozambique until, as it passes Manhiça town, it is flowing south. The coastal hills across the river from the town were a roadless maze, full of hideouts, and, Lina said, the empty beaches beyond them were ideal for resupply by sea.

I wondered why, if the bandits had come from far away, the family of the fighter killed at Ribangue was living in Manhiça. Lina said that the composition of the local Renamo bands had changed over the years. The commanders were still all Ndau-speakers, from the north, but now many of the troops were local men. In fact, Lina believed that there were no longer any large Renamo bases in Manhiça but instead just a number of small bands with excellent radio communications, which enabled them to mass for large attacks and then disperse. She showed me on the map where the bands tended to camp, where they went for water and food, where they attacked at different times of day, where army offensives had secured some areas, where villages had been burned, where others had been abandoned. And as Lina waxed military in her descriptions of the fighting over the years, the tactics and countertactics used in Manhiça, one thing became clear, even to nonmilitary me: Renamo could not be defeated. Even in Manhiça—though it is near the capital, has a railway and a highway running through it, and is, for Mozambique, relatively developed and heavily populated—there were vast, roadless areas where guerrillas could hide. It occurred to me that if the entire army were brought to the Manhiça district—which constituted less than 1 percent of Mozambique's area—its 30,000 soldiers might have a chance of actually securing the district, of making it safe for the people who lived there to grow their crops and live their lives without fear of attack. *Might.*

And Lina, to my surprise, agreed. But the army was not the answer, she said. There would never be enough soldiers to defend Manhiça. No, the answer was militias: local people, well trained and well armed. They were fighting to protect their own property, and so had a level of motivation that soldiers would always lack. What was more, they knew the area, and they often had advance word of Renamo attacks. Many people were disenchanted with the popular militia—the Territorial Defense Force, it was now being called. They said that militiamen were dangerous, drunken, undisciplined thieves. That attitude, which made Lina furious, had been most cruelly manifested, she said, at a meeting in Manhiça the previous Saturday. Local private farmers and shop-keepers had gathered and, at Lina's urging, had agreed to support the reorganized district militia, but at the insulting level of 1,000 meticais (less than two dollars) a month each. Lina was still spitting mad about the outcome of the meeting. "We *must* help ourselves," she said. "The army cannot help us. The security in this district could be much, much better. The bandits are not really so strong here." The Italians, who funded two of the four foreign-aid projects in Manhiça (there were also a West German project and the Korean irrigation work), kept and fed *their* own militias, defending *their* projects. They had considered leaving the district after a series of attacks, but they had been per-suaded to try militia defense; and it, according to Lina, was working. The least that local property owners could do was match the faith of foreigners in local people! Militias, I gathered, had been the subject of some of Lina's columns in *Notícias*.

It was getting late. I had noticed, under the bed where I would be sleeping, an AK-47 Soviet assault rifle, and I asked Lina about it. She said, "That is for your self-defense, in case the militia fails." She checked to make sure that the rifle was loaded, showed me how to set it on auto-matic fire, and said good night.

Thinking about it afterward, I wondered why Lina had said, "in case the *militia* fails." The town was full of regular army. Earlier in the evening, in the commercial district, I had seen hundreds of people bedding down for the night on the canopied sidewalks. They were from the cane town, Lina said, and from nearby villages; they were afraid to sleep in their homes. Every few yards, a young soldier had sat, cradling an automatic rifle, guarding the sleepers. And open trucks full of soldiers were cruising the streets, the soldiers singing lustily. They were letting people know, Lina said, that they were being protected. They had already come past the house several times.

As I was getting ready for bed, I asked one of my housemates, a quiet young man named Alexander, why Lina had not mentioned the army when she left.

Alexander, who had studied animal husbandry in South Africa and, as a result, spoke English, looked at me strangely and said, "You have heard her. She believes that the militia, not the army, must protect us."

I asked Alexander if he had a gun.

"No," he said.

I asked him what he thought about my having one.

He shrugged. "The chap who usually sleeps in that room keeps that gun. I think it is not a good idea."

I poured Alexander a glass of Scotch and asked him why.

He said, "Because when the bandits come, they don't come just one or two. They come one or two hundred. You cannot fight them alone. And if they see you have a gun, they will consider you the enemy."

I found it hard to believe that Renamo ever came to that part of town, much less in a force of hundreds, and said so.

Alexander stared at me. "They come," he said.

I asked him when Renamo had last come into the center of Manhiça.

"The last time they killed many people here in the cement town was January 12," he said. "They broke into the shops on the national road and they killed eleven people. But the last attack we suffered here was three months ago—in June. They came into this road." Alexander gestured at the Fresno-like street outside the window. "I was alone here, and I was sleeping, and nobody came to warn me. When I woke up, I heard the bandits singing and firing their guns. I ran outside. There were hundreds of bandits marching in this road. They were beating drums, firing guns in the air, and shouting. It was very dark, so I just stood next to the house and said nothing, and they said nothing to me. They were singing, and they were shouting, 'Where are the men in this town? Where are the soldiers? We are the men in this town!' They went to the national road, and they looted the shops. They took clothes, and they just left their old clothes there in the road. They even took the curtains from the hotels. No one was killed in that attack. But that was when the last white people living here in Manhiça town left. They owned the hotels, and I think they didn't want to see the bandits next time wearing clothes made from their curtains."

I repeated the bandits' question. "Where *were* the soldiers?"

Alexander waved a hand toward the river. "The bandits came from three directions at once," he said. "Everybody ran in the fourth direction, including the soldiers. Why should they stay and fight? The bandits are so much stronger." Alexander regarded me seriously. "We have a very bad situation here," he said, finally.

We finished our drinks and said good night.

Later, lying in bed, I tried to recall if I had heard anything about militiamen standing guard nearby. Was there even any militia *to* fail? The month before, there had been a major militia failure a few miles south, at an agro-industrial complex called Maragra. Lina had been very upset about it. From 1982 to 1986, she had been the deputy director of Maragra, and she had created and trained the militia there herself. It had repulsed a number of Renamo attacks, and the reputation it gained had caused many people to move to Maragra. But then, in August, a late-night attack had caught the Maragra militia napping. Six hundred Renamo fighters had overrun the complex, killing twenty-one people and wounding many. The most horrifying aspect of the attack was that a number of teenage boys *from* Maragra had joined the bandits in looting the homes of their neighbors and had departed with Renamo. Lina had been lamenting the Maragra militia's fatal overconfidence, but the community's problems clearly went far deeper than that. The war in Manhiça contained a large amount of delinquency, apparently, and nonpolitical banditry, as well as organized military activity, possibly supported by South Africa. The threat hanging over Ribangue sounded like an Appalachian family feud or an inner-city gang fight—"We're comin' back for our Mauser, and we're gonna put flowers on our buddy's grave!"

I decided that, Alexander's wise words notwithstanding, I liked having a rifle within reach. Somehow, perhaps by reducing, if only symbolically, my sense of vulnerability, it made the possibility of sleep slightly greater. Still, I slept poorly. The problem was not so much that I was thinking about a Renamo attack as that my bed's mattress was thin and lumpy and had a horrible odor that seemed to get stronger every hour. Finally, after a long night, roosters began to crow, birds began to chirp. The dawn revealed a small, too blue room—blue walls, blue curtains—and slowly transformed the assault rifle from a dream-dark lifeline into a battered, prosaic old gun.

Manhiça was typical of nothing in Mozambique. Officially, it wasn't even part of "the emergency." None of Maputo province was. There was, therefore, no free distribution of food or clothes in Manhiça. In truth, while no one was starving in Manhiça, there were plenty of unofficial *afetados* and *deslocados*. There was also large-scale unemployment, caused by the cutbacks in migrant mine labor in South Africa. For generations, young men from Manhiça, and from all over southern Mozambique, had been forced to work in the mines for some years before they could start farming and raising a family; it was the only way to earn enough to buy cattle, land, and a house, and to pay bride-price. All the people driven by the war from the remote areas of the district into the towns had, in combination with the legions of the unemployed, created intense pressure on the land. Again, this kind of pressure was unusual in land-rich Mozambique. The highway, the railway, the abundant water, the soil's fertility, Maputo's proximity— all made Manhiça a special case. And the fact that it was in the far south, where the people spoke Ronga and Shangaan, and had been exposed to modern life and ideas, made it, politically, natural Frelimo territory—in contrast to many other parts of the country. And yet, paradoxically, as I traveled around Manhiça, I began to feel as if I were seeing all of Mozambique's problems, and all the patterns of the war, in perfect, murky microcosm.

The murk here, as everywhere, shrouded not only the war but local farming and living arrangements. Lina said that communal villages had been a failure and that the only one still functioning in Manhiça was a model project that received special government support; and yet we visited at least two other communal villages that seemed to be functioning. Both were building schools, and both had militias. I never did find out what sort of operation Ribangue was. Every time I asked someone working there who owned the farm, the answer was "Lina." Lina, however, denied owning it. What had probably happened was what had happened on many cooperative farms: the Ministry of Agriculture had ended up running the show, with little or no formal declaration. In any event, Ribangue was just one of many projects that engaged Lina's attention. Her job description was simple, she said: she was supposed to find out what Manhiça's farmers needed, and then go to the government to try to get those needs met. But her actual work seemed to involve everything from importing bicycles (the trading network in Manhiça, like that almost everywhere in rural Mozambique, had collapsed since independence, and Lina believed that she and the Ministry of Agriculture needed to take up some of the slack), through diagnosing crop diseases, to training militias.

There were many kinds of farmers in Manhiça: subsistence farmers, wealthier peasants, small and large private farmers, Portuguese, Chinese, African, and those on cooperatives and state farms. Lina's decisions about where to focus her assistance were critical, and highly political. Was she still working toward Frelimo's revolutionary goal, "the socialization of the countryside"? Lina seemed impatient with the question. The former economics student pointed out that Marx had never said that agriculture had to be collectivized, and, as for Lenin, "He had his own cultural-historical situation to deal with, and we have ours." Private farmers, she conceded, were a long-term problem, but Frelimo's medium-term goal was simply to reduce the social and economic gaps between farm workers and their employers. And the government's short-term goal was even simpler: to increase production.

This was Lina's obsession as well as the government's. She talked farm talk with every farmer we saw: the tomatoes killed by the frost; the rice that was getting too much water; the ominous yellowing of the onion tops. She constantly rued her own lack of technical expertise. She needed surveyors, a hydraulic engineer, and an agronomist. First, though, she needed vehicles for them. And, since they would probably have to be foreigners, she needed houses. There were no houses suitable for foreigners available in Manhiça, so new ones would have to be built. Lina also dearly wanted to establish a farm-equipment shop in Manhiça, selling seeds, pesticides, and pumps, perhaps offering pump and tractor maintenance and repair. She was very excited about the possibility of growing rice in the bottom of a lush valley she showed me, but she was in despair over a mealybug infestation that was destroying the district's cassava crop—she had no idea how to combat it. She would give *anything*, she said, to have an agronomist here in Manhiça.

Lina's politics did show sometimes. In a communal village called Malavele, we stopped to inspect a school under construction. It was a set of prefab buildings, financed by the Italians, being put up by a crew from Maputo. Later, in another communal village, called Muinguine, we looked at another school under construction. It was being built by the villagers themselves out of bricks made with a simple press from earth found next to the school. Not only would the bricks be more durable than the Styrofoam-core walls being used in Malavele, Lina said, "but imagine how those Styrofoam walls will burn when the bandits decide to destroy that school! This school the people of Muinguine will defend and maintain because they have financed and built it themselves. This is my favorite village in Manhiça!" Lina also loved the Association of Agriculturalists of Muinguine. They were a group of twenty small farmers—not peasants but teachers and shopkeepers and mechanics who had acquired parcels of good land, forty or fifty acres apiece, on the right bank of the Incomati when the white owners fled after independence—and they had pooled their resources and bought a new tractor from the government. When they weren't using the tractor, they rented it out to nonmembers for 4,000 meticais (about seven dollars) an hour. Lina and I spent several hours with some of the Muinguine farmers, bumping around their fields in Lina's van, with Lina asking questions and taking notes.

Afterward, she exulted about the success, the forward-looking self-sufficiency of the Muinguine farmers. Had I seen their tractor, how well it still ran? I had seen it, and the sight had recalled something José Luís Cabaço said: "Our first goal was to promote the self-capacity of the peasants. But our fascination with modern technology led us into a great contradiction. We made a big investment in mechanization, but we forgot culture. The people making the decisions are urban, technically oriented. They have always been around cars, so they know the sound of a motor that's not running right. But if you put a peasant who is thirty years old into a car, no matter how well he is trained, he won't hear the motor the same way an urban person hears it. The relation between man and machine is a cultural relation. The concept of maintenance is not learned in a training course. It takes a generation. So we introduced tractors, creating a dependency on the systems of support for the tractors—exactly what we did not want. And then maintenance was neglected, and we lost most of the tractors!" The loss had been greatest on state farms, where workers felt the least responsibility for the new machinery. There seemed, I thought, no danger that the Muinguine farmers would neglect *their* tractor.

Wandering the back roads of Manhiça with Lina was part celebrity tour. Everywhere we went, the children ran at the van shouting, "Lina Magaia! Lina Magaia!" Peasant women gazed at her adoringly as we sped past. Lina looked entirely unlike any of the other women I saw there. They wore *capulanas* and head scarves; she was now wearing blue jeans, pink elf boots, and a loose lavender knit blouse, the short sleeves of which kept blowing back over her shoulders. And yet she seemed beloved: the longer we drove, the more the back of the van filled with gifts of onions, bananas, lettuce, carrots, sugarcane. Many bundles were placed there by unseen hands while we were out tramping around in the fields.

Not everybody was estatic to see Lina. Several times, we came upon individuals with whom she was unhappy—"these so-called technicians they send me," she called them. They were all young men, and they all looked stricken on being found lounging behind a warehouse when they knew they were supposed to be out building a dam. After two or three of these scenes, Lina began to fume. Her biggest problem, she said, was the difficulty of delegating authority. Nobody wanted to make any decisions, so nothing got accomplished when she was not around. People had such terrible work habits! It was a hangover from colonialism. Because of slavery and forced labor, people had the habit of conserving their energy for their own *machambas*. That was why communalization had not worked. Frelimo had made a huge mistake at independence when it allowed people to start believing that life was going to be easier.

I had heard about the onset of "commandism" in relations between officials and peasants, and Lina clearly had a serious case of it going in Manhiça. Her interactions with people were hard for me to read, though. She seemed to chew out all comers without fear or favor. She was obviously a diva, self-involved and imperious. But most of her conversations were in Shangaan, so I understood nothing that was said, and several times, just when it seemed to me that she was riding roughshod over everyone, some worker would answer her more robustly than I expected, get a big laugh from everyone listening, including Lina, and then press his advantage, getting more aggressive and winning more laughs. Lina's moods were mercurial. While she was driving along in silence and I was watching her from the corner of my eye, I could see expressions of tenderness and ferocity and perplexity pass over her great fleshy features, alternating along with her thoughts.

"Do you see why I love Manhiça?" she said, sighing and waving a hand out the window. We spent most of our time in the floodplain on the right bank of the Incomati or up on the rich green bluff at its edge, but when she asked that question, we were crossing an exquisite open plain known as the Mozambique Valley. A eucalyptus windbreak ran alongside the road, which traversed brilliant fields of rice and sugar-cane. "Only war could cause famine here," she said. "It's a naturally *rich* place. And it all makes me so sad. This farm here used to be João Ferreira's place. He was my favorite farmer. He worked so hard. He was going to be a Mozambican Inácio De Sousa." Inácio De Sousa, a white man, had been the biggest farmer in Manhiça. "But João was killed last year, along with two friends, on the way home from a wedding." Lina pointed out a young *mestiço* man in a battered cowboy hat who was climbing out of a truck. "That is João's brother-in-law. He is trying to run the farm, but he is very, very young. All this unnecessary suf-fering!" Later, on the edge of Manhiça town, Lina pointed to an aban-doned house set back in the woods. "This is where João and his friends were ambushed," she said. "The bandits hid in that house. After shooting them, they slit their throats, and took all their clothes, leaving them naked."

I asked Lina if she had ever been ambushed. She said she had not. Several times, she had come upon the scene of a fresh attack, though, and had ferried dead and wounded in her car. She had also been involved, she said, in the defense of Maragra during Renamo attacks. I asked if she had ever been threatened personally by Renamo. She had once heard that the local bandits were hunting "the lady who wears black and organizes the militias," she said. "That was when I always wore black. But they never found me." Another time, in Tete province, she had heard a captured *bandido* say, "This is a real war. It has even been written in a book." She assumed that he meant a collection of her stories about Renamo atrocities in Manhiça, which had originally appeared in *Tempo* and had then been published as a book called *Dumba Nengue.* "Dumba nengue" was a local expression. It meant, lit-erally, "Trust your feet," and in Manhiça it referred to farming areas that had been abandoned but were sometimes visited by former resi-dents, who came to gather fruit and nuts and were always ready to flee from Renamo. The stories were full of murder, torture, rape; of people burned, beheaded, thrown down wells. Ten thousand copies had been published in Mozambique and had quickly sold out. *Dumba Nengue* had also been translated into English and published in the United States. It was still the only local book about the war. But Lina didn't know whether the bandits in Manhiça knew that she was *that* Lina Magaia.

I got a sense of how Lina might have collected the stories for her book when we asked a farm worker in a field for directions. He had a tiny, hoarse voice, and he had trouble speaking. Lina asked him what had happened. He said that the *bandidos* had caught him near Palmeira and had slit his throat. He lifted his head so that we could see the scars. They went from ear to ear, and were at least an inch wide. It was hard to see how he had survived.

Later that day, while we were on the way to Palmeira—it's a small town on the national highway in the northern part of Manhiça— things briefly got tense. Lina spotted three men with rifles standing on a curve in the highway ahead of us. There were burned vehicles overturned along the side of the road. It was obviously an ambush spot. Lina stepped on the gas, we both slid low in our seats, and we went flying past the men, who did not move. "Those might be bandits," Lina said, as we slowed down to normal speed. "Sometimes they will come out and simply stand by the road, waiting for a truck carrying food, or a bus, or any vehicle they want to ambush. People think they're the militia. There is no way to know." We stopped at the next village to ask around. Eventually, we found an old man who said that the men *were* militia. They had been stationed out there because of all the attacks on the curve. Afterward, Lina grumbled, "But is anyone feeding those militia? Is anyone paying them? If they are not being paid, how will they get food? And what will they do when they get hungry?"

We were going to Palmeira to see José Inácio De Sousa, a son of Inácio De Sousa. Inácio, who died in 1976, had been such a respected farmer, Lina said, that Samora Machel himself had given the eulogy at his funeral, praising his honesty. Most of the white and Asian farmers in Manhiça had left after independence. Others, like a Chinese shop-keeper who owned a big banana farm we had seen near Muinguine, lived in Maputo. The Portuguese farmers in Manhiça had been pros-perous, unlike the illiterate European peasants who settled in, say, the Limpopo Valley, to the north. The most prosperous among them, though, had been Inácio De Sousa. He had controlled the entire banana market in Maputo. And José Inácio—who was popularly known as Zeca—was still here, growing bananas and rice, raising cattle, and running a large mill and rice-cleaning plant in Palmeira, where he lived with his wife and child. We looked for Zeca in Palmeira and were told he was in the fields. We drove out to a large, beautifully laid-out, well-drained banana farm and found Zeca on an access road, driving a new white Japanese pickup truck with a black roll bar.

He joined us, and we took a tour of his farm. Zeca was a trim, unas-suming man of thirty-three, wearing tinted glasses. He had a crooked, modest smile and a quiet voice. Lina and he talked trucks for a while—she needed to borrow some. Then I asked him about how the war had affected his operations. Zeca looked out across his fields. Finally, he said that the farm and the mill in Palmeira had both been attacked many times. The farm, for instance, had been attacked last year by a force of about 150 men. The farm had a good militia, with forty full-time fighters and fourteen part-time fighters, trained and equipped by the army, paid and fed by Zeca. In the early days, Zeca himself had taken the militia to search for *bandidos*. People in Manhiça, he said, tended to believe that the *bandidos* were "bulletproof," and he had wanted to show his men that the *bandidos* were mortal. Fortu-nately, he said, they never found any. But they began to hear about other militias that had killed *bandidos*. Zeca's militia took heart, and Zeca retired from active duty. In last year's big attack, the farm's militia had killed eleven *bandidos,* according to people who had escaped from their camps, and they had gravely wounded many more. Six tractors and two pumps had been burned, but no militiamen had been killed, and only a few were wounded. Most of the great success of the defense was attributable to the fact that the militia had heard about the attack in advance from escaped captives.

Palmeira had suffered even larger attacks, Zeca said. The most recent one, three months before, had involved three hundred *bandidos.* Zeca and his family had just gone to Maputo that afternoon. His wife and child were now staying in the city, waiting until things calmed down. One militiaman had been killed in the last attack on Palmeira, and many people in the nearby communal village had been killed or kidnapped. But the *bandidos* had been repelled before they reached the mill, which they no doubt wanted to loot and burn. Again, the militia had had advance warning. Zeca had since put up an electrified fence around Palmeira, and powerful lights, which shone all night out into the fields. He was thinking about doing the same thing on this farm. It was all very expensive, though.

I asked Zeca about his family. He said that he had two sisters who had moved to Portugal after independence, but that his mother and his brother still lived in Maputo. His brother was a pilot.

I asked Zeca about his relations with Frelimo. He said that he had lost a little land to a communal village and that his taxes had gone up. They were now 45 percent of profits. Otherwise, he said, he had had no problems with the government.

Lina erupted: "I love this man. He is doing so much for my country, and he loves this land."

I asked Zeca if he had ever been approached by Renamo.

He was silent for a minute. Then he said, "Twice." The first time had been in 1984. A well-dressed black man had come to him in Palmeira and asked for a lift to Maputo. He said that his car had broken down in Manhiça town. He had left it there, and, he said, he had come to see Zeca especially. He was cool, Zeca said, but he had nervous eyes. Then he changed his mind and said that he didn't want to go to Maputo after all, but wanted to stay the night. Zeca said he could. Then the man changed his mind again. He wanted to go to the coastal town of Bilene. Zeca put him on a bus to Bilene. Then Zeca thought about it, and sent the militia after the bus in a truck. They brought the man back, Zeca questioned him, and the man gave him a new story. Now he was coming from Sofala. He mentioned several Portuguese farmers and businessmen whom Zeca knew there. Zeca had heard enough. He took the man to Manhiça and handed him over to the police. Someone said the man had a room at one of the hotels in Manhiça, so the police went there. In the room, they found several South African and Swazi passports issued to various black men, some photographs of Samora Machel and other Frelimo officials, and a Renamo document transferring the man from Sofala to Manhiça for "research."

"That means that he was sent to approach white farmers, to see who might support them," Lina said.

The second approach to Zeca had been only five months before. A man had come to him asking for a job. He said he had been living in Matola, a suburb of Maputo. There was something fishy about the references he gave. Zeca had him searched, and, again, the searchers found a Renamo document, transferring him from Matola to Manhiça for "research."

It was all very strange, if only because the De Sousa farm had a big reputation with the *bandidos* in Manhiça as a government redoubt. Among Renamo's captives, anyone known to work for De Sousa was usually killed, because the De Sousa militia was considered a major enemy.

We were passing through a newly planted banana field. Lina stopped the van, and we all climbed out. Lina had been asking Zeca questions about his farming methods between my questions to him about the war. Now she wanted to know how he had dug the large, regular holes in this field, each with a young banana plant growing nicely inside it. Zeca reminded us that we had seen a machine up at the farm headquarters, attached to the back of a tractor. That was a special machine for digging such holes, he said. Somehow that was the last straw for Lina. As we climbed back into the van, she burst into tears. She sobbed and sobbed, while Zeca and I sat and squirmed. Through her tears Lina began to rage against, of all things, government bureaucrats. They sat in their offices in Maputo and issued idiotic orders that did nothing but screw up the people trying to work in the country. They called a meeting to enlist support for the new militias without proper preparation, on the wrong day, undermining the entire project. They set ridiculous production goals that did nothing but oppress the people trying to produce, and they arbitrarily reorganized successful projects, destroying them in the process. They sent her stupid, lazy, so-called technicians instead of a real agronomist who could teach her things like how to dig proper holes for young banana plants. Lina was sad, she was furious, and, for the first time in her life, she was *tired.*

Zeca and I tried to comfort her. She eventually stopped crying, wiped her face with the back of her hand, took three belts of Scotch, laughed lightly, and resumed driving, plainly in a much better mood.

The Cubans thought highly, everybody said, of the Territorial Defense Force. It had worked for them at the Bay of Pigs. Other military advisers in Mozambique were less enthusiastic. Cuba had a strong central government and few remote areas. In Mozambique, creating militias with loyalties that were primarily local—to the farmer or factory owner or administrator who fed and paid them—carried the risk of fostering warlordism. It also seemed like a backward step in the overall effort of nation-building, the struggle to create larger, national loyalties. But, again, this had been Frelimo's deepest political problem since independence: how to reconcile local realpolitik with abstract modern ideals. And the military reality was that, in many places, the regular army was useless. In Manhiça, in March, Renamo had overrun an army training barracks in the southern part of the district virtually without resistance, capturing a large number of weapons.

The army could also be worse than useless. Lina and I went to see the one *cooperante* living in Manhiça, an Italian named Giovanni. We found him at his warehouse, very near the spot where João Ferreira and his friends had died. Giovanni was a dapper-looking fellow about forty years old. When Lina asked him how he was, he said, "Fine. Now." His smile was tight. I thought I saw his hands shaking. Lina asked him what he meant. Giovanni said that he had been driving in from Maputo on the national highway earlier that afternoon and had come upon an ambush. A group of soldiers was looting a truck between Maluana and Esperança. He stopped and made a U-turn. The soldiers spotted him and started shooting at him. He got away without being hit, and reached Manhiça by back roads.

Later, Lina said that Giovanni must have meant *bandidos*, but I had heard him say *"soldados."* Lina sighed hugely and said that it was a major problem: the soldiers were ill fed. She had often had to feed them herself. But the situation was improving. It had been a long day. Lina was right when she guessed that I might want a bath. She was also right when she guessed why I hesitated when she suggested it. She came to check out the facilities where I was staying, and she emerged from the bathroom with her face a mask of fury and shame. She went looking for my housemates, and I heard her out in the kitchen shed berating someone fiercely. All I caught was the word *barbarity*. When she returned, she muttered that she would take me to her friend's house for a bath—the damn Koreans were already back at her place.

We went to an old house on the highway, in the center of town. I got a bath—in water heated over an open fire—and afterward sat talking with some of Lina's friends, including a shopkeeper, a young man who worked for a parastatal agricultural company called Diprom, and a part-Chinese farmer named Abraão, whom we had met earlier in his fields. Conversation centered on business and the war. Like Lina, the shopkeeper and Abraão had their families in Maputo and drove back on weekends. Abraão said that he had 150 acres and a tractor, and employed fifty-eight people, and also owned a fishing boat in Maputo. But Abraão was not a capitalist, Lina said, because he actually worked the land. In fact, he wasn't making any profits from farming and would do better to invest his money elsewhere. I asked Abraão if he was really such a good citizen that he made his investment decisions according to party directives about production, and he laughed. He wasn't a party member, he said. He just loved to work on the land. But Abraão was not against Frelimo, Lina said. She studied him. Abraão grinned. "He prefers to have an independent position," Lina said. (I later learned that Abraão had fought with the Portuguese during the *luta armada*, and that would have disqualified him from party membership even if he had wanted it.) Each time the conversation came around, as it seemed to do often, to the government's failings in agriculture and commerce, I noticed that the others turned to the man from Diprom, taxing him with their complaints, rather than Lina. Lina, meanwhile, was trying to persuade Abraão to open a shop for his workers—he said he would do so if he could get his work force up to two hundred and if he could be assured of security—while Abraão was trying to persuade me to try to interest individual American investors in becoming partners with small Mozambican farmers like him.

Later that evening, we ended up down the street at the Hotel Castro—no relation to Fidel, Abraão assured me, so Americans were welcome. It was a lively bar and restaurant, with drunks falling about, a jukebox, a number of trucks parked out front that had not made it into the last convoy of the day, and soldiers posted at the doors. We ate steaks and mealie pap—a cornmeal mash that is the southern African staple—and drank local beer. The Castro's proprietor, a sharp-eyed woman with big gold earrings, joined us and then entertained us by coolly ejecting some of her more boisterous customers. I inspected the new curtains—the Castro was one of the hotels relieved of their dry goods by Renamo in June—-and met a large number of Lina's friends and associates. At one point, a song by a Brazilian pop singer named Roberto Carlos came on the jukebox, and Lina's face became a vision of bliss. She had owned this record when she was seventeen, she said. She used to have parties at her house and play this record, and she and her friends would dance. Roberto Carlos was singing a Portuguese version of Dion's "The Wanderer," and Lina did a hilarious imitation of herself at seventeen seriously bopping. "You know, Bill, when I am not working, I really love to play," she said.

There were a number of soldiers in the bar, some of them drinking, some of them dancing in front of the jukebox. Few of them looked over eighteen. Abraão studied the crowd critically, then said, "There are only two good soldiers here tonight." He pointed out two older, serious-looking characters, both sober, alert, erect, and well dressed, standing at the edge of the room. One wore a greatcoat. Both wore pistols. I later noticed two young soldiers with pink flowers in their berets, and for no particular reason I pointed them out to Lina. Her smile disappeared. She called one of the soldiers over and spoke to him long and quietly. After he left, she called over one of the watchful officers and spoke to him. He left, and I asked Lina what was happening. She said that the young soldier had said that he and his friend had just completed a British training course in Zimbabwe, and that they had received the flowers in their berets as graduation gifts. That might be true, she said. Or the flowers might mean that the boys were spies for the bandits. The bandits might have told them to wear flowers so that they could be recognized and would not be killed accidentally in an attack.

I was shocked to hear what I had started, and a few minutes later I went outside for some fresh air. I had seen the soldiers with the flowers in their berets go out a minute before, but I did not find them on the hotel steps. The guards in front of the hotel were extraordinarily young—they looked like children—and they wore big, unnervingly cowled East German helmets. I asked one of them where the boys with the flowers had gone. He smiled, held up his hands, and hit the insides of his wrists together. It was the sign for "arrested."

Some hours later, I found myself back on my evil-smelling mattress, still horrified by what had happened. I had heard before about Renamo attacks in which certain soldiers suddenly turned their caps around backward, were not shot at, and, when the battle was over, left with the enemy. People said that Renamo had spies everywhere, even in the army. But the boys in the bar with the flowers in their berets seemed to me so clearly what they said they were. (I later asked a British defense attaché about the course in Zimbabwe. He said that the training officer was from the Fusiliers, who wear a hackle, a red-and-white plume, in their cap badge, and that the training officer did indeed award a hackle, or the best locally available equivalent, to his graduates.)

The incident had led me into a series of bar conversations about the army, some of them even more disturbing than the arrest of the young soldiers. I had asked one of my companions what he thought could induce a soldier to spy for Renamo, and he had said, "To many of these boys, there is no difference, the bandits or the army. They are taken in just the same. They are never let go, even though the army says they only have to serve two years. We hear that the bandits are starving, but we *know* the soldiers are starving. They do not get enough food."

I asked if he had ever heard of soldiers ambushing vehicles on the highway.

He sneered and said, "They do it. And they are the most dangerous, because they don't want to leave witnesses, so they try to kill everyone. The massacre at the Third of February—that was soldiers." The Third of February was the village near the spot where the big highway massacre had occurred the previous October. Rocked by this news, I asked two other solid Manhiça citizens, as discreetly as I could, who they thought had committed the massacre at the Third of February. Neither blamed the soldiers, but only one blamed Renamo. The other said, very sadly, "I don't know." (A number of diplomats had flown by helicopter to the scene of the massacre. When I got back to Maputo, I asked one of them what he thought. He said that the army had provided very poor protection to the convoy that was attacked, and that there was a chance—a *chance*—that soldiers had joined in the looting, which lasted for hours.)

The man who had accused local soldiers of committing the massacre was, at the same time, sympathetic to soldiers. He said, "Not only is the soldier hungry but his family, wherever they are, they are hungry, too. And he knows it. And his wife knows that if he is killed she will get nothing but a pension for six months. The soldier you see is the same man who was struggling to survive, to see his future, to understand his situation before he came to the army. He has not stopped thinking. And so he must ask himself, 'What am I fighting for? So that a few officers, high officials, and the bourgeoisie can eat meat, drive cars, and live in nice houses, while we eat beans, if we're lucky, and our

families starve, must walk everywhere, and sleep on the bare earth?'
Lina loves the soldiers. But have you seen her telling them that they are
the victims of injustice? Have you seen her telling the peasants that?
No, and you won't hear her telling them that. Because there is nothing
that she can do about it, and they will only look at *her*."

Was this what Renamo was telling people in Manhiça?

The man sneered again. "Renamo? Who is Renamo?"

It was a good question. I had been struck by the disparity between
the intrigues Zeca De Sousa had described—the shadowy characters
carrying Renamo transfer papers and engaged in dubious
"research"—and the world of the Manhiça *bandidos*, such as I had
glimpsed it. Although most Renamo fighters were, like most Mozambicans, illiterate—even important commanders, according to Paulo
Oliveira, were illiterate—there were levels of Renamo where written
records were kept, as several captured caches of documents had
shown. But there were other levels, probably including some of the
Manhiça bands, where records were not kept, and Zeca's experiences
suggested that the communication between, say, the Manhiça bands
that battled the De Sousa militia and whoever sent the "researchers"
to sound him out was poor at best. I had been surprised to see, near
Maragra, an undestroyed bridge over the Incomati. It was in an area
where Renamo had been active for years. When I pointed it out to
Lina, she said that the bandits did not try to destroy infrastructure in
Manhiça, but simply tried to kill and terrorize. It made me wonder just
what their orders, if any, from outside Manhiça were.

Local conditions dictated who Renamo was locally. The mass unemployment caused by the cutbacks on the South African mines and the
hopelessness that it bred in many young men were, I had heard, a
major aid to Renamo recruitment in Manhiça. The belief that the *bandidos* were bulletproof was common throughout Mozambique;
Renamo fighters, and especially Ndau-speakers, were believed to have
powerful magic. And yet the main Renamo magician in Manhiça, who
gave the fighters their power, was, according to Lina, a local woman
named Nwamadjosi. She was the widow of a former *régulo*, and she

was considered a great *curandeiro*. The "advance word" of attacks which Zeca's militia always got suggested that there was a steady traffic of local people between the Renamo camps and government territory. Nwamadjosi was an attraction, apparently, helping to swell Renamo's ranks; perhaps she was drawing more ordinary business as well. I somehow doubted, in any case, that her line of goods included extolling the virtues of democratic elections or, for that matter, of Afonso Dhlakama.

Trying to fall asleep, I began to see the war in Manhiça as a battle between two titanic women: Lina and Nwamadjosi. It was a silly idea—and it wasn't silly at all. Beyond the fact that they fought on opposite sides, with very different weapons, Nwamadjosi casting spells and invoking the spirits of the ancestors, Lina importing bicycles and writing books—beyond everything they might be made to represent in the wider world of ideas, politics, values—there was the fact that each of them was a locally powerful individual. Lina was not Frelimo's sole representative in Manhiça, or even, necessarily, its most important one, but she was clearly popular. She was in no danger of becoming a warlord in Manhiça—that wasn't why she favored militias—but in another place, at another time, it would not have been inconceivable. She and Nwamadjosi circled one another like lions in a dim clearing in my head as I drifted off.

In the morning, I discovered that, after our long evening in the Hotel Castro, Lina had gone home and written a letter to the minister of agriculture about the things the farmers needed in Manhiça; a letter to the local military commander about the problem of nonstandard uniforms, with particular reference to the beret-flower incident; and most of her weekly column for *Notícias*. I had seen her houseguests leave for work, so I ventured to her house for coffee and found her tapping on an old portable typewriter at her dining room table. The night before, she had groaned, held her great head in her hands, and said, "I smoke too much, I drink too much, I eat too much, I never sleep, I am *so tired*"—but that morning she looked infinitely fresher than I felt. Her beret seemed set, in fact, at an even more rakish angle than usual. She asked me to give her a few minutes to finish the column. It was addressed to a director at the Ministry of Health who had still not handed over an ambulance that the Mozambican Red Cross had given to Manhiça more than two years before. This was a fantastic modern ambulance, with blood and oxygen on board, and the director apparently believed that it was too good for a little one-horse district like Manhiça. But Manhiça was where the war was *happening*. This was where people were getting wounded, and a high-tech ambulance was needed to keep them alive. The director's behavior was a perfect example of office-bound Maputo thinking, and Lina was flaying him without mercy. She wanted that ambulance!

Lina's house was airy and bright, and crowded with potted plants. Pictures of her mother and her children covered a bureau top; one of the children, I knew, was a war orphan she had adopted. Although the bookshelves were nothing like the shelves in her house in Maputo, which groaned with the works of Faulkner, Camus, and dozens of Portuguese and Soviet authors, they were well stocked with technical books, mostly agricultural science. A mud-caked surveyor's tripod stood in a corner of the living room. The wonderful old map of Manhiça covered one wall. Mozambican pop music was playing on a radio, and in the kitchen Lina's cook was chopping vegetables. I glanced into Lina's bedroom and saw, propped next to her bed, an AK-47. Also, a pistol on the night table. And a very large knife.

The map of Manhiça, which I had consulted several times since coming to the district, had helped me form a picture of the area with sufficient detail in it that, while we wandered the fields and back roads, I rarely worried about the possibility of an ambush. There were places and times of day that were dangerous. Otherwise, the risk was remote. Once, we had come into a small compound on the bank of the Incomati, near Muinguine, and I had asked a woman living there—she was one of several wives of a wealthy peasant—whether she and her family were not afraid. They were in a spot where, from everything I had heard, the *bandidos* were certain to pass at night. She said that the

bandidos did sometimes come at night, and for that reason they sometimes slept at Muinguine. (I had actually been hoping to see a hip-
popotamus in the river there. Lina had told me that tourists on their
way to the beach at Macaneta, which was nearby, used to honk their
car horns, which aroused the hippos' curiosity, to bring them out on
the banks. The tourists were long gone, and salt water had penetrated
far up the Incomati during the great drought of 1983–84, forcing the
hippos, as Lina put it, "to hide themselves," but the water in the river
was fresh again now, and the hippos might be back. I was embarrassed
to ask Lina to honk her horn again, though—and it was getting late in
the day to linger in that area.)

I studied the map on Lina's wall. We were planning to return to
Maputo that afternoon, and Lina had said that she did not want to
take the highway. Apparently, Giovanni's had not been the only report
of an attack on the highway between Manhiça and Maputo over the
past couple of days. Instead, Lina wanted to take a dirt road that ran
along the bluff on the Incomati's right bank. It went through more
heavily populated areas. It was dangerous at night, but in the daytime
there was only one bad stretch, a few miles south of an army training
barracks—not the barracks that had been overrun, Lina said, but
another one. I found the barracks Lina meant, and the dangerous
stretch of road, on the map. The back road did look less vulnerable
than the highway, and the bad stretch looked short.

We spent most of the day running around Manhiça. Lina was planning to go overseas on a speaking tour, and she was worried about Ribangue. The stock operations were poorly managed, and the militia
needed to be ready for the next attack. She and Domingos Jasse went
over his preparations several times. We ran into the local military commander on a road in the cane town, and Lina and he had a talk about
the need for standard uniforms for soldiers, thus obviating her letter.
We went down into the fields at Ribangue, where Lina pondered the
blighted cassava crop. "Sometimes I feel that it's me against the land,"
she muttered. "And I don't know which one will win."

Finally, rather alarmingly late in the day, we were ready to leave

Manhiça. We set off on the dirt road, through the cheering columns of children: "Lina Magaia! Lina Magaia!" We passed through Maragra, Lina's old headquarters, where a vast old sugar refinery stood silent, closed for lack of spare parts, and the rows of worker housing, their residents nowhere in sight, looked like a town still in shock from the Renamo attack of the month before. Lina was driving very fast. Suddenly, in the woods south of Muinguine, she slammed on the brakes. As we slid to a stop, hundreds of young men surrounded the van. They were jogging in the road, running straight out of the low sun—that was why I had not seen them. They were recruits from the nearby training barracks. They were all bare-chested, and they all had their heads shaved, and they came at the windshield in waves, all with hypnotic marathoners' eyes, their skin shining in the dusty golden light. They were singing: a deep, swinging, African chant. The recruits swarmed past the van, and when they saw Lina, they tapped the van's roof, but they did not alter their chant. As the last of them passed, I saw that Lina's face was lit with a beatific smile. She put the van in gear, sighed, and said that she really regretted having left the army. "I think I have the military mentality," she said. She liked the order and discipline of military life, and she believed that military discipline had a role to play in the economic development of Mozambique.

The road turned to sand as we approached the stretch where an ambush had seemed possible. Lina showed me how to release the safety on the pistol and told me to hold it between my knees. I wondered about the wisdom of my blazing away at any attackers—maybe they wouldn't start shooting if they thought we were not armed—but I figured that Lina knew more than I did. The road dropped into a gully, the sand got deeper, and I felt a sense of menace that I had not felt before in Mozambique. Lina was battling the sand, which slowed us to walking speed. It was already dusk in the gully. The crest of the far slope was lined with abandoned houses. Although it probably took less than a minute, it seemed to take hours to climb the slope beneath the houses, the van screaming and lurching in the sand. I didn't need to be told that any attack would come from the houses. The worst moment occurred when we emerged from the gully into a scatter of abandoned, bullet-riddled buildings and had to round a slow, blind corner. Nothing happened, and we were soon speeding down a gravel road, each sending regards to our separate deities.

The Scotch was all gone, but we promised ourselves a stiff drink in Maputo. Lina tried to raise someone on her two-way radio. She was going to be late delivering her column, and she wanted to reassure her editor. I had heard that Lina had sometimes called Samora Machel himself on her car radio. She laughed when I mentioned it, shook her head, and said, mostly to herself, "Samora, Samora." She gave up on the radio. I asked if she ever called President Chissano on the radio. Lina said, "I never have. I have other ways to talk to him." She nodded at the typescript on the seat between us. It struck me that Lins had been producing engagé journalism—writing with consequences—ever since she was the only black child in her class at school and was jailed for three months, at the age of seventeen, for publishing an anticolonial poem. The gravel road curved and came up onto the highway. We were now out of Manhiça, and out of ambush territory. The soldiers at the checkpoints seemed surprised to see us. Lina handed out cigarettes, and we headed for the city.

While the buildings multiplied around us, Lina said, "So you have seen Manhiça. People here in the city will tell you Manhiça is too dangerous. They put their hands on their heads and say, 'Oh, all these tragical things!' " Lina did a good imitation of a Maputo worrywart. Then she said, "Yes, there are tragical things, but that is why we must fight. We must not abandon Manhiça." We skirted the crowded, smoky edge of the cane city, passed the American Embassy, the Hotel Polana, and the South African trade mission, and drove down into the center of the cement city. Outside the editorial offices of *Notícias*, Lina called to a man standing on the sidewalk. She handed him the typescript of her column and asked if he knew where the editor's office was. He said he did. That was all she needed to hear. Lina made a U-turn, and we went to find a drink, agreeing not to talk—at least, not that evening—about tragical things.

from # A Different Kind of War Story
by Carolyn Nordstrom

Anthropologist Carolyn Nordstrom has done field research on wars in southern Africa, southeast Asia and central Europe. Her 1997 book about the civil war in Mozambique explored local communities' responses to the violence.

The Question of Violence and Anna's Story

So, what is violence? I hold with philosophers like Nietzsche who say that all too often theory is a mirror held up to reflect one's own presumptions and worldview, not one positioned to reflect the world outside. Or, as Bacon—ironically, one of the forebears of scientific realism—observes:

> The human understanding is no dry light, but receives an infusion from the will and affections; whence proceed sciences which may be called "sciences as one would." For what a man had rather were true he more readily believes. (1960:52)

This is nowhere more evident than in considerations of violence, a topic so politically loaded and emotionally charged that opinions often speak more to how people want to see the world than how it really is. Violence is a cultural construct, as are the theories intended to explain it. Each is embedded in a spiral of personal, social, and cultural histories and experiences that color one's orientation toward the topic, researcher and informant alike.

Violence fits well with Bacon's list:

> There is no soundness in our notions, whether logical or physical. Substance, Quality, Action, Passion, Essence itself, are not sound notions; much less are Heavy, Light, Dense, Rare, Moist, Dry, Generation, Corruption, Attraction, Repulsion, Element, Matter, Form, and the like; but all are fantastical and ill defined. (1960:42)

The *notion* of violence is an abstracted category, by definition an order of reality altogether different from that of the experience of violence. As a "notion" it is removed from "actuality" as we live it. Moreover, notions are conceived, politicized, even poeticized in ways experiences never are. Many of the definitions of violence I held to be "true" before I began to study it were dispelled as I listened to the hundreds of stories of people living on the frontlines of conflict. I realized that many of the assumptions we take to be valid are more a part of our cultural heritage than a product of scholarly endeavor. To illustrate the complex nature of violence and the questions that accrue to it, consider the story of Anna, whom I met in 1991.

Anna lived on the outskirts of one of the larger towns in Zambezia. She had arrived a year or two before—a refugee from the war in her own village. She had fled an attack, and before fleeing she had seen one of her sons, and a number of her friends, brutally murdered. When she ran, she took her youngest child with her, but lost track of her husband and the rest of her family, who had scattered to avoid the violence. As she paused to look back at the village where she had grown up, she saw flames consume her home, the market where she bought her goods, and the houses of her friends where she went to talk and share chores.

As she tried to reach safety, she was captured by a group of Renamo soldiers. She was raped and beaten, and forced to carry the loot of her own village for seemingly endless days through the bush, heading toward, she guessed, the Renamo base camp. Other people from her village that were kidnapped during the attack shared her plight. One older man could not keep up. He had a cough and the loads were too heavy for him. He was beaten and left to die. She hoped he somehow had made it to safety.

One night when the soldiers seemed to relax their guard, lulled into complacence by the vastness of the bush and the distance from any village or Frelimo base, she and her child slipped off quietly into the night and ran, hungry and full of fear, until dawn. She walked, her child in her arms, for days, living on what little she could scavenge from the land, until they came to a town. There she was told she should try to make it to a larger town several days' walk away—the town where she now lived—for there she would find refugee assistance. Along the way she met several others in her predicament, and they made their way to the new destination.

There was a refugee center, but it was like nothing she had ever seen before. There was food, but not much; there were houses, but they were small huts all crammed one on top of the other, stretching as far as the eye could see. Not long after she arrived, she and her child moved in with a man she had met. He was all right, but he beat her when he became angry or frustrated, which was often. But she told herself it was better than being alone and on her own.

Food was more than a daily preoccupation, one she, like all of the deslocados, worried about hourly. The food made available through the center was not enough. By the time the distributors had their cut and the blackmarketeers had siphoned off what they could to sell, there was little left for the many who were hungry. The village leaders and the military, if present, often took the lion's share of what was left. People were encouraged to make and farm their own machambas, but that was fraught with danger. The townspeople were embittered with the arrival of so many deslocados competing for resources, and fights over rights to farmland often became bloody. The townspeople usually won—they had rights to land that spanned generations and bureaucracies, and they had the force of family and friends to back them up. That meant the recent arrivals like Anna had to go far into the bush, often several hours' walk, to plant a machamba. Traveling so far on one's own left a person vulnerable to attack from soldiers in the bush. For those who had already escaped from Renamo attack or capture once, this was an unbearable possibility. However, so was starvation. The dilemma became whether to risk kidnapping or death at the hands of Renamo while traveling to and from one's machamba, or to procure food in the camp or in town either legally, which was sometimes impossible, or illegally, risking imprisonment. In addition, even if one could procure land to farm, a newcomer had no ancestral rights to it. Ancestral rights were significant because of the traditions that linked lineage and ancestral rights to specific land(s). One's ancestors came to live in the land, ensuring the right of their descendants to live and work the land, and ensuring fecundity. Living on someone else's land meant that deslocados either lived without the protection of their ancestors or, if they chose to perform ceremonies to bring the protective spirits of their ancestors with them, lived on land under the rule of someone else's ancestral lineage. Many people told stories of becoming sick because their ancestors fought with the ancestors who had historical rights to the land, the former hating to succumb to the domination of the latter.

Amid all this, Anna was profoundly troubled by the fact that she had not been able to do a proper burial and ceremony for her son who had been killed in the attack on her village. She worried about what would happen to his spirit, and what that meant for both him and her family. She was never able to express the grief she felt.

Anna was hungry, her child was hungry, and she had nothing; all her possessions had been lost when she fled her village. Many people were in her position: refugees who had lost everything and fled here for safety. Embittered, angry, exposed to too much violence, and unable to work or farm, the more aggressive and desperate turned to thievery and violence to put food on the table. This was especially true in the town areas, where even walking in certain places or at certain times was unsafe. You never knew when someone might catch up with you walking at night and take your last piece of clothing, the few coins you had, or the bit of food you had been able to coax from the ground or another person. As Anna spoke a different dialect from that spoken in the area she now resided in, she feared this might leave her even more vulnerable to the unscrupulous.

The thing that kept Anna going was dreaming of returning to her home village, of finding her husband and the rest of her family, of rebuilding her house and replanting her machamba. But she was pregnant again, and what would her family say to that? In all likelihood, the pregnancy had resulted from the rape she suffered at the hands, so to speak, of Renamo. She had heard women gossiping about other women who returned home with one more child than they had left with, only to be cast out by their husbands.

I met many Annas in Mozambique, and I tell her story here to explore the question of what violence is. The question is complex, and the layers of violence to which people are subjected are stacked one on another in an experiential whole that can be understood only by investigating all the strata. Military assault is the most compelling font of violence, but from where Anna stands, violence extends out from her world in many directions. The layers of violence in her daily world are manifold and indivisibly intertwined:

• There is the violence that extends into her home. Probably most immediate to her is her child's hunger, a product of a world of inequalities whereby some can feed their children and some cannot. Yet it goes deeper than this: her child's normal destiny has been taken from him. Her son does not play lightheartedly with the other children of his birth village, grow strong on the stories and the food of his extended family, delight to the tales told by his grandparents. He does not learn the landscapes, the animals and the plants of his village, but the harshness of a town of strangers and how to listen for the attack of soldiers or thugs. There is the violence done to her murdered son, and to her in watching him killed—an unresolved pain for Anna because she has never been able properly to express her grief, conduct the ceremonies necessary to ensure his place among the dead, and to mourn him and his spirit in a healthy way. Then there is the violence of her home life: her partner who beats her and has little respect for her traditions and values.

• There is the violence unleashed on the community: of people competing, at times viciously, for insufficient food and goods; of crime and feeling continually unsafe.

• There is the violence of being a *deslocado*, a person of a different language group, of being an outsider. This is an everyday fact of life that ultimately impinges on her very identity: to be dis*placed* is to be uprooted from that which grounds notions of self and self-worth, suddenly to confront a world lacking in signifiers that give meaning and sense to being-in-the-world.

• Then there is the violence of her memories. As she describes it, each thought of her family, of not knowing if they are dead or alive, is like a knife wound. Her yearning for her once-happy home life is, she says, like a crippling pain. Her nightmares of her village burning make her physically sick.

• And then there is the physical violence of the war itself, both that done to Anna and all those like her, and that which they were forced to witness. It is a violence, Mozambicans tell me, that goes far beyond the physical bloodshed to injure family stability, community sustainability, and cultural viability. The continuity of the historical present is obliterated, respected traditions are dismantled, values rendered moot. Psychological peace and emotional security are bygone memories. Tomorrow, once taken for granted, now becomes a tenuous proposition.

Multiply Anna's story not by the thousands but by the hundreds of thousands, even the millions, and a picture of what the war in

Mozambique was like for the citizens begins to emerge. Widely accepted figures demonstrate that fully one-half of the population, more than eight million people, were directly affected by the war.

Nuancing Our Understanding of Violence

What does this say about Mozambique? In terms of sheer overt violence how do we compare the experiences of the people who are mutilated in individual acts of terror; the villages that are totally destroyed; the communities that bribe paramilitary soldiers not to harm them; the districts on the margins of the fighting that have never seen actual warfare but slowly starve because of ruined infrastructure; the children kidnapped and forcibly trained to become soldiers; the refugees who continually flee war and never see it but lose family members to it; the traditional healers who treat the devastating wounds of war but are then placed at the center of fighting as targets and booty for both armies alike; the people who make fortunes selling information and acquiring loot; the war orphans who have seen their parents killed; and, finally, the experiences of the soldiers and political leaders themselves? How do we successfully juxtapose the violences Anna has endured to those of the woman who told me:

> I love this country and I hate it. It is my country, its blood flows in my veins. No one who has not lived like this can understand. The war has gotten into us all, it lives in us, affecting our every move and thought. If I walk outside, I wonder if today is the day I will die. If my brother is late coming to visit me, I wonder if he has been kidnapped or killed, and the terror lives in me. I have not heard from my mother—she lives in an uncertain area behind Renamo control—and I live daily not knowing if she is dead or alive, whether her spirits are calling for me to do a proper ceremony for her, or if her body is calling for food and family. You do not have to see the war to live the war, and the war lives in all of us.

Each story, each experience, is as personal as its narrator; but all, taken together, begin to make up the cultures of violence and survival that shape the lives of Mozambicans. And this culture of violence is inserted into the daily life-worlds of people on myriad levels, from the actual to the symbolic, from parable to representation, from personal interaction to dream. It is less about actual institutions of violence than about the reality of violence as an inescapable fact of life. It is the knowledge systems made necessary by war and threat; it is the site of resistance. This culture of violence is not activated only during or near actual encounters with physical violence; it does not disappear when the physicality of violence ceases. Violence becomes a cultural fact, a persistent enduring dynamic. This cultural force of violence maintains the reality of violence beyond its mere physical expression.

Because violence was so widespread in Mozambique, stories about violence—stories of suffering, of compassion, of survival—circulated constantly in everyday conversation. These discussions were a survival skill intended to take care of the victims of violence and to warn others how to avoid victimization if at all possible. But to accomplish this, an accurate understanding of how violence is experienced was crucial, and thus many discussions revolved around the many "casualties" of violence, the many ways it could harm. This knowledge was essential to understanding how the harm could be ameliorated.

Readers may have noticed that the songs, the stories, and the quotes so far presented in this book do not often deal solely, or even mainly, with actual physical acts of violence, but rather with a type of violence that is much deeper and enduring. This perspective stands in contrast to the more official accounts of violence in global culture. In journalistic reports, official statements, academic publications, and popular movies physical acts of brutality are the main focus, and stories of gruesome mutilations, rapes, and murders abound. The stories that most violate notions of human decency tend to be the most circulated. Yet when I listened to average Mozambican civilians discuss the war, these barbarous accounts, while present, were not the focal point. The destruction of home and humanity, of hope and future, of valued traditions and the integrity of the community resonated throughout these conversations.

To illustrate these nuanced perspectives of violence, I start with a classic example of violence, and move on to examples of some of the more common themes surrounding the experience of violence Mozambicans frequently discussed. Lina Magaia's well-known book on the war in Mozambique, *Dumba Nengue—Run for Your Life: Peasant Tales of Tragedy*, contains what many consider classic accounts of violence, no matter what culture or position one holds. Magaia's book is a compendium of accounts of military (Renamo) attacks against non-combatants, each a story she collected in the course of her work with the Ministry of Agriculture. Magaia is careful to point out that these stories are not the worst or most uncommon, but just the opposite, the most commonly heard war stories of the most average of civilians. Her book opens with the following account.

Classical Example of Violence
It happened at night, as it always does. Like owls or hyenas, the bandits swooped down on a village in the area of Taninga. They stole, kidnapped and then forced their victims to carry their food, radios, batteries, the sweat of their labor in the fields or in the mines of Jo'burg where many of those possessions had come from.

Among the kidnapped were pregnant women and little children. Among the little ones was a small girl of nearly eight. . . . And the hours went by and dawn broke and finally there was a halt. They put down their loads and the bandits selected who could return home and who had to carry on. Of those who had to keep going, many were boys between twelve and fifteen. Their fate was the school of murder—they would be turned into armed bandits after training and a poisoning of their conscience. Others were girls between ten and fourteen, who would become women after being raped by the bandits. Others were women who were being stolen from their husbands and children.

To demonstrate the fate of the girls to those who were going back, the bandit chief of the group picked out one, the small girl who was less than eight. In front of everyone, he tried to rape her. The child's vagina was small and he could not penetrate. On a whim, he took a whetted pocketknife and opened her with a violent stroke. He took her in blood. The child died. (Magaia 1988:19–20)

Nuancing the Classical

Such stories as this have come to be associated with the very nature of violence. They have come to define it. But violence is not so easily rendered. While Magaia lived with the truth of this violence in her everyday life, readers outside Mozambique do not have this same depth of knowledge. If we take this description alone, as journalist reports and anthropological vignettes are wont to do, what do we learn about the ontological dynamics of violence? How did the act described above reconfigure the definitions of self, the lives, and the daily realities of the people present? What does it convey about the nature of grief and fear? How did this act of violence insinuate itself into the society and culture of those who witnessed it or heard of it? How did it reconfigure cultural truths? What is it that is so powerful about this kind of violence that it is found in virtually every war taking place in the contemporary world? If war is about hegemony and control, and violence is fundamental to the carrying out of war, what is the relationship between violence and the abuse of power and control?

We also need to ask: would we as readily see violence in the plight of the mother whose son works in an area behind Renamo lines, who has no way of knowing if he is kidnapped or safe, dead or alive? Would we label as violent the situation of the child who may never have seen bloodshed, but listens, in both fascination and fear, to the stories told around the cooking fires at night of the treachery and terror the war has brought to the child's land? And whose definitions of violence do we take to be most true?

> The war brings many types of violence, and some we can
> deal with better than others. The physical mutilation and
> massacres are horrible. . . . There is no excuse for this, no

easy solution to the suffering it causes. The foreigners, the government representatives, and the journalists all talk of this as if it were the only kind of violence there is—when you see the blood run. But this may not be the worst form of violence. We have seen people hurt and killed in our life-time. We know there are dangerous people in the world. We have seen people mutilated from war and accidents. We know there are sorcerers in our midst who wish us harm. Our traditions teach us how to deal with these difficult aspects of life. This war has elevated death and mutilation to a terrible level, worse than anyone should have to live through, it is true, but these things we have seen before. But you want to know what I think is the worst thing about this war, the worst violence I suffer? It is sleeping in the bush at night. The Bandidos come at night and attack while we are sleeping, so we all sneak into our villages, our homes, during the day to do our work and tend our crops, and then sneak back into the bush at night to sleep hidden by isolation in some distant location covered only by the sky at night. Ani-mals live in the bush, not humans. Forcing us to sleep out with the animals makes us no better than them—these Ban-didos, they take away our humanity, our dignity, they make us like animals. My marriage bed is the center of all the things I hold dear. It is the center of my family, my home, my link with the ancestors and the future. This war, these soldiers, have broken my marriage bed, and with that they try to break my spirit, break what makes me who I am. This is the worst violence you can subject someone to.

Violence reverberates across personal and social landscapes in ways that move beyond the sheer physicality of the act of harm. Adding to Magaia's stories, consider the following perspectives on violence I found common in Mozambique.

Grief as a Weapon

One day, during a visit to a town that had recently shifted control from Renamo to Frelimo, several Mozambicans and I walked past a hut where a man's body was being carried out. We had been talking about the fact that more than a score of people were dying each day in the town, and the many ways war kills. One of my compatriots turned to me and said:

> His child died some days ago, and now the war has taken him too in its own awful way. You see it all the time, a young child will die, and in a few weeks the parent will be dead. He had to watch his child waste and die in his house before his eyes, unable to do anything, unable to get medicines or food or help because the war has made all this impossible. And he sits and thinks all during this time, "I am the father, I am supposed to take care of my family, to protect and nourish it; and yet here I sit watching my child die and I can do nothing." And then when the child dies, he just locks himself in his house and his grief, and he doesn't come out—and pretty soon we must perform another funeral.

Attack Against Hope and Normalcy

This is a particularly insidious form of violence. One day, I was speaking to a child of five or six years of age who had walked hundreds of kilometers with his family after his own village had been attacked and burned. He had the countenance of an adult and the weakened body of a child half his age, and he spoke with the detached seriousness of an old man about the violence he had witnessed. At one point I asked him about a wound on his leg, the type of injury children are prone to get. My question was intended only as a demonstration of concern—the wound was not serious. I was quite shaken with his response, a pronouncement delivered with the utmost seriousness:

The wound? I will die of it. We walked here many days, and we had nothing while we walked. I watched my brother die during that time. We had to leave our home because the Bandidos attacked it, and I saw them kill my father. Now we are here and I watch my mother dying slowly, because we have nothing. I will die too.

Tactical Use of Contradictions

Consider the all-too-common scenario related by Mozambicans who have been attacked by Renamo. When the soldiers came, as they often did at night, they sometimes broke into a home and raped the wife in full view of her husband and children. In fact, they often commanded the husband to remain and watch, or be killed. Sometimes family members were forced to hold the wife down during the assault. Both soldiers and victims know all too well that this is a broad-spectrum form of violence intended to undermine personal integrity and family relations in their most profound sense. Trust, normalcy, power, and control over one's life are all attacked. It is a spectacle of violence. The injustice is made worse by the actions of some of the FAM troops. I have been told by a number of FAM soldiers that if they hear of such a rape, they immediately assume the husband must be a Renamo collaborator—for how else could he sit and watch such a scene? So the violence is carried one step further, compounded layer upon layer. If the husband is incarcerated or killed by Frelimo troops because they assume he is a Renamo supporter, his wife and children suffer yet another assault in a spiral of violence—the survival of their family.

Thwarting Solutions

When chaos comes to define a person's life-world, Mozambicans seek to remedy the situation by returning order and meaning to the world through ceremonies. A constant refrain I heard among people was that, precisely because of the war, they could not perform the ceremonies they needed to. Ceremonies were usually performed at night, and the noise would alert soldiers in the area, potentially eliciting reprisals or attacks. For many Mozambicans, one of the greatest violences they were forced to endure was that they could not perform these ceremonies in order to begin healing the violence in their lives.

Emotional and Existential Violence

These rank equally with, and in many cases outrank, physical violence. The following is an excerpt of a conversation I had with a man in the interior of Zambezia the day after he arrived in town after having escaped from the Renamo band that held him. He was middle aged, his speech was halting, and his affect undermined. He was both a strong and a broken man. The first attribute had allowed him to escape; the second was a product of what he had to escape from. Speaking to him was like conversing with someone who is simultaneously present and looking off into the far distance.

> We were under Renamo control for several years. They came and took everything, including us. We were forced to move around a lot, carrying heavy loads for Renamo here, being pushed there for no apparent reason. People died, people were killed, people were hurt, assaulted, beaten—there was no medicine, no doctors, no food to help them. My family is gone, all of them. Only I am here. But the violence and the killing is not necessarily the worst of it. Worst of all is the endless hunger, the forced marches, the homelessness— day in and day out a meager and hurting existence that seems to stretch on forever.

Ongoing Violences

But what the above quote does not capture is the fact that the man's suffering is not over. An acquaintance had taken me to see the man, who was staying on the outskirts of town in a bombed-out and deserted quarter that had seen the ravages of the war come and go. Someone was sent to find him, and we spoke to him outside, on the border of a field lying fallow. At the time, I thought it unusual:

Mozambican etiquette normally involves making one's introductions, and then sitting and talking inside, on a verandah, or on a patch of ground under a tree or in a clearing. In this case, no introductions were made, and we stood, isolated from paths where others might appear unannounced or rooms where others might overhear. In the harsh sun and on a flat plain, we could see anyone coming from a distance.

Only slowly did I realize that the man's ordeals continued. I remembered a phrase I had heard repeated frequently, both by civilians and soldiers: that one was never sure about these people who had been with Renamo for such a long time, kidnapped or not—for the violence and the way of life, maybe even the ideology, under Renamo might become absorbed, become a habit, become reproduced. Soldiers and civilians grappled with this dilemma in different ways. The soldiers said they investigated the person to try to determine if he or she might have become a Renamo collaborator. If the evidence was strong, the person might be shot or taken to prison. Sometimes this was done even if no apparent proof of collaboration existed, or if there was evidence the kidnap victim had been forced to participate in raids. The soldiers explained these were not necessarily punitive actions. They justified their deeds by arguing that most kidnap victims escape far from their homeland, and without money or family connections they have little means of returning to safety. Should such a person fall back into the hands of Renamo, he or she will certainly be killed, the soldiers say. So for their own protection, they may be incarcerated. For others' protection they may be killed. Personally, I did not find the soldier's actions to be so reasoned. I encountered a number of towns where FAM troops had arrived and shot Curandeiros, village leaders, traders, and people suspected of being collaborators on the flimsiest of reasons. *Deslocados* were often suspect merely because they were "dislocated," and even for the most innocent victims of war the fact remained that soldiers and officials kept a close eye on *deslocados*.

Civilians have a different means of dealing with the recently escaped, means generally far more grounded in creative resolutions than in violence. Fluent in the realities of life under war, they recognize that the violence to which people have been subjected can remain with them, capable of erupting at a later date, and that this violence can ruin normal sensibilities. The solution, however, is to recommend African medical therapy from a curandeiro or curandeira who specializes in war trauma. Such a professional is adept at recognizing the psychological and emotional as well as physical wounds of war, at treating them, and at helping the patient begin to reintegrate into a normal community life.

But the end point was that everyone was concerned with those who have suffered under Renamo, and were watching them carefully. Because the man I spoke with had just arrived, and had not been interrogated by the troops, embraced by the community, or treated by local methods, his position was volatile. And because he had not undergone these rites of passage, he had not learned how to respond appropriately. As is often the case with people in this condition, they are extremely honest about their ordeal, almost carelessly so—they have not yet learned to "edit" their conversations to fit social and political requirements. It seems clear that my acquaintance felt for the man and was concerned with his protection, but also thought it important that his story be known, and for that reason he took me to see him. So we stood at the edge of a field in an isolated area talking and watching for anyone to approach. I have often wondered if that man finally made it to the safety of his home village, if he languishes in prison, or if he is dead. I never heard of him again.

Destruction of the Future

One day I was speaking with a man in the clinic who had just had his testicles cut off by a contingent of Renamo soldiers he had the bad luck of running into. Although bandaged and clearly in pain, his concern was not with the overt violence to which he had been subjected, or with the wound itself, but with what this wound meant to his future.

> I have two wives. What will they say to me when I return home? I am not like I was before, now I can give them

nothing. How will they want to stay with a man who has
no sex?

Is the cutting off of the man's testicles the violence? Is it the cutting
off of his identity as a man and a husband? Is it the cutting off of his
lineage, of the children he will now never father? Or is it something
more profound and enduring? The Mozambican scholar Sergio Viera
once said to me that the aim of the war was to create a *nonsociety*, and
that is why tactics like castration are employed. The spectacle of violence cannot be detached from its experience, its aftermath, its
enduring reality. Dirty-war specialists know the actions of today define
the truths of tomorrow.

One of the most insidious and powerful targets of violence is the
very sense of future that gives definition and direction to people's lives.
In an uncertain present, a future is impossible to determine. But to be
human is to have a future, and this lack of future, people said, can fuel
further violences:

> People do what they do, the atrocities and responses,
> because they do not see a future. They have no sense of
> themselves in the future. Thus a man who kills doesn't think
> of the repercussions of his act—that the spirits of those he
> has killed will return to harm him, that the society he has
> violated will hold him responsible.

The assault against a viable future carries a great weight in everyday
life. When a friend who lived in a different province asked me to stay
a while longer during a visit, I told her I had to go, but that I would
return. She responded:

> Don't talk to me of the future, don't talk to me of coming
> back. Maybe I'll be dead, killed by the soldiers, maybe I'll
> have had to flee and no one, even me, will know where I
> am, maybe they'll blow up this damn town with everything

and everyone in it and then what will you have to come
back to? No, don't talk to me of tomorrow—stay here for
we may only have today.

The reverberating effects of violence projected onto uncertain
futures is nowhere more evident than with people like Anna, whose
story opened this chapter. Her chronicles of violence, from watching
her village burned and her son killed to the indignities of life as a *deslocado*, will not be over with the end of the war. In discussing Anna and
the people like her that have come to populate the desperation of the
Mozambican landscape, Joaquim Segurada, a Portuguese anthropologist working with Action Aid in Mozambique said to me:

> So what happens when these women go back to their
> homelands? Still they are missing their husbands, their
> families. Who will want them? Maybe they return to find
> their lands missing—that they have lost the rights to
> them when they lost their husband, or maybe some avari-
> cious person or enterprise has taken their land over, and
> the women have no means, no strength to fight this. But
> worse than that, they will have lost "normalcy": the con-
> text of their family and home can never be the same again—
> it has been irreparably destroyed. Healthy culture, as they
> knew it, is gone. How are they to live and thrive, to find new
> husbands, to find land to work, to build a home where
> they can raise their children well, to reestablish family
> ties with a family that has been shattered? Unfortunately,
> isolation is their plight now, and it will be their ongoing
> plight in the future; and for Africans, isolation is an
> impossibility.

I had just heard a woman's account of her experiences that gave
tragic illumination to Segurada's words and am reminded with this
story that it is not just this woman's, this family's, future that is a

casualty of war. This is a stark example of the conditions necessary to reproduce violence across generations if left unsolved.

> I was kidnapped by the Bandidos Armados several years ago when they attacked our village, and forced to march back to their base camp. Life was awful: we had only the clothes on our backs, a fist in our face, heavy loads on our heads to carry, nothing in our bellies, and a soldier with his penis out coming at us every time we turned around. I was "given" to many men, and in the way of nature, shortly became pregnant and gave birth at the Renamo camp. It seemed like I was gone forever, for a lifetime. Sometimes I could not believe I was still alive. Times were always hard for us at the camp, but it became hard for the Bandidos as well. Food became scarce, and there were some attacks a distance away which forced some of the soldiers to leave and lend help in other places. With the confusion, some of us saw the chance to make our getaway, and slipped off one night into the bush. All those long days walking back to my village, all I could think about was how happy I was to be returning to my home, my husband and family, my machamba, my parents, and the land of my ancestors. Little did I know another war was about to begin. When I arrived home, my husband had taken up with another woman. I was disappointed but not surprised, I had been gone away a long time. I still expected to live with him [her society is polygamous], but he could not stand the fact that I had a child by another man, even though it had been conceived in rape. He hit the child and called it filth, and threw me and the child out. My parents were still alive, and I moved back with them. But my father felt much as my husband had. He would hit my child and call him Renamo dirt, and tell me I was dirt to have produced him. He would con-stantly say, "You should take this filth back out to the bush

and leave it there along with the rest of the Renamo garbage." No other man will consider me now. I see no future for me. I live with my parents now, but they are growing old and will die someday, and then I have no idea what will happen to me. I cry, and my child cries. But it is worse for him. He is treated like dirt, and he is starting to act like it: he is angry and aggressive, withdrawn and difficult. He does not play and grow and learn normally like the other boys. What will he grow up to be? This war has killed so much, and it is killing generations to come.

from Martyrs' Day
by Michael Kelly

Michael Kelly traveled throughout the Middle East during
and after the first Gulf War. His reporting included a visit
to Kuwait in the aftermath of the Iraqi occupation. Kelly
was killed on April 3, 2003 while covering the U.S. invasion
of Iraq.

The hall at Kuwait University's school of music and drama was a
place of conspicuous civilization, a big cantilevered room with
blue cloth seats trimmed in gold. The walls were paneled in
some rich wood, and a deep, broad stage surmounted the
orchestra pit. The first discordant signs of barbarism were feathers and
bones. The building was of modern design, with an exterior ramp that
led several stories up to a broad concrete platform, which in turn led
to the doors that opened into the top tier of the auditorium. The Iraqis
had used the platform as a pen for chickens and sheep, and what the
beasts had left behind made a rotting, malodorous mess underfoot.

Inside the hall a British television crew was videotaping the statement of twenty-nine-year-old Abdullah Jasman, Kuwaiti citizen, University of Pittsburgh graduate, and victim of a torture session in this
unlikely setting. The crew had set their camera up on the balcony, and

Jasman stood a few feet away, facing it. When I walked in, the producer in charge motioned with his finger to his lips for me to be quiet. I stopped, and the place was still and silent except for the man standing in front of the camera, talking and crying. He was a square-built black man, with strong, homely features; not the face of one for public weeping. But this sort of thing no longer surprised me. In normal life, you hardly ever see grown men cry; in war, it is a commonplace. Between the beginning of things and the end, I must have seen twenty men cry, not counting myself.

Near where the camera stood, there lay a broken rubber-handled truncheon. In a corner was a pile of academic robes, trimmed in azure and gold, sodden and reeking of wet rot and urine. Here and there the tile floor was spotted with drops of dried blood, little trails that went nowhere in particular.

"One day on the highway the Iraqis stopped us," the black man began.

"Could you just come forward a bit, Abdullah?" said the producer. "Need to get you in frame properly."

He moved forward a step. The producer said, "Now, that's a good chap. Where were we, hmm?"

"I was with a group of people. They covered our eyes and roped our hands and put us in a line and walked us up here." A door cracked suddenly shut, and he jumped in a rabbity little hop.

"Oh, sorry, Abdullah," the producer said. He gestured to his Ministry of Information guide. "You there, keep that door shut." Turning back to the black man: "Now then."

"They hang us upside down. Naked, no clothes; we are not allowed to sleep or eat. They try to get us drunk, but we do not. So they started torturing us. The three days passed like years. [He was crying hard now.] Human beings can't resist. You hear people screaming next to you and then you think you are going to be next. You can't resist. What are you going to do? [Now, racking sobs] You can't sleep. You don't know, if you sleep, if you will ever wake again. . . . All the people screaming, begging, screaming."

The producer interrupted him, to prompt him toward the thing that made for television. "Abdullah, could you tell us what happened to you in particular, here in this theater?" he said.

The victim pointed to the stage, on which stood a big section of steel set scaffolding. "On this stage, you can see the metal frame. They put both legs on that and they open them wide and they put a sort of wood on you that comes from one knee to another and they spread you open all the way. When you are open wide, it hurts you. It hurts you bad. They raped one of my friends here. They raped him. They were laughing. They said, 'This is what your president did to you.' I heard later he was dead."

He drifted back into hideous reverie. "You sat in these chairs, waiting to be tortured. You can't see anything. You can hear the voices loud and screaming. . . . They wanted to know where is my brother. I didn't tell them; I didn't know. . . . My family gave them five thousand Kuwait dinars and videos and a TV. . . . They let me go. . . ."

The producer gave him another little push. "And what did they do to you besides putting you on the rack, Abdullah?"

He pulled up his pants legs and showed the camera his calves, mottled with ugly deep black burn wounds. "They put electricity on you with batteries. They would put wires on your legs and your feet in water, so your whole body is electricity. They would put you with the electricity in the water twenty seconds, thirty seconds, and you would go unconscious and they would throw water on you and revive you and then do it again."

As he was finishing, he offered an observation on the nature of torture. "Torture not only hurts at the time. It will hurt all your life. You get up at night and you think that you are in a torture room, not in bed. You are in a safe place, and you think that you are not safe. It is like a fingerprint for the rest of your life." He shivered when he said this, as if fevered.

The producer thanked him, and motioned for the cameraman to turn off the machine. "Well," he said, "I must say, your story is really something." The black man stood silent, with one trouser leg hiked up to the knee and tear trails streaking the dust on his face.

• • •

All over Kuwait City after the Iraqis left, people talked of murder and torture and disfigurement and rape. Over the seven months of the occupation, they had become involuntary experts in these things. Familiarity had not bred contempt—pain and death command respect—but morbid fascination. They could not get over with what eagerness and thoroughness the Iraqis had hurt them. It was something almost beyond comprehension, something vastly out of the run of their experiences. They were an unusually insulated, unusually pampered people. For more than two hundred years, they had lived in a stable oligarchy, peacefully prospering since their beginnings in 1752, when Sabah bin Jaber became the first emir of the small seacoast town that had grown up around a fort (*kut*, in Arabic, from which comes Kuwait) built by the bedouin chieftain who then held sway over northeastern Arabia. The town of Kuwait, set on a firm coastal beach in the Bay of Kuwait, enjoyed two local rarities, sweet water and a good protected harbor, and was geographically well placed to trade between the interior of Arabia, the eastern coast of Africa, and the western coasts of India and Indonesia. It quickly became the dominant entrepôt of the region, with a large fleet of *dhows, boums* and *baghlabs*, trading in, wrote a British observer, "Bengal piece goods, Coromandel chintzes, Madras long-cloth, cotton yarn and various cotton manufactures of Malabar, Broach, Cambay, Surat and Gujurat; English woolen goods; silks, Arabian coffee; sugar and sugar candy; spices, condiments and perfumes; indigo; drugs; chinaware; and metals." It became as well the leader in the Gulf pearl trade, and by the turn of the twentieth century it supported a fleet of more than eight hundred diving *dhows*.

In 1938, the Kuwait Oil Company (one half Gulf Oil and one half Anglo-Iranian Oil, now British Petroleum) tapped the Burgan oil field twenty-five miles south of Kuwait City, the second-largest field in the world. Interrupted by the Second World War, drilling began in earnest in 1946, and by August 1990, Kuwait had 950 wells pumping out 1.5 million barrels of oil a day, with proven reserves of 94 billion barrels, enough to last at those production levels for more than 130 years. The oil money converted Kuwait from a country of slowly accumulating wealth to one of super-riches; by 1990, the little city-state had a per capita income of $14,700, up there with Abu Dhabi, the United States, and Liechtenstein. The unemployment rate was zero; the inflation rate was about 3 percent. There was so much money, and so few Kuwaitis, that for most people work was something other people did. Of the two million people who lived in Kuwait, 60 percent were non-Kuwaitis, guest workers and their families. Foreign workers made up 70 percent of the labor force. Palestinians managed the government agencies and the businesses, Indians ran the hotels, Filipinas served as maids (and sometimes as forced mistresses), Egyptians built the roads and houses and glass towers of the new downtown, Sudanese and Senegalese and Algerians swept the streets and picked up the trash. Eighty percent of the nation's 3,200 physicians were foreigners, 90 percent of the ten thousand nurses. Except for the topmost level of deal-cutting and decision-making, foreigners did everything that needed to be done in Kuwait.

In return, Kuwait gave its guest workers a standard of living that was well beyond anything most of them could enjoy at home, with one of the most comprehensive social welfare programs in the world. Medical treatment was free, for everybody, and of sufficient quality to produce a death rate of only 2.4 per thousand, with a life expectancy for men of seventy-one years, for women, seventy-five. The public school system was well funded and free through the secondary level. University and technical schools maintained high standards and low tuition and were open to non-Kuwaitis. Seventy-four percent of the population above fifteen was literate.

A tiny, interconnected group of well-satisfied men ran everything. Only 6 to 7 percent of Kuwaiti citizens had the right to vote: literate adult males who had lived in Kuwait before 1920 and their literate adult male descendants. Of this group, only half, or 3.5 percent of the total population of citizens, had voted in the last election. The 1962 constitution gave all real power to the emir, Sheikh Jaber al-Sabah, who was chosen by members of his family; other important government positions were filled by Sabahs or by men the Sabahs chose from the small, shallow pool of the oligarchy. There had been some experiments in participatory democracy, but they had not set well with the ruling class; in 1986, the emir had dissolved the young National Assembly and announced he would henceforth rule by decree.

In two hundred years, the Kuwaitis had never fought to protect their wealth, preferring to deal with predators through shifting treaty arrangements and allegiances, and through generous payments of protection money. Since 1973, when Iraq made a tentative land grab turned back by British pressure, Kuwait had given its big, belligerent neighbor a great deal of money, including $12 billion in loans for the war with Iran. In 1990, Kuwait's armed forces amounted to a little more than twenty thousand troops, about one-fiftieth the size of the Iraqi armed forces.

You could see the difference between Iraq and Kuwait simply by the way the young men of each nation carried themselves. Young Iraqi men, in their black vinyl jackets and pegged trousers, moved like Marseilles toughs, with hips rolling in subtle insolence and shoulders squared in puffed-up counterpoise above. The young Kuwaiti men walked tough too, but there was something distinctly off-note about it; it seemed an imitation, the swagger of a rich kid forced to walk home through the bad part of town because the chauffeur forgot to pick him up at school. To a country like this, a people like this, the nature of the Iraqi visitation was an astonishment and a bewilderment and a shock.

After I left the theater, I drove to a gas station in a middle-class residential neighborhood. Gas had been largely unavailable since December 2, when the Iraqis forbade its sale to Kuwaitis, but here and there stations were getting their pumps working again, and word of where there was gas circulated around the city every day. There must have been three hundred people and a long line of cars waiting on a crew of four or five men who were working with portable pumps and generators to get the gasoline up from the underground tanks. I put my cans in line and went into the little office of the gas station to escape the heat. There was a man behind the desk who looked in charge. He said that, actually, it wasn't his gas station, but he knew his way around pumps and engines, so his neighbors had made him boss. He was a tall, skinny man, with features that were all crags and hollows. He handed me his card, which identified him, in fancy script, as Basim Eid Abhool, Assistant Electrical Engineer, Kuwait International Airport. When I gave it back to him, I noticed his fingernails, or rather the lack of them. They had been removed, and what was left was just the barest baby beginnings of new nails, little strips of cuticle as soft and fragile as the shells of the smallest shrimp. "Ah, you notice my fingers?" the man said. "Iraqis, of course."

He told his story in a matter-of-fact way, leaning his forearms on the desk, and with his hands folded so that his fingernails were tucked away. A group of men gathered around while he talked, but they were quiet, so that all you could hear was his voice and the buzzing of flies. I sat in a hard little yellow plastic chair and wrote down what he said. He spoke slowly, so it was easy to get it all verbatim.

"It was on January 19. They arrested me outside, while I was walking. They took me to a prison. They say, 'Are you in army?' I say, 'Yes, but not anymore. Now I work at airport and am an assistant engineer.' They put me in a small room and they say, 'Exactly what do you do in the army?'

"I say, 'When I am in army, I am a writer, not a soldier, and now I am not in army anyway.'

"They say, 'You have friends, cousins, in army?' I say, 'I don't know.' They say, 'Do you know that your president, Sheikh Jaber, he is no good?'

"I say, 'I don't know.'

"They say, 'Do you know what your president do to your people?'

"I say, 'I don't know. What do he do to my people?'

"They say, 'He marry two hundred women and he take all your money.'

"I say, 'I do not know that. Thank you for telling me.'

"They say, 'The Iraqi people have come to give freedom to people of Kuwait.'

"Then a man comes in who has no uniform. He says, 'Put him in jail.' I stay in jail until Thursday. All the time, behind me in the other room, I hear screaming, 'No, no, please, no, I don't do anything, please.' I listen. I am afraid. On the second day, they come back and they say, 'Put your hands on the table.' I put my hands on the table and they take a stick and hit my hands. They say, 'Can you feel?' I say, 'Yes.' They say, 'Good.' Then two guys take my hands and hold them and they tell me to close my eyes and they take pliers and one by one pull out all my fingers [fingernails]. Then they put them in salt water. And go away.

"You know, the first day and the second day and the third, I feel terrible. But after that I cannot feel it. My hands, my arms, my head, all feels numb. On the third day, Thursday, they take me back to the room. They take my fingers and where the nails were, they take pliers and crush. It is too much. Much too much. I faint. When I wake up, they say, 'You have Kuwait money?' I say, 'No.' They put me back in jail.

"On the fourth day, they say, 'Don't tell anybody what we do here. If you tell anybody, we will kill you.' And they let me go. I go home. My family is all gone out of Kuwait, but my friends say, 'What happen to your fingers?' I say, 'It was an electrical accident at work.' Two weeks later, I see the Iraqis who did this to me at supermarket. They are shopping. One of them says hello to me and he says, 'How are your fingers? Are they good?' I say, 'No, they are not good.' He says, 'Come back to the police station and we will make them good.' And then they laugh.

"But now—*hamdililah*—I am good again."

A thin man, squatting on the floor, picking his teeth with a bit of wood, spoke up. His name was Wael Yusef al-Moutawa, twenty-three years old, an employee of the Kuwait National Petroleum Company. He said: "One day the Iraqi soldiers arrest me. I was carrying a gun because I was a resistance fighter. A Kalashnikov. They beat me, and after that, they take a rope and tie my hands behind my back and tie the rope on the ceiling and pull me up by my hands tied behind my back. They kept me hanging there. The first hour was not so bad, but then it got very bad.

"My father and mother came and they brought two thousand dinars to free me. They took the money and said to my parents, 'Soon, he will get out.'

"The next day, an Iraqi man comes to me and he says, 'You love Mr. Jaber? Okay, you watch this. This is what Mr. Jaber does to your people.' He brings in a girl twenty years old, maybe. I am staying on the wall tied up. I try not to see. The soldiers pull my head and say, 'You must see.' One soldier holds the girl hard and the other fucks her. She tries to stop them. She says, 'I am a virgin.' She says to the soldiers, 'You are a Muslim. You must be polite to me. You must be a good man. You cannot do this to me. I am a Muslim. I am your sister.'

"He says, 'I am not a Muslim.'

"She says, 'You do not believe in God?'

"He says, 'You have a God? Where is your God? There is no God. Who is Muhammad? An old man.'

"Then they rape her and I watch and I can see the blood going out. They put her on the floor of the room and do it. And then they take her out, like a sheep. It was very shameful."

He thought about it for a minute and then he said, "I think there are no Muslims in Iraq. Not at all. Really, they are all crazy."

A smiling middle-aged man with a grocer's figure interrupted to disagree slightly. He introduced himself as Ali Zamoon, general manager of the Kuwait National Real Estate Company. He had been educated in America and had married an American woman. He had an American sort of theory. The Iraqis were not precisely crazy, but were brainwashed, a nation of Manchurian Candidates.

"One time I was stopped by some Iraqi soldiers while I was driving my car. They asked me why I had not changed my license plates from Kuwaiti plates to Iraqi. I said I forgot to do it, or something. But they could not get over it. They could not understand how I could have failed to change the plates after Saddam had told me to do so. They said, 'How can you disobey an order from Saddam?' This made me think about it, and I realized that there was something wrong with these people. Everything they did and thought was all about Saddam. It was Saddam! Saddam! Saddam! all the time. They were like robots.

They would follow this man anywhere, doing whatever, because they could not imagine disobeying him. They could not see any point to disobeying an order, even if they knew it was wrong. One day I had a talk with an Iraqi officer I had come to know a little. I asked him, 'If they tell you from Baghdad to kill me, would you kill me?' And he said, 'Yes.' I said, 'Why?' He said, 'Because if they ask me to kill you and I say no, they will kill me and then kill you anyway."

The men who had dealt most directly and most often with the horror—the emergency-room doctors and morgue-keepers and ambulance drivers—had tried to make sense out of it by quantifying and classifying its various permutations.

At Mubarak Hospital, the fourth-largest in the city, Dr. Abdullah Behbehani, a small man with that perpetually harried air that you often see in doctors, sat with his hands neatly folded at his desk. He had occupied his mind—perhaps saved his mind—by charting the plague of murder and torture and rape in the same methodical way he would plot a plague of cholera or influenza. He spoke in a small, dry voice.

"All told, we saw approximately four hundred executions at this hospital, and from the beginning I kept careful track of the trends of atrocities. In the beginning, in August, they didn't practice any atrocities against the civilians. They were just interested in invading the country and destroying the army and annexing Kuwait. . . .

"However, it was clear from the beginning that they were very quick to kill. I give you an example. On August 3, the day after the invasion, the Iraqis came here to supervise the evacuation of Iraqi soldiers wounded in the first day of the invasion. We had taken in some of them and treated them, the same as we would a Kuwaiti. As the evacuation was going on, my anesthesiologist, a Kuwaiti lady doctor, was standing next to me and she said, 'God curse the devil,' which is a well-known saying in our culture. An Iraqi officer heard her say this and he said, 'You mean the devil with the beard?'—which was of course a reference to our emir. And she said, 'No I mean you Iraqis, because we were sitting here in peace and you invaded us.' So the officer immediately called over some army men and he told them to hold her and said, 'I will execute you on the spot.' He pulled out his pistol and pointed it at her.

"I had to beg him to spare her. I said, 'Look, we were invaded just now. We were Kuwaitis when we went to sleep last night and now we are Iraqis. You must give us some time to accept this.' After my begging, he said he would forgive her and let her live.

"This was the way it was always. You could not say anything, even a word, of rejection. The only punishment the Iraqis know is to kill. No trials. No prison terms. Just kill.

"When we, the civilians, started to resist and show that we did not like being annexed, the first thing we did was demonstrate peacefully— women, young men, and children. We would raise the Kuwaiti flag and pictures of the emir in demonstrations; we did this to show the Iraqis we did not accept annexation and we wanted our government back and we wanted them out. They immediately opened fire on the demonstrators. I personally had to amputate the leg of a thirty-five-year-old Kuwaiti female because of her bullet wounds. I saw young children killed. The Iraqi soldiers did not try to end the demonstration peacefully or anything like that. They just immediately opened fire against the demonstrators, many of whom were women. This was one week after the invasion.

"The atrocities began soon after that, in reaction to the Kuwaiti people refusing to go along with the annexation. They did this by refusing to go to work, refusing to open their shops, refusing to change their IDs, refusing to do anything except sit in their houses. Soon we began expressing our opinions on walls. Either by putting flags on them or by writing signs of rejection and refusal and signs saying that we wanted our government back. The Iraqis started shooting anyone they saw participating in this. They would shoot them immediately, on the spot. No trial. My sister witnessed two children shot dead in this fashion.

"The most serious atrocities began in the next phase, when the Kuwaiti resistance started trying to carry arms and kill Iraqis. The Iraqis responded with great force. They sent in a new governor, Ali Hassan Majid, and he brought in execution squads from Iraq. The execution squads were not regular soldiers, and they were very brutal. They began executing young men on a systematic basis. We started to see a lot of men between the ages of seventeen and thirty-two brought in here, not as patients to care for, but as bodies to bury. They were brought in in groups of five to ten. This happened almost every day for two to three months; every day we would see another group of bodies. In the beginning, the executions were straightforward—bullets in the head, bullets in the chest. At first they were killed in front of their houses. They would take the young man out of the house and blindfold him, and stand him up in front of the house and then shoot him in the head or the chest in front of his family. This method accomplished two things. One, it meant that they didn't have to deal with the body; they just left it for the family. Two, it contributed to the atmosphere of fear. These executions began in late August and lasted throughout September and October.

"In late September, there started something more severe. We started getting mutilated and tortured bodies. These were bodies that had not simply been shot, but had had their eyeballs taken out, their heads smashed, their bones broken. It was very painful for us as doctors to see this. We could not imagine how anyone who thinks of himself as a human being could do this to another human being. The injuries were very bad. You would see heads completely unvaulted, that is, with the top of the skull sawed off or cut off with an ax and no brain left in the skull pan. Or you would see multiple fractures, legs that had been broken four or five times. Or you would see severe burns on the face and body. Or fingernails that had been extracted.

"When the mutilations began, the Iraqis stopped bringing in the bodies of those killed. They started dumping them in the streets and then calling us and saying, 'There are bodies in such and such a street,' or 'near such and such a police station. Come get them.' And we would send out an ambulance and pick them up.

"We didn't know what these people had done to be killed in this manner. There were old people among those killed, at least fifty of them.

"Then, in November, worse atrocities began, involving women. We started getting numerous women brought in who had been raped and tortured. Rapes became very common after the first few months of the invasion. They would kidnap women, detain them, rape them, and then either kill them or let them go. I personally was on call when three cases of rape came in. I treated all three women. One, I recall, was a young woman who had been raped by three soldiers. They came into her home and hit her husband and smashed his face and broke his ribs with their rifle butts. Then they assaulted her sexually. I was very careful in documenting this by direct examination of her. The awful thing was that she had her period at the time, so they took her from behind—anally—the bastards. The poor woman. What made it even worse was that when the soldiers first came in and attacked her husband, he actually was able at one point to get his hands on a gun and he was going to try to shoot the soldiers, but his wife and his mother told him it was not necessary and got him to give the gun back to the soldiers. You see, they thought the soldiers were just there to beat them and question them, but after the soldiers got the gun back, then they raped the wife.

"I knew one particular woman. The top of her head was gone and bullets were in her chest when they brought her in. She had been picked up and detained for a month and a half. I knew her well. I think she was involved in a lot of resistance activity, principally in sending messages to the government in exile. She was less than twenty-four years old. She was married and had two children. Her name was Asrar al-Kabany. We knew she had been kidnapped right in front of her door, when she was taking out the garbage. She was—my God—she was completely mutilated! They dumped her on the street and the ambulance brought her in here and I saw her—"

As he was talking, the doctor had lost, bit by bit, the voice of the scientific observer, and now he was suddenly overwhelmed. He put his face in his hands and wept, and it was a minute or two before he could recover himself sufficiently to speak. "There was no brain inside her skull. Why should you take the brain out, for God's sake? I am sorry. I get emotional whenever I speak of this." The tears streamed from his eyes, really heavy crying, although silent; the sobs shook his shoulders.

At Al-Sabah Hospital—a big, crowded, dirty place, the hallways lined with various sitting and lying specimens of the hurt, the sick, and the lame—a surgeon named Ali Nassar al-Serafi invited me into a small office, where we sat in the dark and drank sweet coffee.

"From the very beginning, the Iraqis brought bodies in here. Most of the people were killed by a single bullet shot to the head. They brought them in here not to treat but to dispose of. They forced us to write fake death certificates for some of them, saying they had died in car accidents or something. Some people, before they killed them, they removed their eyes. In other cases, there was physical evidence that people had been mistreated by electricity or by cigarettes, or had been beaten badly. We saw people with multiple fractures of the hands or legs. The fractures appeared to have been caused by blows with heavy objects. Sometimes they would bring in people whom they had mis-treated, and ask us to make them better, so they could take them away again for more. This happened seven or eight times to me.

"One man they brought in had massive bruising all over his chest and shoulders from beatings. I said, 'What happened to you?' He said, 'A metal door fell on me.' He was really very sick. I knew they had mis-handled him and hurt him and that he was obliged to lie about it. I wanted to help this man. He was my countryman and he was begging me to admit him to the hospital for just two or three days, so he could get a rest from his suffering. But the Iraqis wanted me to examine him and make sure he could survive more beating so they could take him away again. I had to have a legal excuse to admit him, so I asked him if he had vomited or had lost consciousness and he said he had. I was able to tell the Iraqis he had suffered a concussion and must be admitted for several days. The policemen let me admit him.

"Later, two Iraqi security men came to see me. They said, 'We are investigating a case and we need this man back to continue our inves-tigation.' I told them he was in need of admission for twenty-four, forty-eight hours. They said, 'Give him medicine and we will take him back with us.' I said, 'There is a danger if you do that that he will lose consciousness because of bleeding in the brain and die on you.' So they let me keep him for two days.

"On examination, I found he had been beaten with great severity. When I opened his shirt, I thought at first a tank had rolled over his chest. He had been beaten so hard that I found the symbol of the Iraqi army from belt buckles imprinted on his skin. He was conscious, but very, very sick. He got a little better over the two days, not much, and then the security men came and took him away and I never saw him again.

"They got someone in the information office to give them some death certificates, which they filled out however they wanted, and then forced me to sign. They liked to say the people had died by automobile accident, and when I protested that it was clear from the bullet wounds that they had died by gunshot, they thought of something clever. After they were finished with an interrogation of a person, they would take him outside and hit him with a car, and run over him. Then they would bring him here and say he had died from being hit by an automobile, and that was certainly true.

"We are still not sure of the total number of dead brought here. There were so many we lost track, and just now we are still doing autopsies to determine the cause of death for people we have in the morgue. There were a lot of people who were buried without autopsies, and without identification. We would just label them 'Unknown.' "

We walked out in the cool dusk air, around back of the hospital to the charnel house, a good, modern morgue, surrounded by a large courtyard, with white speckled tile floors and walls so that the blood and fluids of putrefaction could be easily washed away. The longest wall, opposite the door, was at least forty feet long and was lined from floor almost to ceiling with refrigerated drawers of stainless steel, twenty-two of them. The whole room was refrigerated, actually, which was a good thing, because the week's fighting had produced an overflow crowd. At least a dozen dead Iraqi soldiers were lying bloated and twisted in the peculiar positions of death, all entwined together on the floor, with blankets here and there cursorily covering them. Most of them had no shoes on, and their feet, puffed up from the gases, swelled out of their pants legs. Their skin was yellow-green. Even with the refrigeration, the stink of half-rotted flesh and formaldehyde was something awful. I lit a cigarette, and the smell was much worse mixed with hot smoke.

The morgue boss came in with us. He was also the hospital's chief ambulance driver, and he said he had picked up more bodies from more street corners in the last seven months than he could even guess at. There were times, he said, when the entire morgue and the entire courtyard would be filled with bodies. He was an old man named Subi Younis, shabby in dress and rough in manner, and very much at home among the dead. He talked slowly—I don't think he was very smart—and spent a lot of time thinking over each question I asked. He spoke in Arabic, and the doctor translated.

"Well, I would say we had more than four hundred bodies here during the occupation, and probably as many as seven hundred. They were all civilians. Some of them were Kuwaitis and some of them were foreigners. They would bring them in bunches. Just dump them here. Many times, the whole yard was covered with bodies. We buried a lot of people in mass graves. Maybe thirty, forty people in each grave, up at the Sulaibikhat Cemetery."

He pulled open drawers at random and slid each metal pan out halfway on the runners, so that the bodies were exposed under the bright white lights, and I looked at them, and wrote down the particulars in a child's composition book I had bought in Hafar al-Batin, the paper cover of which was decorated in gay blue and red and purple flowers.

The corpse in drawer 16 was of a handsome man in his thirties. He had a full black beard, which was stiff with dried, caked blood. His formerly white shirt was blood-dyed a rusty brown, and blood had coagulated in purplish gobs, like horrible raisins, at his nostrils and ears and mouth. He had been shot twice, execution-style, in the chest and head. He had been brought in on February 19, and he was labeled "Unknown."

As we stood looking at him, two men came in. They were middle-aged, both of them, fat around the middle and dressed in clean, pressed clothes. They seemed quite out of place, but they were in the right spot; they had come to look, they said, for a cousin who had disappeared the week before. Since drawer 16 was already open, Mr. Younis said they might as well start with that one, and the men peered over my shoulder and looked down. "No, that is not who I want," said one. "No, it is not," said the other. "But the funny thing is, I know him. I can't remember the name, but I know the face. He lived in the neighborhood." He shrugged. "What can you do?"

Mr. Younis sighed. "So many killed, in all areas of the city. Why, I remember we had forty-five bodies one day. In one massacre. Came in from the police morgue in a truck."

His assistant interrupted him. "That is nothing," he said. "On August 3, you remember, the day after the invasion, we take in eighty people on one day."

"Oh yes, that is true. I had forgotten," Mr. Younis said.

The corpse in drawer 3 had its yellowed hands tied behind its back with a strip of white rag. It was naked and it had belonged to a young man. When he was alive, he had been beaten from the soles of the feet to the crown of the head, and every inch of his skin was covered with purple-and-black bruises. His shoulders and chest were crosshatched with the marks of an additional beating from some sort of stick, or rod, or whip. His legs were striped with deep black bruises six inches or more long. Such torture would most likely have been sufficient to kill him, but he had probably died from one particular, terrible blow to the head. The whole right side of his skull was caved in, like the way a pumpkin gets several weeks after Halloween, rotting and gently folding in on itself.

The man in drawer 12 had been burned to death with some flammable liquid. His body, found in a suburban street on October 9, was shrunken and slightly mummified and curled fetus-like. The hands were claws, and what remained of the head was still barely recognizable as a head, but a head that seemed to have been slathered in some brown, viscous liquid—molasses, maybe—and then baked. The features had disappeared in the process, and the body was also labeled "Unknown."

The corpse in drawer 4 was hardly damaged at all, just one round little hole in the neck where the bullet had gone in and a messier, bigger place on the other side, where it had gone out again. "No, no, that is not him either," said the man looking for his cousin.

Corpse 17 was another fire victim. This one had been burned so badly it no longer looked like a body at all. It looked like something you might find on the beach on an early-morning walk, in the smoldering remains of a driftwood fire. It was only about four feet long and had no legs or arms; it was just a husk with something round stuck on one end that presumably had been a head. November 3; Unknown.

Corpses 18 and 19 had names. They belonged to the brothers Abbas. On January 20, the Abbases had gotten excited by reports of the war and had led a small, bloody insurrection against a police substation in their suburban neighborhood. The rebellion had failed and the bodies of the Abbas men had arrived at the morgue with those of five of their neighbors, rounded up and killed for the sake of good measure and collective reprisal. All of the dead had been shot in the head, and the eyeballs of the elder of the Abbas brothers had been removed. The sockets were bloody holes. "We believe the eyeballs were plucked out with fingers while he was alive," Dr. al-Serafi said, with a sad little shake of his head.

There were more in other drawers, but Mr. Younis said I had seen enough, and I didn't argue the point. We all went outside and I offered around my cigarettes and we all smoked in the cooling dusk breeze.

"You cannot imagine how it was," the morgue assistant said, after the silence. "It was easy to die. I remember, in my neighborhood, someone one day put up a poster of the emir on the supermarket window. The police saw it and soon the security men came around and they said to the manager of the supermarket, 'Who did this?' He said he did not know, which was true; he did not So the security men took him outside right then and there and made all the people in the store and in the street gather around, and the one in charge said, 'We are going to have a demonstration today. The demonstration is called How to Kill a Supermarket Manager.' And then he pointed his pistol at him and shot him in the head."

"It is true," said Dr. al-Serafi. "No one can believe what we have seen. No one can believe that such things happen in the twentieth century. It is beyond human thinking. I could never have imagined this before, and I still do not believe it now. But I know it is true because I have lived with it every day for seven months." Many people in Kuwait City, he said, never fully grasped the horrors of what was going on, because they were not exposed to the daily evidence that those in the medical community saw, and because they did not want to believe what they heard. "I would tell people outside the hospital what I was seeing, and they would say, 'You are exaggerating.' And I would say, 'No, I am saying less than it is. I am only telling you I have seen today a man shot in the head and his eyes removed. I am not telling you about the man I have seen who is burned alive.' "

The Iraqis I had met in Baghdad had seemed to me to be generous, likable people—this had been true even of most of the bureaucrats. I had a hard time reconciling my memory of them with the overwhelming evidence of how the Iraqis had behaved in Kuwait. At first, thinking about it, I speculated that the horror inflicted on the Kuwaitis had been largely a professional job, conducted by the torturers and executioners of the Iraqi security forces, for practical reasons. There was some truth in this. The Iraqis did have what you could fairly call a rationale for conducting a campaign of terror—that is, to subjugate a hostile, numerically overwhelming population. When the Kuwaitis resisted, the Iraqis employed the methods they had found effective, over the past twenty-five years, in quelling dissent at home: arbitrary arrest and detention, widespread torture, frequent murders and public executions.

But the evidence was overwhelming that while the worst torture and the greatest number of executions and rapes had been committed by the security forces, there had also been many instances in which ordinary soldiers and officers had committed these acts, and for no evidently logical reason. A lot of people I talked to held to the view that the Iraqis were simply, fundamentally evil. I heard this again and again: the Iraqis were not normal, they liked inflicting pain, they liked brutality and destruction, they liked killing people. The subscribers to this belief pointed to history, which they said showed the Iraqis were a bloodthirsty people, even by local standards.

It was true that the Iraqis had an exceptionally violent past. The Assyrians, sweeping out from Nineveh, in what is now north-central Iraq, to conquer everything from northern Saudi Arabia to Turkey, had set a standard of behavior remembered three thousand years later. "I built a pillar over against the city gate, and I flayed all the chief men," wrote the Assyrian king Assurnasirpal II, recalling one victorious campaign. "And I covered the pillar with their skins; some I walled up within the pillar, some I impaled upon the pillar on stakes . . . and I cut off the limbs of the officers. . . . From some, I cut off their hands and their fingers, and from others I cut off their noses, their ears . . . of many I put out their eyes. . . . Their young men and maidens I burned in the fire."

Throughout Iraq's history, violence had served as the principal means of exercising political will and effecting policy. In his book *Republic of Fear*, the Iraqi political scientist Samir al-Khalil (a pseudonym) compares Saddam Hussein's reign with that of al-Hadjadj ibn Yusef al-Thaqafi, the governor of Iraq in the late seventh and early eighth centuries. Al-Hadjadj brought order to Iraq, then a chaotic, independent-minded province of the Damascus-based Umayyad dynasty, and established a bureaucracy that laid the foundations for the great Abbasid dynasty. Al-Hadjadj's inaugural speech, al-Khalil says, is known to every Iraqi schoolchild, and is regarded as a truthful depiction of the exercise of political power in Iraq:

"I see heads before me that are ripe and ready for the plucking and

I am the one to pluck them, and I see blood glistening between the turbans and the beards. By God, O people of Iraq, people of discord and dissembling and evil character . . . For a long time you have lain in the lairs of error, and have made a rule of transgression. By God, I shall strip you like bark, I shall truss you like a bundle of twigs, I shall beat you like stray camels. . . ."

"The special problem of Baathi violence," writes al-Khalil, "begins with the realization that hundreds and thousands of perfectly ordinary people are implicated in it. Even Saddam Hussein's torturers and elite police units who do the dirtiest work are by and large normal. There are too many of them for it to be otherwise. From being a means to an end, violence has turned into an end in itself, into the way in which all politics (finally no politics) is experienced by the public in Iraq."

Corrupt regimes corrupt those who live under them, and in their own particular way of corruption. A regime corrupted by a lust for money creates a society sickened by greed and selfishness. A regime corrupted by a lust for violence creates a society sickened by an appetite for the true sins of the flesh, the violation and desecration and destruction of it. The young men who came from Iraq to Kuwait—some of them, by no means all—found they had the appetite to do to the Kuwaitis the terrible things that the Mukhabarat did back home. And there was no one to stop them. Indeed, the masters of the evil, the professional sadists of the security forces, were among them, doing the worst of it; Ali Hassan Majid, the governor of the new nineteenth province, was known, by previous exploits among the Kurds, for his approval of the harshest measures. An astonishing and terrible thing: to be nineteen years old, a country boy, to find yourself in the richest place you had ever seen, a city filled with weak and trembling people, and to realize that you had within you terrible desires—to hurt these people, to rape a pretty girl and then throw her in the trash, to stomp a man's face under your boots—and that you had, as it were, permission to do so. It must have been blackly exciting at first, and then sickening, and by the end a descent into Conradian self-horror. All the physical signs of the occupation—the filth, the destruction, the garbage and shit even in the Iraqis' own quarters—spoke of men sinking deeper and deeper into rottenness. No wonder they had fled in the night. They must have been ashamed to think they would be caught in the place of their sins; they must have yearned to run with their backs to the awfulness, to get home to Iraq and never admit to a soul what they had done.

from Hazardous Duty
by David H. Hackworth

David H. Hackworth spent 26 years in the U.S. Army, and holds more than 100 U.S. or foreign decorations. He visited Yugoslavia in 1992 as a Newsweek correspondent to report on the conflict there between Serbs, Croats and Muslims.

Serb mortars had turned the airport at Sarajevo into a hot landing zone. The pilot couldn't descend the normal way because Serb snipers up on the hills took potshots any time they felt like it. I had bummed a ride on an Italian C-130. The freaked-out pilot came down like a fighter jockey in a gut-churning pedal-to-the-metal combat dive. The plane started falling like a paratrooper with a bad chute. Adrenaline pumped through my body. I took a look at a young *Newsweek* photographer named Antoine Gyori who was sitting across the aisle. The look on his face showed he felt the same electric current sizzling through me.

The plane nosed over even steeper.

"Do you feel it?" I said.

"Oh yeah, man, I feel it. I love it. I'm an adrenaline junkie!"

No wonder war won't go away. Young guys get off on it.

The plane pulled up with the engines screaming, skimmed across the runway, and landed. The second we stopped, the cargo door slammed down and the cargo pallets shot out. Antoine and I jumped down and the C-130 was gone, wasting no time hanging around that killing field. As we tore across the landing strip, incoming dropped on all sides of us. CRUMP, CRUMP, CRUMP. Hot steel whizzed past our ears. We piled into a bunker. I hit the floor wondering what the hell I was doing here: *Welcome to the Balkans, motherfucker.*

Tito was dead, the Soviet Union was in ruins, and Yugoslavia was being hacked apart by the inmates running the asylum. In the spring of 1992, the Serbs, Croats, and Muslims began carving up the carcass, and that August I decided to see how far they really meant to go. I flew from New York to Frankfurt and caught a plane to Zagreb, where I set up my base of operations. While I was standing at the car rental agency, a rangy young guy named Jim Bartlett walked up.

"Are you David Hackworth?" he said.

"Yeah,"

"I got your book. Man, I love you."

He told me he was a freelance photographer. He had been on the ground for a couple of years. One look and I could see he was an action freak.

"Can I buy you a beer?" I said. After a couple, I had a new sidekick. Jim knew the roads, the fighting positions, the back ways out in the countryside and he had good contacts among all the combatants. I hired him as my stringer and we were in business.

Civil wars are always rotten, and this one was the craziest I had ever seen. The first morning I took a walk in Zagreb's main park. The city was as clean and pretty as a botanical garden. The people were as fat as the pigeons. It was late August; the sun filtered peacefully through the trees. You couldn't even tell a war was going on, although only a few weeks earlier incoming had been falling like hail on Zagreb. But if you drove out of town, in less than half an hour the country looked like Vietnam in the middle of the war. Villages were blasted, buildings and homes gutted, everything bullet pocked, shrapnel torn, shell blackened. Out there the people were already chopping down trees for firewood.

Jesus, how are they ever going to get through the winter?

Everywhere you looked you saw a fresh graveyard.

It was plain nuts. The rules of war had all been blown away along with everything else in sight. But the people were incredible. They were rebuilding, working their gardens, trying to grow their corn, patching up what had been trampled or destroyed. Even as they went about these chores, they were being mortared. I felt as if I were in a disjointed time warp. In some areas rich fields of corn, pastures, orchards, stretched off as far as you could see. It was like being back in Pratts, Virginia, in 1700. Mules and horses were pulling wagons. Since there was little fuel and the tractors couldn't go, people were back to farming the way they had done it three hundred years earlier. So far as I could see, there was no military logic to the war, no real front, no artillery exchanges across the lines at opposing breastworks. But the mayhem wasn't really guerrilla fighting, either. What was happening was pure butchery—random, exotic, bloodcurdling. The Serbs were the most efficient killers in the slaughterhouse, but the Croats and Muslims were also standing in blood up to their waists. When the Yugoslavian Army fell apart, the Serbs grabbed the keys to the supply depots and snatched the best stuff. They were able to put together a well-equipped military force with modern tanks and artillery and plenty of ammunition. What was left, the Croats seized. Any remaining scraps went to the Muslims.

To get a fix on the balance of terror, I paid a visit to the headquarters of General Anton Tus, the Croatian Army's chief of staff, a four-star who also served as minister of defense. The interview was at nine o'clock in the morning. As I was setting up my tape recorder, we began to lay out the ground rules. The general looked tough and I needed to break the ice.

"You know," I said. "I've seen your army once before because we fought against each other. I was in Trieste from 1946 to 1950."

General Tus was a big man and he suddenly looked very interested. He got up and grabbed a tactical map and slapped it down on the desk in front of me.

"Where were you?" he said.

I studied the map. I hadn't seen that area for nearly half a century, so it took some time to place everything. Suddenly I could pick out where the old American defensive positions had been near a little village named Banne. The rocky high ground stretching between Yugoslavia and Italy had been my nursery as a soldier. In 1946 I had started out as a private in a recon unit of the 88th Division. We were deployed along the Morgan Line to keep Tito from gobbling up Trieste. The setup was World War II Army surplus: foxholes, bunkers, and big-titted easy girls.

Near the end of the war Tito's partisans had taken Trieste. Earmarking everyone who had been a Fascist or supported the Germans or just got in the way, the partisans lined them up against a wall and wasted them. As a kid soldier, one of the first things I did was go to Garibaldi Square to see the bullet holes in the execution walls. That taught me all I needed to know about Communists. They were bad, worth fighting against. After the war, Trieste went back to Italy. But the Yugoslavs were still right outside town. I also knew from my personal encounters with them along that mean border they were goddamn good soldiers. They were not going to back off from a fight.

My recon platoon regularly patrolled the Morgan Line. I was just a little kid, 135 pounds with my 9.5-pound M-l rifle locked and loaded, a basic load of ammo and hand grenades hanging down, and my steel helmet on whenever Captain Kenneth Eggleston was around. I had a good friend, who was also fifteen, Jimmy Sparks from Indianapolis. Jimmy had taken reconnaissance basic with me at Fort Knox. Since we were both little kids, we paired off, stuck together, went out on patrols both for pussy and adventure.

The terrain was rocky—high hills with sparse vegetation, some trees and brush, but mostly stony ground and many rock walls. Ducking along behind those walls, Jimmy and I would work our way right up to the border where we could hear the Jug patrols advancing. We used to make a popping sound with our mouths, then lob a rock over the wall. In the old days, a hand grenade popped, then made a fizzling sound. A spark came out when the firing cap popped. The Jugs in diamond formation moving forward in the rain, ponchos and pots on, heard us. *"Granate,"* they yelled and hit the deck. THUMP, CLATTER, BANG. They had to smack down on the rocks, skinning their hands and puncturing tender places, and they would get up covered with mud. No explosion. Then there would be nothing. They knew they'd been had. You could hear them swearing all the way to their patrol base. And we lay back behind the rock walls laughing up a storm.

It wasn't all fun and games. While my unit was deployed on the Morgan Line and around Trieste—1945–1954—it took about twenty-five dead and over a hundred wounded or captured. But to two 15-year-olds in steel pots—when Captain E., as we called him, wasn't watching—it was a Huckleberry Finn and Tom Sawyer adventure in olive drab.

The memory flashed through my mind.

"Here, right here west of Banne," I said, stabbing the map with my finger. "I was right here."

General Tus looked at me and a huge grin spread across his face.

"I was there, too," he said. "My regiment was four miles from you, opposing you, right across from you."

Was this good or bad? A little defensively, I said, "I was only fifteen."

"Good," he said, thumping his chest with his big hand, "I was fourteen."

He came over and grabbed me and gave me a bone-crushing bear hug.

Among professional soldiers there is seldom hate down at the dying level. We don't blame the man in the foxhole across the line and he doesn't blame us because we know that something or someone up above us has caused the war. We must kill him, of course, before he kills us. That's only common sense as well as our duty. But when the shooting is over, most grunts always have more in common with other grunts, even old enemies, than they will ever have with the politicians who sent them.

General Tus was of the old school and he wanted to talk. He sat me down and told me everything about his army and how he was fighting his enemies. He was outgunned and he seemed pessimistic until he started talking about armor.

He had a secret weapon.

"We have killed six hundred Serbian tanks and captured two hundred twenty," he said.

He wouldn't tell me how. The numbers were outrageous. It sounded so much like William Westmoreland's old razzle-dazzle with the Vietnam body count that I had to suppress a laugh. But something about the face of the former CG of Tito's air force said he wasn't just bullshitting the troops. I made a mental note to look into the claim.

"Can I do anything for you?" he asked at the end of the interview. I thought for a second and I remembered a trick or two from Desert Storm.

"Yes, General," I said. "Would you give me a letter so I won't have to go through all the hassle of finding spies to take me into your positions."

"Good," he said with a laugh. Then he called in a general and directed him to give me the letter right there. The officer wrote out a document that basically said, "This is a friend from *Newsweek* magazine. He can go wherever he wants. He can see whatever he wants. Help him."

Not even "General" Clifton had been quite so precise—and these orders were real. From then on, whenever I was stopped by the Security Police or a hard-nosed officer as I was whipping around the front, all I had to do was pull out that letter. The cop or soldier would take one look and snap to attention.

Then he would salute me.

I called it "my magic letter."

The countryside outside Zagreb was Ambush Alley—rolling hills with forests, roads that twisted through woods, rivers and creeks snaking under light bridges that couldn't handle armor—ideal turf for guerrilla war. One glance at the landscape and you were transported back to World War II. Everything was shot to shit. Walls were pock-marked by bullets, houses blown away by artillery or air strikes. Debris and mines covered the ground. No logical military purpose explained the havoc. It was chaos. In battle, the normal course of things is to start pounding the enemy's main line or trying to break up his logistical network or to blow apart his artillery. When you apply military force, you are supposed to have a rational purpose and clear objective. But there was nothing normal about this war. This was about firing for its own sake. The targets were villages and cities. The targets were civilians. The point was terror. The Serbs were on one side of the Sava River trying to drive back the Croatians on the other bank. But it didn't really matter in this sector whether you were a Croat or a Serb. The idea was to blister the other guy so badly he would never dare to return.

Every day was an orgy of wild gunfire. Plums were plentiful, and for the locals plum brandy was the drink of choice. In the morning a guy got up, had his breakfast, popped off a few rounds from his mortar or machine gun, then stopped for a little eye-opener. As the morning pro-gressed and his alcohol count increased, the shooting got crazier and crazier. By noon everyone was out of his gourd.

Eilhys had given me a silver cowboy buckle embossed with a horse for my Chinese birth year. The belt had zippers in the back where I could tuck in a thousand dollars' worth of bills. I used the buckle as a character tester on those cutthroats, pirates, and crooks; Muslims, Croats, and Serbs. Every time I stopped at a checkpoint, I would see how long it took them to scope out the belt. The average was about fifteen seconds. After one guy started pointing to it and talking to his mate and monkeying with his AK, I began thinking, *These guys are so bad they're going to knock you off just for your belt buckle, especially after they've had a couple of plum brandies.* So I stuck it in my pack and let my pants ride low.

The drunkenness made me look twice at the ammo supply of these gunslingers. I had never been on a field of battle where the supply of ammunition wasn't rationed. Usually you are told to restrict yourself to just so many rounds per day, be it rifle, mortar, or artillery—unless you are about to be overrun. Here nobody held back. The drunker these guys got, the more stuff they threw. It was mindless shelling and mindless killing with no purpose other than to terrorize people or to take revenge. The erratic shelling was like nothing I had ever seen before. In Korea and Vietnam you got thumped all the time but you knew where it was coming from. When you moved, you moved fast. You always kept your eyes peeled for the next good hole to jump into. In the Balkans the incoming was completely unpredictable. You never knew where or when it would come crumping in. In the Army I came from, a stud would never consider wearing a flak jacket. But in Bosnia I couldn't get the thing on fast enough. Man, I almost *showered* in that flak jacket. I wasn't trying to prove anything to anybody anymore. Luckily, most of the houses in the Sava River sector have deep cellars. Every night before I fell asleep I would think how much I loved my cellar. It was safe and the rent was free.

Now I had another visit from my guardian angel.

I know it sounds nuts, so let me explain. Throughout my life, I should have been killed a bunch of times. But whenever I've come right up to the edge, something has pulled me back. Being face-to-face with death no longer upsets me. Besides, my Gram, who was convinced I'd be hanged like my horse thief great-uncle from Missouri, would always assure me, "If you're born to be hanged, don't worry about drownin'." But sometimes I wonder why I've been snatched back so many times when I should have died.

One morning Jim Bartlett and I set off for the battlefield in our little Hertz rental. Jim had arranged with a friend of his, a Croat sergeant, to meet us, escort us up forward, and infiltrate us through all the checkpoints and into a front line unit. We drove down the highway leading due south of Zagreb until we came to a crossroads. To the left ran the main freeway; to the right was a small one-lane secondary road that meandered cross-country to the village that was our objective. One road was fast; the other would take three or four more hours.

"Your choice, Hack," said Jim.

If we went straight we could move fast but we would have to pass through Serb territory and the Serbs could screw us. Or we could take the meandering little road through Croatian territory and we would be cool. We would get to our rendezvous but we would be cutting it close in terms of the time we were supposed to meet up with our sergeant.

"We'll go the fast way," I said.

The expressway was empty. A lot of heavy fighting had passed this way. Shrapnel was lying all over the road. We had to drive about seventy miles. We were going so fast the poor little Toyota was shaking. I heard a thump and then a clump, clump, clump, and the car went all spongy. A flat. So we took out the spare, put it on, resumed our high speed for another two miles before it was clump, clump, clump again. By now we were only about eight miles out from our goal.

"Let's just ride the rim," I said. I knew the accountants would be upset when they got the bill for new tires, new rims, new wheels, the works. But I wasn't going to stop and get stuck out there in the middle of a killing zone.

It didn't work. Riding the rim never does. By the side of the road I saw a little village, so we stopped.

"I'll hike over there," I said. "Who knows, maybe there'll be a wrecked car we can crib a tire from."

Just as I was ready to start, a truck drove up.

It was a big ice cream truck.

We waved it down. The driver spoke no English, but we got by with my fractured German and hand and arm signals. I went around to the trunk where I had stashed several cartons of Marlboros for just this kind of emergency. Cigs always make the best trading materials on a battlefield. I laid a couple of packs on him. Then I took out a 100-deutsche-mark note. I ripped it in two, gave the ice cream man half, pointed at Jim and the tires, signaled for him to take them over to the village and bring them back, at which point I would give him the other half of the banknote and some more smokes.

He got it. I had found his button.

"You go with him," I told Jim. "Get the two tires fixed and I'll see you as soon as you get back. I'll stay with the car." The driver gave me a couple of ice cream bars.

The two of them set off. I crawled into the backseat, turned on the BBC, and munched ice cream as I started reading a favorite book, Sun Tzu's *The Art of War*. Time passed. No Jim. More time passed. Still no Jim. We were cutting it right down to the microsecond on making the hookup with our sergeant and hauling ass out of that bad place before dark. Finally, Jim came back. He had two tires, used, but plenty good enough for us. We slapped one on the car and headed down the road toward Slavonski Brod, a town across the Sava River from our destination.

The closer we got the hairier things looked. As we were entering the town, I noticed that all the trees were blown away.

Shit, they've received a lot of incoming.

A farmhouse was the meeting point. We drove on slowly. All the houses were shot to hell and several were burning brightly.

Man, some bad stuff has just happened here. We pulled 'round a corner and up to where our farmhouse was supposed to be.

And there it wasn't—totally destroyed, still smoking.

We got out and made our way through the ruins to the cellar. Six people were lying there dead—including our sergeant, who was now reporting in to Saint Peter.

It turned out the Serbs had just shelled the holy shit out of the town. Then an air strike had smacked it. Then a large missile had crashed down.

"Jesus," Jim said. "Thank God we were late."

"We weren't supposed to be here," I said.

"What the hell are you talking about?"

"All my life I've had this guardian angel," I told him. "Every time I get myself in a real corner the angel rolls me over, turns me around, and changes whatever is going to happen. That's why we got the two flat tires. We weren't supposed to reach this place."

Jim looked at me like I had lost it, became very quiet, and walked away, probably his way of dealing with looney tunes. But this sort of thing has happened to me so often I don't know how else to explain it. An hour earlier and we would have been as dead as the six folks in the cellar. In my mind's eye, the guardian angel is a woman. Maybe it's my grandmother, who raised me. Or my mother, who died when I was a few months old. Whoever she is, she always changes the dice and let's me walk away from death with a big pile of chips.

The Croatian field hospital near Bosanki Brod was well marked with red crosses. Serb gunners were using them to draw a better bead. From up on the high ground they were lobbing in the heavy stuff. The pin-striped politicians had declared a cease-fire in London a week earlier, but if anything the incoming had only gotten hotter. I hadn't seen such a relentless attack since the Korean War.

Parked outside in the firestorm were a couple of tanks and a flak wagon with four antiaircraft guns that fired in unison. The field ambulances looked as if they had been working downrange at a turkey shoot. As soon as I pulled up, the hospital started receiving a lot of heavy incoming artillery fire. It had taken at least a dozen hits or near misses. The first floor was all blown to shit—shrapnel had slashed every wall—and the Croats had it barricaded. The operating room was in a deep cellar. You came down through a sandbagged entrance to where the doctors and nurses were working.

While I was standing there watching, the medics brought in two young guys who had been badly shot up earlier in the day. They were both kids, about nineteen. One guy had taken a six-inch sliver of steel in the forehead, the other had a sucking hole in his chest. Dying material. Obviously they were not going to make it through the night. One of them had a nice Austrian pistol tucked down in his belt. A Croat officer reached down and took it. Pulling out a cloth, he wiped the blood off and stuck it under his jacket.

"You got a good pistol there," I said.

"That's eight hundred dollars on the black market in Zagreb," he replied, not missing a stroke.

Jesus, I thought. *What kind of army is this?*

The artillery fire lifted for a few minutes. Then a Serb MiG-21 came in really hot and started strafing us. Around the hospital, there were just enough military vehicles along with my poor little rental to justify the place as a target, I guess. I began keeping score. *Let's see. We've been here thirty minutes and we've been shelled, we've been mortared, and now we're being strafed.*

With that, Major Kincl Miroslav, the surgeon, came running up the stairs. The flak wagon was one of his personal weapons. When he wasn't cutting you open to dig out steel, he was throwing as much of it as he could at the Serbs. As the MiG-21 came in for a second pass, he jumped into the gunner's seat and started blasting away until the pilot thought better of it and turned tail. He also had his personal tank. Between operations and air raids he would get in, cruise the front and zap any Serb who had the bad luck to get in his sights. I was looking at an army of renegades with a surgeon-warrior everyone loved because of his gut and caring.

While all the boom boom was roaring over me, I looked over at a Croat captain who was crouched up against the stone wall next to me. He had been wounded in the face, not badly, and he had come in to have the mad doc pull out the splinters of steel and stitch him up. His name was Derislau Sipicky and he spoke English. In civilian life he was an architect.

As the barrage continued, we started shooting the shit and I pulled out my notebook. To get his attention, I showed him the letter from General Tus.

"That's an important letter," he said.

I told him how pleased the general had been with the score against Serbian tanks but added I doubted the numbers.

"No. They're correct," he said. Reaching into his pocket he pulled out a worn notebook. In it he had written down the performance of his own tank hunter-killer teams. The first note covered the previous forty-eight hours.

"Killed eight tanks," it said. He leaned over and translated the notes for me. During the month that had passed one team alone had "killed thirty-two tanks." Another had blown away forty-five Serbian armored vehicles.

Then came a fascinating scribble. "Eight missiles killed two T-72 tanks, one Praga track vehicle with 30-millimeter antiaircraft guns and five T-55 tanks. No friends hit. Average kill range, 1,500 meters, 95 percent first-round hits."

General Tus did have a secret weapon. But what were those missiles? I pressed the captain.

"Top-secret antitank missile," he said. "It creates a radical pressure change inside the struck vehicle." Sounded better than anything we had. The weapon was "fire and forget," meaning the gunner could duck after he shot. The missile locked onto the target and cut through the protective armor with a double warhead. During Desert Storm our own tank busters had to guide our TOW weapons with a wire to the target. That meant the gunners were fully exposed for at least ten seconds, forever on a hot battlefield, more than enough time to be blown away.

The captain wouldn't tell me what the weapon was or where the Croats were getting it. When the shelling slowed down, I asked him to show me some hard evidence. His driver, no Rambo, wouldn't come back to pick him up because of the shelling.

"I'll take you in my Hertz," I said. "Anywhere you want to go."

He got behind the wheel and whipped down the shell-torn roads toward the front.

We kept driving until we came to a Croat position that had just taken a direct hit from the Serbs, a house fronting the Serb lines. One of the captain's men was dead and two were wounded. But before the Serbs crippled the five-man team, they had taken out a T-55. I could still see the tank smoking and there were three other dead tanks nearby.

When I examined the tanks, I found each had been killed by a missile that had burned a hole through the armor. The hole was about the size a pencil would make if you stabbed it through a sheet of paper.

The front of the building that had been the Croat position was still smoldering. I was standing in the smoke, glass all around, not knowing exactly where the fire was coming from.

"Where's the Serb position?" I yelled.

"On that knob," the captain said, pointing to a ridge about seven hundred meters away. I could just make out the green silhouette of a pair of tanks that from the distance looked like giant turtles.

"Shit," I said, ducking quickly into the back bedroom and behind the fireplace.

When I caught my breath, I joined the captain, who was patching up one of his guys. When finished, he held something up to show to me.

"This is a Serb antipersonnel mine," he said. He was holding a Bouncing Betty.

And the captain dropped it. He accidentally dropped it right at my feet.

All I could think was, *This is it. Holy shit, it's landed between my legs. I'm really gone. There go the family jewels, and there go I.*

It didn't go off. Perhaps my guardian angel saved me. But there was no limit to how reckless these guys were, drunk or sober. Working our way around to the back of the building, we put his wounded in a shot-up car and raced hack to the field hospital.

After a few days, I knew I had a good thing going with him. We went back up to the front. I was still skeptical about the kill count and I wanted to find out what the secret weapon was.

"You're knocking out all these tanks," I said. "But I only see a few tanks. How can you be knocking out so many if I'm seeing so few?" What I was really angling to see was the antitank weapon. All the tank talk was smokescreen. Then he said something that knocked me out.

"We are pulling them back and rebuilding them."

"Great. Let's go look."

Jim was with us, so I slipped him one of those tiny pocket cameras.

"See if you can get some pictures of this tank rebuild factory on the sly," I told him, not knowing what we would find.

Four miles behind the line, the captain showed us the workshop— and it was for real. Inside he had about twenty Serb tanks at different stages of repair. The mechanics were cannibalizing one tank to refit the others. They were not soldiers, but they were at the front, working right under the noses of the Serbian gunners.

In any American operation the same sort of factory would have been fifty to one hundred miles behind the lines, with a sophisticated maintenance depot, all the proper spare parts and equipment, probably air-conditioned. Not the Croats. When they finished rebuilding a tank, all they did was stick their own flag on it and send it up to fight with a new crew. These kinds of fighters don't play by our rules. Yet we always assume they do. That's why we so frequently get our asses kicked.

When I examined the tanks, I found more of the little holes. The missile had melted its way through the armor, changing the air pressure. That alone was enough to kill the crew inside. The metal from the hole is called spalling. It's melted, it's hot, but the minute it's forced into the tank it hardens again and starts zinging around at a tremendous velocity, slicing through all those young, tender, fleshy bodies.

This was General Tus's secret weapon.

It had to be a modified French Milan missile. I had seen those same telltale holes on Iraqi tanks in the French sector during Desert Storm. But that still left the question of where General Tus was getting them.

The next day I was sitting with another Croatian officer in a cafe just behind the lines. I bought a bottle of the local rotgut and we killed it plus a couple more. When we were both hanging onto the edge of the table, I showed him my magic letter from General Tus and told him how much the tank killer program impressed me.

"It's the Milan," he said.

The system cost $80,000; each missile cost $20,000. They were getting them from South Africa. The officer raised his glass.

"The South Africans hate the Serbs," he said. "And they love the profits."

The real winners in this civil war were the gunrunners. The United Nations blockade had more holes in it than the New York subway system. Everywhere I went I saw stacks of military equipment: Russian Sagger missiles, new T-72 tank engines still in the crates, grenades, mortar shells, bullets. The weapons came from every country in the world: from Japan, from Italy, from the United States, from Germany. You could read the origins on the sides of the crates. Only the Muslims were short of ammunition, but the Iranians were helping them play catch-up. While I was there, an Iranian transport plane was nailed in Zagreb loaded with four thousand AK-47s and millions of rounds of ammunition. The Croatians and the Serbs both had plenty of hardware and were building the support systems a modern army needs. *Where is all of this coming from?* I wondered. *How come that big blockade we are hearing so much about isn't working?*

Finally, I met an officer from NATO who explained everything.

"The blockade leaks like a sieve," he told me. "It's a joke."

We weren't boarding ships. Any captain could say, "Hey, I've got a load of bananas," and he would be waved through. The reply was, "Fine. Pass." And another shipment of rockets or mortar shells was on its way to the killing fields.

No one could keep the peace under these conditions. The French and the Canadians both sent crack regiments under the United Nations flag only to see them become targets or hostages. In this crap game the locals had loaded the dice. The mission of the UN troops should have been peacemaking, not peacekeeping. There was no way to execute a peacekeeping mission because there was no peace. The UN troops should have had the tanks and artillery they needed to separate the warring parties and rules of engagement that had teeth. As one sergeant put it: "If that son of a bitch shoots at you, we want to blow him out of the saddle."

To test my theory I hitched up with the men of November Company, a unit from the elite 22nd Royal Canadian Regiment that had arrived in the spring of 1992. In mid-April, the company had come down into Croatia from Germany, where they were doing NATO duty. The first night they formed up in their assembly area, expecting to be greeted as peacekeepers. Most of the regulars, the NCOs, and the older officers were veterans of other UN missions around the world. They had just gotten off the train and were standing around wondering when they were going to eat. And suddenly, PLOMB, PLOMB, PLOMB, PLOMB, PLOMB, a dozen 120-millimeter mortar rounds landed all around them.

They had no foxholes, no prepared positions. Hey, they didn't need them, weren't they peacekeepers? In some cases it was the first incoming fire the regiment had received since the Korean War. So these guys were a little bit rusty.

"It was one hell of a wake-up call," said Sergeant Major Richard Clark, who herded the 235-man rifle company to safety. Later I met Platoon Warrant Officer Hall, who was stoic about it all. "The shelling was a blessing in disguise," he said. "It told us that this wasn't peace-keeping as we'd known it and that we were going to be up to our eye-balls in a very hot war." From that night on, the company was all heads up and tails down and alert. "In the long haul," he said, "that incoming fire saved a lot of lives."

Sergeant Major Clark was the only man wounded in the shelling. Flying shrapnel nicked his thumb. He had the cut bandaged, and the men renamed their outfit Lucky Company.

The Canadians moved out into Sector West near the city of Pakrac in central Croatia, where they might as well have been in the middle of World War II. Incoming artillery and mortar fire mixed with plenty of small arms fire to scourge the rolling countryside night and day. Snipers, ambushes, and mines added to the danger of patrolling the rugged, heavily forested terrain. Every turn on the road offered a potential ambush. Most of the Canadian armored vehicles I saw wore scars from bullets and shell fragments.

The Canadians were particularly good at peacekeeping. Many of the NCOs had done tours in the Sinai Desert and Cyprus. Peacekeeping is not an infantry role, but only the infantry can do it because the infantry is down on the ground and in position to see and control things. The job is a bitch. These troops were looking at ill-disciplined militia gangs posing as soldiers. The Balkans were a patchwork of deadly ethnic hatreds and no two sectors were the same. One day Lieutenant Kevin

Cameron's platoon was manning a roadblock on the Serbian side of the line. To while away the time they were listening to the music and propaganda of Croatia's Zagreb Zelda. A drunken Serb soldier walked up and thrust his weapon in Cameron's face and said, "If you no shut off, I kill you."

I would have whacked the son of a bitch but Cameron, good peacemaker that he was, zapped Zelda, slammed a tape of Guns 'N Roses into his ghetto blaster, and offered the drunk a cigarette. They wound up looking at each other through tobacco haze instead of gunsmoke while Axel Rose kept the peace.

On another patrol, a second soused Croat accidentally fired a burst of submachine gun fire into Lieutenant Cameron's armored vehicle, wounding Corporal Lloyd. The lieutenant disarmed the drunk, patched up the corporal and evacuated him, and went on with the patrol. This kind of work took great discipline. The sad part was good efforts could restore peace here and there but sooner or later the winds of war blew elsewhere and everything withered.

One day I was out in no-man's-land when I ran into a young woman, half-Serb, half-Croat, who was visiting her father near the temporary safety of a UN roadblock. She looked up at Corporal Nick Dorrington, twenty-five, a young guy from Halifax, Nova Scotia, and said, "Thank God for the UN. You are saving us from ourselves."

Next to staying alive the biggest problem for the UN soldiers was staying neutral. "If we took sides we'd be caught in the middle," Sergeant Jim MacDonald told me during one break between patrols. "We'd become a target for every side and we'd lose our effectiveness at getting all parties to the table to talk." He might as well have been a prophet. The first reports on the shelling that greeted November Company blamed the incoming on the Serbs. Then another report said the Croats had done the job. The troopers discovered that they were trapped in a beaten zone between cunning enemies who had spent decades stacking the deck and hoodwinking neutrals. Brave men from Canada were giving candy to kids from all sides. All sides were giving them the finger.

There is something in human nature that seduces us into reducing war and its offspring to clearly divided teams of good and evil. Sometimes, as with Adolf Hitler, the division is accurate. In the Balkans, ethnic cleansing was also evil, no matter who practiced it. But on any given day it could be hard as hell to tell the good guys from the bad guys. Hatred was passed down to the children by their grandmothers. The mom and dad were out in the fields or in the cities working, but granny was at home telling stories to the kids, educating them from two generations away, reminding them of what they might have seen if they had been in Sarajevo when the archduke was killed and the First World War came, or what happened in World War II. To change the mind-set of these people you would have to get rid of all the grandparents. I've never seen hate run so deep.

White-hot emotion made it very hard to be fair to all parties, to report objectively. It surprised me to discover how hostile the Canadians were toward the press, the international press, not just American reporters. They complained about reporters taking sides. Their home base in Germany was only a few hours away by air. One corporal told me when he went "home" he would see TV reports from the Balkans and think he was watching a different war. Another Canadian said, "The press wants a clear-cut good guy and a clear-cut bad guy. They won't dig deep. They just grab what's on the top." Warrant Officer Joe Parsons told me he had been in the middle of one fracas in the morning, flew to Germany that afternoon, then flicked on the tube for the evening news. "I couldn't believe what I saw," he said. "It was mind blowing. I had just lived through that event and the distortion was incredible."

I returned to Sarajevo in mid-August. Landing under fire was the easy part of the trip. It didn't take long to see everything else would be a lot more complicated. The ancient city sat dead center in a valley. Serb artillery and snipers commanded the high ground. It was not like Dien Bien Phu or Khe Sanh, where trained armies fought until one side or the other pulled out. This was a killing zone where mad butchers were blasting away at anything and everything that moved. The Serbs rained death on all living things in the city and villages below. The people were like goldfish in a glass bowl. A drunken lout with an AK-47 was leaning over them, peering into the bowl and shooting them. They couldn't run, they couldn't hide, and they couldn't make the relentless fire go away.

On my first trip I spent equal time with the UN peacekeepers, Muslim troops, and the Serbs. Sarajevo was a zoo. To cover all sides fairly you had to move from the UN peacekeepers—the Canadians, Malaysians, Swedes, and French—to the Muslims and over across the lines to the Serbs. There were no tidy front lines. The battle area was like a checkerboard with the reds and the blacks crazily intermixed. To the eye of a regular soldier, nothing made Army sense. I wasn't looking at World War II-style warfare; nor was it the Desert Storm, Air-Land Battle of fire and maneuver; nor was it guerrilla irregular war. Something deadly new and corrosive was at work. The city was turning into a crater within a valley the way Beirut had turned into a crater by the sea.

To me the oddest thing was that people did so little to dig in or protect themselves. They went about their daily lives as if the war were just a bad dream that would be gone when they awoke. One afternoon I was drinking coffee with a Muslim commander in his rose garden. The day was sunny and warm and I had almost forgotten that I was at ground zero. Suddenly five 82-millimeter mortar rounds crunched in and exploded not more than fifty meters away. The commander and his staff calmly set down their fine porcelain cups and moved with the grace of ballet dancers, behind trees and walls. Saying to hell with pride, I crawled inside a French armored carrier and looked thankfully at the thickness of its steel skin.

I spent a lot of time with the Muslims, a lot of time with the Serbs. When I traveled with the Muslims, I was on my own hook. Then I would join the French. The French commander was an old paratrooper who had trained in the United States. He had also served in Desert Storm and he said this duty was far more dangerous than anything he had seen in the Persian Gulf. As the high sheriff, he could drive through all the lines, and when I was with him so could I. We would stop and talk to a Muslim colonel at one position, then move on and check in with a Serbian colonel a little farther down. One day I ran into a Serbian commander who said, "We pray to God the war will be over by winter. If it were up to us, we'd stop this hour, but the politicians at the top won't let us stop fighting. They have their own secret agenda."

We were standing at a spot overlooking a Serbian village. During the previous three days the village had taken five hundred rounds of artillery and mortar fire.

"Before the war we played football with them," the commander said. "Now we throw mortar bombs."

No one could be pro-Serb given the murderous way the Serbs practiced ethnic cleansing. But I couldn't be pro-Croatian or pro-Muslim, either. The Serbs were so violent they no longer gave a rat's ass if the rest of the world saw them as murderers and rapists. But the Croats and the Muslims were no slouches either. They had worn Nazi black during World War II. They were responsible for a million Serbian, Jewish, and Gypsy deaths in that round of ethnic cleansing. They had gotten along with Adolf Hitler just fine. Even the Nazis were startled by their brutality. The irony now was that Washington and Berlin were both supporting them, that NATO was on their side.

The Bosnians were excellent propagandists. The first people I met in Sarajevo were enormously friendly, well educated, sympathetic. The press briefer spoke English and had a doctorate from an American university. I liked him at first, as I was meant to. Then, when he was taking me around, I noticed we were not going along any direct routes. We would stop by a cemetery where I was told ten people had been killed and buried the previous night. Then there would be a stop where a woman had been raped. Then a school nursery vignette with children and their books and their teachers while their mothers were supposedly out in the fields digging trenches to stop the barbarian Serbs. And so on. He had choreographed the whole tour. If I had not been streetwise, I would have been saying to myself like so many naive visitors did, *Oh my God, look at this. Fresh graves. Mortars coming down. We have to do something.*

Stringing along a visiting reporter was innocent enough but some of the other situations I saw were far more sinister. While I was in Sarajevo, people were saying that the Serbs were behind a mortar attack that had killed several dozen innocent civilians. I went down to examine the physical evidence. When a mortar hits concrete it leaves a very clear signature. But I couldn't find any signs of mortar shells, even though all the reports said the bloodshed had been caused by a couple of 120-millimeter rounds. I found something completely different: the big, roundish, unmistakable scar left by the concussion and backblast of a large claymore mine. A claymore can be fired by command or by trip wire. From twenty or thirty feet away you can press a firing device and BANG. No evidence, unless you know how to look for it. Someone had set the thing off. I suppose a Serb could have sneaked in, planted the mine, and then triggered it. But why go to so much bother and take such a risk when all you had to do was lob in mortar rounds? Some of the Canadian peacekeepers suspected the Muslims had zapped their own people to draw sympathy and blamed the Serbs. No one could prove it, but given the past record of all the warring parties it was enough to put me on my guard. Nothing in this sump of violence could be taken at face value.

On another outing with the Bosnians, I went to a military command post in the sandbagged cellar of a ruined house. I found a group of soldiers watching television. It was noon and I wondered what they were watching, so I slipped up behind them and looked over at the tube. It was a Mozart concert. I thought, *What a war. The Muslim soldiers are so civilized, cultured, incredibly decent. When I was a soldier and back in the rear we would be seeing who could get laid or who could get drunk. And here they are listening to Mozart.*

Then I walked outside. On the roof of the bunker a sniper was lying underneath a camouflage net. Just as I appeared, BAM, he fired. I turned and saw his face and his rifle sticking out. Then I whirled around and saw a man go down in a field about four hundred meters away.

The next day I happened to be out with Serb troops just across the demarcation line from the Bosnian bunker.

"Yesterday I was over there and I saw a guy being shot," I said to the Serbian commander. "What was the deal with him? Was he one of your soldiers?"

"No," said the Serb. "He was an old man, eighty years old, out gathering plums for his lady love. They shot him in the gut, not the head, so he was out there moaning. But we couldn't reach him because of the sniper. He was dead when we finally got to him."

A very old sniper's trick. The Japanese were very good at it; so were the Viet Cong. You cut a guy down so everyone's trying to help him and if you are lucky you can zap eight or nine more. The target had no military value. He was just an old man, a plum-picking lover. Murdered by the sniper on duty above all those civilized Mozart lovers four hundred meters away.

Not long afterward I went out on another patrol to a little Serb village a few kilometers outside Sarajevo. At one point as we were walking along, we stopped at a cemetery. The patrol leader shouted a few directions to his troops and they started digging up a grave. At first I thought they must be looking for weapons. It is an old trick to cache weapons in a grave. It looks like you are going to dig up Omar but what you are really after is a case of AK-47s. While they were digging, I wandered around the graveyard. Checking the marker they had thrown aside, I saw the guy had a Muslim name and had died in 1944. This puzzled me.

Finally, the shovels hit a coffin. The soldiers scraped away the dirt and climbed out. Then they all lined up around the hole and pulled out their dicks and pissed on the coffin. After that, the patrol leader snapped an order. This time the troops slammed rounds into their chambers and emptied their magazines into the disintegrating casket.

"What goes on here?" I said to the patrol leader.

"That man was very, very bad man," he said. "He killed many, many Serbs during World War Two. He is being punished."

If you go to that kind of trouble to punish the dead, I thought, *what are you doing to the living?*

I left Sarajevo the first week in September, just as the politicians in London announced another cease-fire. The same day thirty-eight people were killed. Any way you looked at it, the only growth industry in the Balkans was laying out new cemeteries. These people were mean as junkyard dogs. I thought we should stop trying to housebreak them.

from The Tenth Circle of Hell
by Rezak Hukanović

Muslim journalist and radio announcer Rezak Hukanović

was an inmate at two death camps during the Serbs'

"ethnic cleansing" campaign in Bosnia. He wrote in the

third person to describe the experience.

E very morning the prisoners awoke to fear and horror. There seemed to be not even a hint of an end to the savage cruelty—the nightly roll calls, daily interrogations, torture, beatings, screaming, and howling. But what got to the prisoners more than anything else was the complete indifference of their jailers to their misery and pain.

The prisoners were filthy and lice-infested; their wrinkled skin hung loosely from their bodies, barely covering their ribs. The suffering made everyone equal; they even all began to look alike, as if they'd just been taken out of coffins, hardly moving. An unbearable stench nipped at their nostrils, getting under their skin and leaving a slimy taste in their mouths. The guards only opened the doors every now and then. When they did, the prisoners all turned toward the door to catch a breath of air, to feel like they could still breathe. As the doors shut, they would be beaten. And so it went, for days on end. Prisoners still pushed themselves as close to the door as they could, just to take a single breath of real air, even if they paid for it with a blow to the back from a club or a rifle butt.

For days a man named Muhamed lay by the door; he was thirty-one years old, from Čejrek. He'd had diabetes for several years. His brother, who lived and worked in Germany, had sent him a two-year supply of insulin, figuring things might get bad in Bosnia. Muhamed's younger brother and father were in the same room. They begged the guards in vain to make some kind of arrangement for his medication to be brought to the camp. Muhamed was slowly fading away. His face turned an odd, pale hue. He soon died quietly in his brother's arms. He just stopped breathing. His eyes stayed wide open, gazing upward. As four men carried Muhamed's lifeless body outside, everyone stood with their heads bent for a long time, expressing their impotence in silence.

Later the prisoners stood the same way as the bodies of Safet Ramadanović, Čamil Pezo, Suljo Ganić (a Croat from Ljubija), Habibović, and others were taken out. They were carried to the lawn in front of the building before being loaded onto a yellow van and taken away. Only the families of Safet Ramadanović, a distinguished restaurant owner from Prijedor, and Suljo Ganić were allowed to come and collect their bodies so they could be properly buried at the city cemetery.

Dying was easy at Omarska, and living was hard. Not even a glimmer of light could be detected at the end of the tunnel. At least in those days, no one found a four-leaf clover in the meadows at the foot of the Kozara Mountains.

The horrendous conditions gave natural selection free reign. Only the strongest and healthiest survived, those who endured the suffering on their own two feet, or those lucky enough not to be called out. Although the math teacher Abdullah Puškar was strong and healthy— built like a boxer, he was almost six feet tall, a hulk of a man—he had the bad luck of having a former student among the guards, a guy who didn't have the fondest memories of school. "Oh, professor, what an honor to find you here with all these hot shots," his old student said cynically the first time he saw Abdullah coming back from the canteen. "I listened to you long enough, now you'll listen to me for a while." He took Abdullah upstairs and, sneering spitefully, ordered him to clean the toilets.

Later, when the former student worked the night shift, he would call Abdullah quite often, leading him out into the night and bringing him back bruised and bloody. Once he just kept beating Abdullah on the head with a club. "I'm gonna beat that math out of you or die trying!" he exclaimed, dumping Abdullah back in the dorm like a sack of potatoes. Abdullah proudly endured the insults and injuries and beatings without complaining, trying to maintain his dignity even under such conditions. His companions in misery nursed his wounds in the hope that the beatings would end one day and he would recover. But late one night his former student called him out once again. Abdullah left a few things behind in the place where he slept. No one ever came for them.

Idriz Jakupović, a well-known public figure in Prijedor, was tortured for days on end. After each interrogation—and there were many—he came back beaten and bloody. Once the guards broke his left arm above the elbow; the end of the broken bone ripped through the muscles of his arm. Another prisoner, Hassan Ališić, tried to adjust the bone, and his efforts seemed to work since Idriz's unbearable pain began to diminish. Hassan made a splint out of a few sticks he found and bandaged the broken arm with a dirty T-shirt. Late one night a guard called Hassan to the door and told him some people from the Omarska "Red Cross" were looking for him. He went out and never came back.

Others not lucky enough to survive the horrors of Omarska included Jasko, who loved motorcycles, and his friend Emir, a policeman, both from Kozarac. They were taken out one evening, stripped, and then beaten with iron rods. Two more prisoners were taken out and, with a knife at their throats, ordered to bite off the genitals of the two young men from Kozarac. As these two died an excruciatingly painful death, the camp resounded with frantic screams.

Equally painful deaths, due to unheard-of abuse and torture, were met by Miro Šolaja, Ilijaz Drobić, Gogi Kardum, Professor Fikret Mujakić-Šicer, Silvo Sarić, Nihad Kadić, and over one thousand other civilian prisoners brought to the Omarska torture chamber from the region of greater Prijedor. "These guys could even give Hitler a run for his money," Dr. Eso Sadiković used to say. "This can't be called Omarska anymore," Djemo would say to himself. "We have to rename it." Each of his words carried the weight of judgment.

Two brothers of Halid Muslimović, the well-known singer from Prijedor, were in the hangar; their names were Senad and Nedžad. Senad was beaten several times. Once, as he was being brought back from interrogation, a guard kept striking his hands with a hammer. Another guard pierced his back with the point of his knife. They forced his feet into two nooses made of electrical cable. Then they hung him by the feet and beat him with truncheons and rods. Senad endured all that and even recovered quite well, although he lost over sixty pounds.

Nedžad was younger, only twenty-three. He was tall and good-looking, with his hair nicely styled. One of the guards scalped him with a knife in the middle of the runway and then made him sing his brother's song, "Bosnia is weeping, weeping. . . ." After the two brothers were transferred to Djemo's dorm, the guards stopped harassing them.

Not all the guards found their nourishment in blood and hatred. A few were good men, honest Serbs. But after a couple of days at Omarska, most such men were sent to the front lines, toward Derventa or Gradačac. That was the last anyone would hear of them. One of them who stayed in the camp the longest was Stole; he was from town, and everyone in Prijedor knew him. He helped his compatriots out as much as he could, even though he knew full well that Serbs who helped Muslims and Croats were punished most severely.

Three Serbs who had been accused of helping "those others" were brought to Omarska: Igor Kondić, his wife Jadranka, and Draško Lujić. Jadranka was let go after two months. After just fifteen days, Draško was transferred to a prison in Banja Luka before going to trial. Igor, whose father happened to have been born in the town of Omarska, underwent horrible torture for a few days before the guards killed him.

The best of all the guards was Željko, also known as Džigi; he was forty years old and a partner in a gas station at Omarska. He never once hit anybody. His post was under the window of Djemo's dorm. He often threw a piece of bread or a freshly picked plum through the window. Djemo knew him from before; they had even been friends. On his first day as a guard at Omarska, Džigi had called to Djemo and said openly, in front of all the prisoners, "Djemo, you're the prisoner and I'm the guard, but you were my friend before, and that's how you'll stay." As he said it, he gave Djemo a firm handshake. "I'll do whatever I can, just don't expect any miracles." Djemo thought he saw a tear roll down Džigi's unshaven face. Later Džigi brought food from home and secretly passed it on to Djemo. Sometimes he took Djemo to the canteen and let him eat a lot more than his ration. He even brought messages from home, from Alma and Deni. He was the first to let Djemo know that his son had been released from the camp at Trnopolje.

Once he knocked on the window frame over Djemo's head with the tip of his rifle and, speaking softly so the other guards wouldn't hear, told Djemo to put his head out through the broken window because he wanted to tell him something. The window was rather high, just below the ceiling, so Djemo put one foot on the radiator, held on to the window frame with his healthy hand, and stuck his head out through the broken glass. "I'll call you again in about fifteen minutes. I've got something for you," Džigi said, winking at him. Soon enough, he knocked on the window again and handed Djemo a big plastic bowl covered with a lid. "Here, share this with your friends, and then give me back the bowl." The bowl was filled with macaroni and meat in a thick broth. Džigi told Djemo later that the food was meant for the guards, but since it was a Serbian holiday all the guards, according to custom, were having roast meat and plum brandy. So their dinner went to warm up some of the shrunken stomachs of those on the inside.

"Make sure you give some of this food to Balada," Džigi used to say whenever he had something extra for Djemo. Balada was a young man from Djemo's neighborhood; he lived in the third house down on the left from Djemo's building. He was a great guy, always there when his friends needed him. One afternoon the guards called Balada, Hućo, Emir, and Šabo and took them over toward the White House. The next day someone from the other dorm told Djemo: "I loaded Balada's body onto the yellow van today." When Djemo told Džigi what had happened, the news really got to him. The next day, as soon as Džigi came on duty, he called Djemo over and said, "Watch yourself, Djemo, all right? I'll tell you straight out, the first thing I do whenever I come in is to look at the lists. If I ever see your name, they'll have to get by me first."

As it happened, Džigi was in the most notorious group of guards; it was called "Krkan's shift," after its potbellied leader. It was also known as "the terror shift." The worst of the group were Paspalj and Šoške, as they were called by the other guards. They killed people for the hell of it, without the least pretext. If they didn't like a prisoner's face or the way he moved, it was all over. They once gave Bajram Zgog, who used to coach and play for the famous Rudar soccer club, ten minutes to collect two hundred German marks from the other prisoners. (Even they themselves put no trust in the money printed up by their self-appointed "Serb Republic.") Ten minutes later they came back and told him to give them the money.

"I don't have it," Zgog said. He hadn't even tried to get it, knowing that the poor wretches in his dorm couldn't possibly have still held on to that kind of money. The prisoners standing near him were ordered to move back. Soske stayed near the door, with his rifle cocked and his finger on the trigger. Paspalj came up to Zgog and began beating him so viciously that everyone watching felt like their hearts were being ripped apart. Suddenly Zgog leaped over the crumpled-up bodies of the dazed prisoners. He got to the window and, raising his hands high over his head, took a swing at it. Shattered glass fell all over the place. He grabbed a piece of glass and tried to slash his wrists with it, preferring to put an end to himself rather than fall into the hands of the brutes. A few prisoners jumped him to stop him from going through with it. After that, Paspalj and Šoške took him out. None of the prisoners ever saw Zgog again.

Another time, in the heat of passionate hatred, one of the guards went up to Braco Burazerović as he sat with some other prisoners on the runway after a meal. Braco used to work for the Yugoslav army in that district. The guard asked, "You the same Braco that used to do recruiting for the army?" "Yes, that's me, Braco," he answered, his voice betraying a strange foreboding. "You motherfucker! When I was there, you didn't want to send me into the armored division. So, Braco, now it's time to meet your maker!" And Braco was led off in the direction of the White House.

When new prisoners were brought to the camp—and there were new arrivals almost every day—they were given a bloody welcome with all kinds of truncheons as soon as they stepped out of the bus. Many never made it as far as the dorm: the guards would have smashed their heads against the brick wall of the building. That was truly a horrible sound—a skull being smashed, the bones splitting and breaking. That sound, intermingled with shouts and painful screams, penetrated deep into the guts of the people inside, scorching their very eardrums. It circled and hovered, like a flock of black ravens, high over the entire region of Kozara. This bloody reality, like a frozen apparition, became sealed upon their very souls. Fear got under their skin, penetrating deep into their bones, traversing their veins, then breaking out all over their bodies in tiny beads of sweat. It was as if evil had been buried in every clump of this border land.

All may be fair in love and war, but practices such as those at Omarska were the most perverse forms of physical and psychological torture—a militarily enforced prostitution of people, supplied by a huge arsenal of pain and suffering. Mujica, a well-known musician from Prijedor and a real card, spoke a bitter truth: every morning when he got up, as he touched his face and body with his fingers, he'd say, "It's okay, I woke up alive again!" Two or three months after he finally got out of the camp, Mujica died in Prijedor in his own house. His kidneys gave out. He couldn't get the medicine he needed, and he couldn't get out of Prijedor. He had just turned thirty.

"Their souls are steeped in atrocities and hatred, so they feed on our blood and our bodies," people said. "But they can't possibly annihilate all of us." The picture of a man made to drink dirty motor oil is unforgettable. Or a guard firing into the back of a defenseless man's head and forcing every witness to applaud. The fear petrified upon the scorched face of Durat, who used to be a goalie on the Prijedor soccer team, as the guards pushed his head through a burning tire. A scrawny, dried-up skeleton of a man tearing apart a dead pigeon for food. A son weeping as he is forced to watch the bloodthirsty monsters plunge daggers into his father's body.

Their suffering found a place to reside between sunset and sunrise. The stench of dead and decaying bodies. No, none of this could ever be forgotten. Djemo remembered a poem by the Bosnian poet Izet Sarajlić:

> *There were twenty-eight*
> *There were five thousand twenty-eight*
> *More than there'd ever been*
> *In a single poem there were lovers*
> *Who'd now be fathers*
> *But they're gone now*
> *Now in Lover's Lane*
> *They await the grave*
> *Oh my little one*
> *My great love*
> *Tonight let's love each*
> *Other in their name*

Prisoner of War

by Scott Anderson

Like other young men, Scott Anderson was drawn to war by the promise of excitement. He found it, along with crippling confusion and guilt.

've never known precisely what to call it, but this is how it begins: heat, thick tropical heat, still air that smells of sweat and paddy water, and Athuma being led into the hut, the afternoon sun behind her so that she is only a silhouette against the hard light. She moves toward me, emerges from shadow, and I see her, always as if for the first time, a slender woman with long black hair, a floral-print sarong, and that is where I stop it—I've become quite good at stopping it there. But if I am not vigilant, the scene continues. Athuma is in the wicker chair, just four feet away, and then she leans toward me, looks into my eyes—hers are brown with flecks of yellow—and is about to speak, and if I am not vigilant, I hear her voice again.

What I can say is that this remembrance comes when it wants to. I can be content or unhappy, on a crowded street or standing alone, I can be anywhere at any time, and I will suddenly be resumed to that hut, all the sounds and smells and tastes there waiting for me, the black silhouette of Athuma fixed in my eye like a sunspot, and until I close off the vision there is the peculiar feeling that I am being asked to try again to save Athuma, that the evens of that day ten years ago have yet to be lived.

The sensation comes on this night, the second of November 1995. I am in Chechnya, standing in the courtyard of a house, trying to count off the artillery against the sky. Normally, this is not difficult—you see the flash and count off, five seconds to a mile, until you hear the blast—but on this night so many shells fall their flashes are like sheet lightning against the low clouds, the roar rolling over the land, a steady white noise of war.

But I am patient when it comes to such things, and I wait for my moment. I spot three quick, nearly overlapping, pulses of light streak out along the base of the clouds, and I begin to count. I count for a long time, so long I imagine I've missed the moment, but at fifty-five seconds I hear it: three soft knocks, little more than taps amid the avalanche of sound.

Fifty-five seconds. Eleven miles. They are shelling Bamut again. It is a small village up in the mountains, a place I think about so much I no longer even refer to it by name. They have shelled it every night I have been in Chechnya—just a few dozen rounds some nights, several hundred on others. The shelling has never been as heavy as tonight.

As I have done many times these past few days, I travel the path to the village in my mind. Not eleven miles by road, more like thirty-five. The paved road cuts across the broad plain until it climbs into the foothills. After a time, a narrow dirt track appears, and it leads across the river and into the mountains. At some unmarked spot on this track, perhaps an hour or so past the river, neutral ground is left and the war zone begins. One is then quite close to the village, maybe just another half hour, but there are mines sometimes, and sometimes the heli-copter gunships sneak in over the hills to destroy whatever they find.

The road ends at the village. It is built along the exposed flank of a mountain valley, and the Russians are on the surrounding heights with their tanks and artillery batteries. The way in is also the only way out, but any decision to leave is up to the rebels, and they do not trust outsiders. Since this war began eleven months ago, a number of people have vanished in the village, and there are stories of torture, that some of those missing were buried alive. I have been frightened of the place since I first heard of it. On this night, its name sounds like death to me.

I am both astonished and appalled by what is about to happen. I have come to Chechnya to look for a middle-aged American man who disappeared here seven months ago. He was last seen alive in the village. I did not know this man, and he is dead, of course, but there is a part of me that has not accepted this, that holds to the fantastic notion that he is still alive and I might save him, and in the morning I will go to the village in hopes of finding him.

But this is nothing; who cares if I choose to do something stupid? What is appalling is that I have maneuvered four others into sharing my journey, and on this night, I can no longer ignore the fact that I have done this simply because I need them, each of them, that in the very simple moral equation between my needs and the safety of others, I have chosen myself. Not that this changes much; even now, I feel incapable of stopping what I have engineered.

If I wanted to keep things simple, I would say that this is a story about war, about modern war and the way it is fought. Or I would say that this is a story about obsession, the dangerous lure of faith and hope. What would be harder for me to explain is that this is also a story about truth. Not the truth of the mind—rational, intellectual, able to make order out of chaos—but emotional truth, what is known before the mind takes over, what seeps in when the mind relaxes, the truth your heart believes.

Rationally, I know I did not kill Athuma. I was in a difficult situation, and I did what I could under the circumstances to save her. I remind myself of this often. The few people to whom I've told the story reassure me of this.

But there is something about that day I have never told anyone. Before Athuma was led into the hut, I believed I was the one they meant to kill. When the vision comes and I am sent back to that after-noon, my very first sensation upon seeing Athuma is relief, a profound relief, because it is only then I understand that I am to live, that it is she who is about to die. And in that moment, there is the blossoming of my own private truth. Emotional, irrational—to anyone else, per-haps absurd—but whenever I see Athuma's silhouette, I believe that she is coming forward to die in my place, that once again I am being called upon to play a part in her murder.

I don't wish to make too much of this. What happened to me is nothing compared with what happens to other people in war. And, of course, what happened to me is nothing compared with what hap-pened to Athuma.

Yet the events in that hut carved a neat division in my life. Before I was one way, and afterward I was another. And just as my life before made it inevitable that one day I would come face-to-face with Athuma—some Athuma—so after her it was inevitable that one day I would come to this night in Chechnya.

I first went to war because I thought it would be exciting—and I was right. It is the most exciting thing I have ever experienced, a level of excitement so overwhelming as to be impossible to prepare for, impos-sible to ever forget.

This attraction is not something to be discussed in polite company, of course. Yet I know I am hardly alone in my reaction. For a great number of people, and perhaps especially for those who traditionally have been called upon to wage it—young men—war has always been an object of intense fascination, viewed as life's ultimate test, its most awful thrill. Of all the easy, comfortable aphorisms that have ever been coined about war—that it is hell, that it tries men's souls—I suspect the odd utterance of General Robert E. Lee, made at the Battle of Fred-ericksburg in December 1862, may come closest to capturing the com-plicated emotions of those who have actually experienced it. "It is well that war is so terrible," Lee said, gazing over a valley where thousands of soldiers would soon die, "or we should grow too fond of it."

But if the guilty attraction endures, it now comes with a heavier price. This is because the modern war zone bears little resemblance to that of 130, or even 50, years ago. What were once the traditional inhabitants of a battlefield—soldiers, or journalists like myself—today represent only a tiny minority, their numbers overwhelmed by the purely innocent, the civilians who find themselves trapped in war's grip. On this modem battlefield, comparisons to the Fredericksburgs and Waterloos and Guadalcanals of history—ritualized slaughters between opposing armies—are largely useless. For a true comparison, one must reach back to man at his most primitive, to the time when barbarous hordes swept over the countryside laying waste to everything and everyone in their path, when a "battlefield" was defined simply by the presence of victims.

A few simple statistics illustrate this regression. In the American Civil War, civilian casualties were so low that no one even bothered to count them. From 1900 to 1950, civilians constituted roughly 50 percent of all war-related casualties. By the 1960s, civilians represented 63 percent of all casualties, and by the 1980s, the figure was 74 percent. For every "conventional war," such as Operation Desert Storm, that pushes the percentage down a fraction, there is a Bosnia or a Rwanda that sends it ever upward. The world has seen many of these wars. Since 1980, according to World Military and Social Expenditures, a periodic compendium, 73 wars have raged around the globe. "War," of course, is a relative term. According to human rights groups, last year alone there were 22 "high intensity conflicts" (defined as 1,000 or more deaths), 39 "low intensity conflicts," and 40 "serious disputes." The 250-odd wars of this century have taken a collective toll of 110 million lives. There are those who say that the truest mark of the last hundred years is not industrialism, or the rise of America, or the moon landing, or the computer, but the waging of war—that war is the greatest art form of our century. Human ingenuity, it appears, has perfected the technologies of death and, like a kid with a new slingshot, cannot help but find targets everywhere.

The result is that today's "hallowed ground" is not at all like the pastoral valley Robert E. Lee gazed upon at Fredericksburg, is barren of the trappings of heroic folly that can be immortalized by poets and painters. Instead, this hallowed ground is a ditch or a filthy alley or a cluster of burned homes, and it is inordinately populated by the elderly, by mothers and their children, by those not quick enough to escape.

To be sure, there are the lucky few who are able to traverse this landscape with a degree of physical immunity (journalists, most obviously, but also soldiers and guerrillas now that most "battle" means the risk-free killing of the defenseless rather than fighting other combatants), but even they cannot arrange an immunity for the soul. If for them war still holds an excitement, it is an excitement that the healthy conscience recognizes as obscene. And if war can still be viewed as life's greatest challenge, it is now less a test of any concept of courage or manhood than of simple human resiliency.

As a child, I always thought of war as something that would eventually find me. The youngest son of an American foreign-aid officer, I was raised in the East Asian nations of South Korea and Taiwan, briefly in Indonesia—"frontline states," as they were called in the 1960s, in the global military crusade against Communism. Although culturally very different, there was a certain continuity to these places: in each, the people lived in thrall of a venal American-allied dictatorship, soldiers ruled the streets under martial law or state-of-siege decrees, and the long-awaited Red invasion, we were constantly told, could come at any moment. In South Korea, soldiers rounded up and imprisoned student demonstrators, then labeled them Communist provocateurs. The entrance to my elementary school in Taiwan was guarded by an enormous antiaircraft gun, two soldiers constantly scanning the skies with binoculars for some sign of the marauding Red Chinese. Every October 10—Double-Ten Day—Chiang Kai-Shek amassed tens of thousands of his troops in Taipei's central square and exhorted them to war, crying, "Back to the Mainland!" as cheers rang and artillery sounded.

This spirit of war was all around me. My father had fought in World War II, had been an eyewitness to the attack on Pearl Harbor.

My godfather was an Air Force major. As the Vietnam War escalated in the late '60s, our small American enclave in the hills above Taipei became home to the families of army officers fighting there, their children my new playmates. When I was seven, the first G.I. I knew, George, gave my brother and me green berets from Saigon and took us to the Taipei zoo—this was on his last R&R visit before he was killed in the Mekong Delta.

War, then, came to seem like a natural phenomenon to me, a cyclical storm always massing on the near horizon. Eventually, I was sure, the right conditions would develop, the winds would shift, and war would come to where I was. Because this was in the natural order of things, I was not frightened; if anything, I awaited it with impatience. I looked forward to Double-Ten Day the way other children did Christmas, and each time I watched Chiang Kai-Shek raise an enfeebled fist in the air and squawk his call to battle, I felt a shivering thrill and thought to myself, "This time he means it, this time it's really going to happen."

But as fate would have it, war never did come to me. Instead, I had to go find it. I was twenty-four and it was August of 1983.

For five months, a girlfriend and I had traveled through Europe, hitchhiking and backpacking, slowly going through the money we had saved from a year of working in restaurants. In Athens, we were down to $300 and our return tickets to the United States. Neither of us wanted to go home yet, but we differed on how best to forestall it. She was leaning toward picking grapes in Italy or hanging out on a kibbutz in Israel. I was leaning toward Beirut.

Beirut had been in the news a lot that year. Since the Israeli invasion of Lebanon the previous summer, the city had sunk ever deeper into chaos, a free-fire zone for a bewildering array of armies and private militias. Four Western nations—the United States, Britain, France, and Italy—had sent in troops, the Multinational Peacekeeping Force, to restore order, and now they were being attacked as well; by August, the American Embassy had been torn in half by a car bomb that killed sixty-three, and a dozen-odd Marines had been killed or wounded at their isolated outposts around the city.

I'd heard vague stories about how news agencies and wire services were always looking for "stringers" in dangerous, newsworthy places, and Beirut seemed to fit the bill. Just what "stringing" entailed, I hadn't a clue, but I managed to convince my girlfriend otherwise.

From the moment we stepped off the plane at Beirut airport and I saw the shell-pocked terminal building, the ring of tanks and armored personnel cars, the soldiers holding back a huge throng of civilians desperate to find some way, any way, out of the city, I felt l was in a familiar place, the place of my childhood visions.

And, I must admit, it was just as thrilling as I always imagined it would be. At night, I lay in bed and listened to the crack of sniper fire and the peculiar feline scream of Katyusha rockets, the low rumble of artillery from the battles taking place in the Chouf foothills some fifteen miles away. By day, I was a tourist of war. Most mornings, I would leave the relative safety of our hotel on Rue Hamra, a main commercial street of West Beirut, and walk the mile down to the shattered old city center around Martyrs Square, inch my way as close as possible to the firefights that periodically sprang up along the Green Line, the no-man's-land separating Muslim West Beirut from the Christian East. Walking the ruined streets, past buildings that had been blasted so many times they resembled melting houses of wax, hearing the occasional gunshot echo from some unseen sniper, I felt exquisitely alive. It was as if I had supernatural powers: I heard the slightest sound from blocks away, my vision seemed telescopic, I could isolate the faintest scents in the air. And through it all came a strange, ethereal quality, a sense that I wasn't really there but viewing everything from a remove, through a lens; and this quality rendered pedestrian issues—of self-preservation, of what was bravery and what was stupidity—moot. I was invisible, invulnerable; a bullet could not find me.

I could justify my tourism, of course: I was looking for a job. As I made the rounds of the different news bureaus, I was greeted with puzzlement, mixed, I imagine, with contempt—the same contempt I would later feel when meeting dilettantes in war zones. Some journalists urged me to leave Beirut. Others were quietly encouraging: the level of violence was not yet to a point where they needed another hand, but I was to check back if something big happened.

I had been swept up in the madness of the place, but my girlfriend had not. To her, Beirut was just an ever-unfolding tragedy. The sight of the amputees hobbling along the waterfront promenade, the white fear in the faces of the young Marines guarding the new American Embassy saddened her to tears, and after a few days she stopped accompanying me on my walks, would stay in the hotel reading books and writing letters.

One day, a firefight that had started down at the Green Line in the early morning gradually moved up the hill toward us; by noon, I estimated it to be about a half-mile away, the concussions causing the hotel room to shake. I had learned to temper my enthusiasm around my girlfriend—it disgusted her—and for an hour or so I pretended to read, trying to invent a plausible excuse to go outside.

"I think I'll check in with Reuters," I said, tossing my book aside. "Want to come?"

She looked up from her letter writing. She was not the least bit fooled. "Go ahead."

With guilty pleasure, I left the hotel and started down Rue Hamra, which was oddly deserted, in the direction of the shooting. When I came to Clemenceau Place, I stopped.

The small park had once been beautiful but had long ago been destroyed, most of its trees shorn to stumps by shellfire. I had walked through Clemenceau Place many times on my wanderings to the old city center, another half-mile on, and there were usually vendors and children, old men lolling on the grass. On this day there was no one.

The gunfire sounded very close, and I studied the buildings on the far side of the park for snipers. For the first time since arriving in Beirut, I felt a glimmer of dread, made stronger somehow by the bright sunlight and heavy stillness of the leaves in the few remaining trees. I decided to go back, but as I fumed, I saw an Arab man standing perhaps twenty feet away. I was startled that I hadn't noticed him before. He wore a long white robe, appeared to be about forty, and he, too, was staring across the park, as if waiting for some sign.

I don't know who stepped first, but without words passing, we started through the park together. We walked at the same speed, separated by some twenty feet, and out of the corner of my eye I saw the white of his robe, and it encouraged me.

We had gone only a very short distance, maybe thirty paces, when the white of his robe slipped from my vision. I stopped and looked over to him. He was standing still, his head bent forward, and I saw that he was working his lips furiously, licking them, biting them, the way some insane people do. Then he began to walk in a small, tight circle, his left leg kicking out, his right dragging slightly, his lips still moving but producing no sound. After his second or third turn on the walkway, I noticed a small red spot on his robe, over his heart, and I saw how this spot grew each time he turned to face me. After five or six circles, he abruptly sat down on the concrete, the force causing his head to jerk, his legs splayed out before him. With the thumb and forefinger of both hands, he pinched the fabric of his robe on either side of the spreading red spot and pulled it away from his chest, as if it were a stain he did not want to have touch his skin.

I felt rooted to the ground. I knew that I should either go to him or run, get out of Clemenceau Place, but I was incapable of deciding. Then the man fell onto his left side, his hands not breaking his fall, his fingers still clutching the fabric, and I knew he was dead from the way his body settled on the concrete. I turned and walked back the way we had come.

As I returned to the hotel, I tried to find meaning in what had happened. I had just watched a person die, and I knew it had to mean something, but no matter how hard I tried, I simply could not imbue the event with much significance. We had walked together across the park, and a bullet had come, and it had found him and it had not found me, and he had died and I had not. That was all.

It took me some time to realize that this—the sheer lack of meaning in what had happened—was the lesson. War's first horror is not that people die for perverse reasons, for a cause, but that they die for no discernible reason at all. They die because they guess wrong. They seek shelter in buildings when they should flee onto open ground, they stay on open ground when they should hide in buildings, they trust in their neighbors when they should fear them, and none of it is knowable—nothing is revealed as foolish or wrong or naive—until it is too late. All that the death in Clemenceau Place meant was that the Arab man should not have attempted to cross the park that afternoon, and it was this very paucity of meaning that stunned me, that I wished not to see.

Others have likened the sound of an artillery bombardment to the sky being ripped apart. I don't know. What I can say is that after a time it no longer even seems like a sound but something animate. It travels through the ground, and you first feel the ache in your knees, then in your upper chest, and before long you can start imagining that it is inside you and will not leave. I wonder if this is why people go mad during bombardments; not the fear of a quick death, of a shell finding you, but the fear of a slow one, the sense that the constant thrumming through your body is inflicting violence from within. And in Chechnya, these thoughts are from eleven miles away, from perfect safety.

The courtyard I am standing in is an expanse of concrete enclosed by an eight-foot brick wall. Along the far wall is a fallow flower bed. I cross the concrete and step onto the bare earth. The vibrations are much softer here, barely noticeable. I lean my back against the wall, soothed by the stillness.

Ryan comes out of the house. I realize by the way he peers around the courtyard that he can't see me in the dark. For a moment I think he will go back inside, but then he sits on the steps, leans onto his knees.

I am not in the mood to deal with Ryan. He is twenty-two—a kid, really, considering where I have brought him—and a couple of years ago he left his native Southern California to scratch out an existence teaching English in Moscow. When I offered him $150 a day to come to Chechnya as my interpreter, he jumped at the chance. He is a good guy, intelligent and sweet-natured, but he left behind a pleasant life in Moscow, a girlfriend he wants to marry, and he has no idea what he has gotten himself into. I have not told him that he was chosen to make this journey simply because no one else would.

I should feel grateful to Ryan, but I don't. Rather, he irritates me. I have attributed this to his talkativeness, his fierce determination to fill every minute of his days with words. When we first arrived here, I tried to explain that the most important safeguard on a battlefield was to listen, but Ryan has either been unwilling or unable to heed this advice—and on this matter I have not been patient. Now I tell him to be quiet fifteen or twenty times a day, and the more he talks the less I do.

After some minutes, I step from the flower bed and walk softly across the courtyard. I'm only a few feet away when Ryan jumps, startled by my presence. "Whoa," he says. "Where were you?"

I don't answer.

He moves over on the step, clearing a space for me, but I remain standing, lean against the stair railing. I feel the ache in my knees again, the vibrations in the metal rail against my shoulder. "They're really blasting the shit out of it, aren't they?" Ryan says.

I don't answer.

"It's never been this bad before. Are they doing air strikes?"

"Tanks and artillery," I reply. "No planes."

I'm quite sure he doesn't like me—how could he like someone who tells him to shut up twenty times a day?—but Ryan maintains appearances. More than anything, I think he is impressed by how I watch and listen out here, imagines me to be something of an idiot savant when it comes to gauging danger.

He has no way of realizing that, in fact, I know very little. Even though it is elementary physics, I do not know, for example, if the sounds I hear, which I carefully count off each night, come when the shells are launched or when they explode. I don't know if the count is thrown off by wind or topography. I don't really know if what I am hearing are tank or artillery rounds. And I still imagine that knowing these things could be important, that knowledge alone might somehow keep us safe.

"Do you believe the stories about them burying people alive?" Ryan asks.

"They're rumors," I say.

"I know, but do you think they're true?"

He is apprehensive, of course, as we all are, and it would take very little from me to reassure him, to at least take the edge off.

"How would I know?" I say. "How in the fuck would I know?"

One night six weeks ago, I sat on the back of a houseboat on a Texas lake with the twenty-nine-year-old son of the man I have come to look for. We sat there for many hours, drinking beer and talking—about women and football and Mexico, only occasionally about his father. At around 4:00 a.m., after a long silence, both of us staring out at the black water, he turned to me.

"I don't want you to go to Chechnya," he said. "It's not worth it. My father's dead. It's not worth someone else getting killed."

The son had recently ended his own four-month search for his father in Chechnya, and over the course of a few days in Texas we had become close. Now he stared down at the beer can clasped in his hand, then took a gulp from it. "At least promise me you won't do anything crazy."

He was not used to talking to another man in this heartfelt way, and neither was I. I drank from my beer and looked out at the water. "I promise."

In the six weeks since that night, I have offered a number of variations on this promise. To my family and friends, it was that I would be careful, that I would not do anything foolish. To those who knew the details of the story, it was more specific, that I would not attempt to reach the village. I was asked to make this promise so many times that I began to deliver it preemptively—"well, I'm certainly not going to take any chances"—reinforcing the point with an incredulous little laugh, as if the very idea was bizarre. And the truth is, before I came here I believed my promises.

"What if they start shelling while we're there?" Ryan asks.

I turn to him. He is looking up at me, moon-faced. This is something I haven't considered. In the time we've been in Chechnya, they have never shelled the village during the day, always at night, and we have planned our journey to be well away before dark. But they've never shelled the village as they are doing tonight, and it finally occurs to me that it might be the prelude to a ground assault.

"Get into a ditch," I say. "If there isn't a ditch, get to a low wall, the closest low wall you see."

I think of telling him more—of explaining why he should go to a low wall instead of a high one, that if he can see the explosions it means that he is against an exposed wall and needs to get around to the other side—but know he won't remember any of it if shells start coming in. I doubt he'll even remember the little I've said, and I have an image of him standing in the middle of a road—slack-jawed and paralyzed—as the world around him disappears.

"You have to understand something," I tell him. "You will be on your own. In an artillery attack, everyone is on their own. If you freeze and stay in the open, I won't come out for you, no one will come out for you. It's not like in the movies. Do you understand?"

Ryan nods, but in his eyes I see a hint of bemusement, as if he is trying to be respectful and suitably grave but not really buying any of it. I am reminded of what I must have been like at his age, politely enduring the lectures of the correspondents and photographers in Beirut. I'm sure I had the same reaction, the same expression. At twenty-two, you can't conceive of dying.

But this is a different situation than Beirut—Ryan is here because I am here. He is following me—and his expression means quite a bit more. In his eyes, he is saying, "I know you won't leave me out there, I know you'll come out for me," and that smugness, that juvenile conviction that I will protect him, angers me.

It is then that I understand the deeper source of my irritation with Ryan. I am irritated by how easily and blithely he left his girlfriend, his happy, pauper's life in Moscow, and placed his fate in the hands of someone like me for $150 a day. I cannot possibly blame him for this—I would have done the same at his age—but I am infuriated by his trust in me.

For a long time, I did not learn anything worth knowing by going to war, and then, finally, I did. It happened on a November evening in

1986 in Uganda, maybe an hour before dark, when, glancing out the window of a moving car, I saw an old man, thin and bare-chested, standing in an overgrown field, swinging a machete.

I think what I first noticed was the intensity with which he worked. In Uganda, as everywhere in the tropics, people laboring in the fields pace themselves for the heat, maintain a slow, steady rhythm, but this old man wielded his machete with a passionate energy, arcing it high over his head, swinging it down hard. I asked my driver to stop the car and, from the open window, watched the old man for a few minutes. Then I got out and started across the field toward him.

The grass was very high, almost to my chest, and I remember thinking it odd how uneven the ground was, how it kept crunching under my feet. Hearing my approach, the man stopped his work and watched me. I saw that he was not as old as I had thought, perhaps only forty-five or so, his face and body aged prematurely by peasant life. I couldn't read his expression—not friendly, not curious, really no expression at all beyond a steady stare. I came to the space he had cleared and saw the two piles he was making—one of clothing, another of bones—and I understood then that we were standing in a killing field, that the crunching I'd felt under my feet had been the breaking of human bones.

I had come to Uganda because my older brother, Jon Lee, and I were writing a book together. We had already collaborated on one book, and this time we decided to compile an oral history of modern war by spending a year going from one war zone to the next interviewing soldiers and guerrillas and the civilians caught between them. With a meager advance from a publisher, we packed our bags and set out, to Northern Ireland, to the Sudan, now to Uganda, where one cycle of civil war had recently ended and another had just started.

Beginning a few miles north of the capital of Kampala was the Luwero Triangle, a verdant patch of farmland that had once been home to one million members of the Baganda tribe. Between 1981 and early 1986, it had been the vortex of a civil war that drifted into genocide; the Ugandan military had sealed off the Triangle and tried to erase it from existence, razing villages, murdering an estimated quarter-million people, and sending the rest into the bush or to concentration camps. When Jon Lee and I arrived in October 1986, the old government was gone, the rebels were in power, and the survivors were starting to return. They came back to a place where nature had reclaimed the fields, where their shattered homes had settled to mud, and in every village they built a memorial to the horror that had been visited on them, a display of the bones and skulls of their fallen.

For several weeks, we made periodic sojourns into the Triangle, interviewing survivors, chronicling the atrocities, watching the harvest of the dead. Everywhere were people carrying bundles of bones on their backs, on their heads, hauling them to communal places, where the remains were laid out with mathematical orderliness—tibias in one row, spines in another, skulls arrayed in descending order of size. The survivors then walked among these displays, studying first one skull and then another, hoping, it seemed, that they might somehow recognize those that belonged to their own families. It was as if, in their state of suspended shock, they had reverted to what they knew: gathering from the fields, carrying to market, examining the yield.

With Jon Lee up north, tracking the newest cycle of war, I had decided to make one more trip into the Triangle. It was while leaving, heading back to Kampala with another tape collection of atrocities, that I noticed the man in the field with his machete.

There are things about that evening I cannot explain. The man and I never spoke, but I intuitively knew a good deal about him. I knew he had just resumed to the Triangle, that the killing field was his land, that he was looking for his family. I began to help him.

This was not easy, because there is nothing mathematical or orderly about a killing field. Amid the weeds, bits of rotted cloth were strewn like garbage, tamped into the earth by the rains, and the bones lay scattered without pattern—a pelvic bone here, two skulls there. I remember thinking that it was pointless, that we would never be able to find what the farmer was looking for, but then I saw that he had a system. The bones he ignored, just threw them onto the pile. It was the clothes he studied. Each time his slashing revealed a piece of cloth, he would lift it with the tip of his machete and scrutinize it for a familiar pattern before throwing it on the pile and going on.

I found a stick and began to do the same. I would poke at the cloth until it came free from the earth or the bones it encased, then pick it up with the end of the stick and carry it to him. He would stop his labors to look it over, maybe scrape off some dirt to see the pattern, and then he would turn away without a word, and I'd drop the cloth on the pile and go back to my spot.

We went on like that for a long time, maybe thirty or forty minutes. The sun dropped to the tree line, and the land started to get that heavy gold light that comes to the tropics in the evening. I remember thinking how beautiful it was out there, how peaceful despite what had happened, as if the land were trying to heal itself, and then I realized I wasn't hearing the thrush of the machete anymore, and I straightened out of the tall grass and fumed toward the farmer. He was about thirty feet away, standing stock-still and staring at me. A piece of brown and white cloth hung from the tip of his machete, and even from that distance I could see it was part of a woman's dress, that he had found his wife's dress. In his eyes was a hatred deeper than any I had ever felt, a rage without end, and I realized it wasn't passing through me, it wasn't as if I happened to be where his eyes were fixed: the hatred was directed at me, meant for me.

I didn't know what to do, so I didn't do anything. I didn't go to him, I didn't speak, I don't think I even looked sad for him. The most I could do was avert my gaze, stare off across the field. Then I fumed and went back to the car and told my driver to take me to Kampala. I know I didn't look back, but sometimes I imagine I did, and in this false memory, the farmer is watching me go, the scrap of his wife's dress dangling from his blade, and across the expanse of the sunstruck field I feel the burn of his hatred.

And here, finally, was something worth reaming. War is all about hatred, and the hatred between combatants is only the easiest kind. At that moment of discovery, I believe the farmer hated all the world, not just the men who had murdered his family: he hated me for being a witness, hated himself for having survived, hated his wife for dying and leaving him alone. After that evening, I understood that it is impossible to go through a war and not learn how to hate.

Every morning in Chechnya I awaken with a start, instantly alert, and this morning is no different. Out the window, I see the blue-black of dawn. I stare up at the ceiling and listen. Somewhere far off is the sound of a rooster. The shelling has stopped. I think of who will be making the trip today, three of us in this house, two others sleeping a half-mile away. I estimate the time to be 5:00 a.m. We are to leave at 8:00.

I go to the basin and throw water on my face, then walk through the house. All is bathed in the milky wash of first light. I pass Ryan. He is sprawled on the bed, snoring. Nothing interrupts his sleep.

The front room holds a table with four chairs and the narrow cot where Stanley sleeps. He is on his back, perfectly still, his hands folded on his chest. Every time I've seen him asleep he is in this position, as if he doesn't move at all during the night. Stanley is forty-six, ten years older than I am, an American living in Paris. He arrived in Moscow two weeks ago wearing an all-black outfit—black hiking boots, black jeans, black shirt, black jacket, black knit cap—and he has not changed out of it since.

Our first meeting was marked by a certain mutual wariness. I knew Stanley had a reputation for taking chances, a war photographer who liked to get as close as possible to his subject matter, and his manner at that first meeting—his low-pulse calm, the watchful stare of his eyes—made me wonder if he might get us killed in Chechnya. I knew he was wondering the same thing about me. I think we both saw reflections of ourselves in the other, and this was both good and bad: we could count on the other to watch and listen, to know what to do in a bad situation, but it wasn't like there was going to be safety in numbers on this trip. Whatever affinity exists between us does not translate into a need to share personal information. What we talk about, when we talk, is the wars we have been to and where this one is headed.

Before we got to Chechnya, I had no intention of trying to reach the village; the journey was impossible, insane. But, as often happens in these sorts of situations, there occurred a confluence of events, of coincidences, that began to make it seem possible—and then, quite quickly, what had seemed merely possible began to feel like destiny. I happened to meet a rebel liaison who said the journey could be arranged, who even wrote out a coded message of introduction for me to present to the village commander. Then I happened to meet Alex, a relief worker with a four-wheel-drive ambulance and a stockpile of medical supplies, who agreed to attempt a "mercy mission" into the village, with us—Stanley, Ryan, and me—going along on the pretense of documenting the humanitarian effort. With such an extraordinary convergence of good luck, how could I not go?

Of course, riding this wave of good fortune meant overlooking certain details. The man I was looking for had also gone to the village with an interpreter and rebel credentials. He, too, had gone in an ambulance laden with medical supplies. And he had gone with an insurance factor I could not hope to arrange: two doctors who were known in the village. None of it had helped; the doctors and the interpreter had simply disappeared as well.

As the days here pass, though, it has become increasingly easy to forget all this. A kind of resignation has settled upon us. Events are happening of their own accord, momentum has built to such a degree that there are no longer any decisions to be made. Whether due to destiny or some kind of group psychosis, we are being propelled forward; the time for debate and reason has slipped away.

In the front room of the house, I quietly pull a chair out from the table. It makes a creak when I sit, and I glance over at Stanley. He is a light sleeper, given to popping up at the slightest sound, but the noise doesn't rouse him.

My notebook is on the table, and I flip through the pages until I find the encoded letter of introduction from the rebel liaison. It's not really a letter but one word written in blue ink on a yellow Post-it note, with a couple of odd, Arabic-looking symbols at the end of the word and three quick dots above it.

It suddenly occurs to me that the code's meaning is unknown to us, that our "safe passage" note to the village commander could actually say something very different, could even be our execution order. In this new light, I study what has been written. Why three dots? Maybe three dots mean "friend" and two mean "foe." Or maybe it's just the reverse. Maybe the liaison meant to make only two, but his hand slipped and left a mark that wasn't supposed to be there. Maybe the dots don't mean anything at all and what I should really be focusing on are the Arabic-looking symbols. I find it both remarkable and humiliating that my future might be decided by a word hastily scrawled on a Post-it note, but there is no choice in the matter and finally I give up.

I turn to a blank page in my notebook and take up my pen.

Many years ago, my brother, far more experienced in war than I, tried to teach me to calculate the risks before going into a battle zone, to arrive at a percentage chance that something bad might happen. "Your cutoff should be 25 percent," Jon Lee had told me. "If it's higher than 25 percent, you don't do it."

It wasn't a true equation, of course—just hunches and intuition, guesses contrived to look like math—and I'd never had much faith in my ability to weigh factors properly, but on this morning I try.

I try to imagine the chance that the Russians will attack the road while we're on it and decide on 10 percent each way: 20 percent. I try to imagine the chance that the rebels in the village will think we are spies. Here, at least, there is some empirical evidence to work with—those who have gone to the village and disappeared. I decide on 50 percent.

Seventy percent. I have never done anything anywhere near 70 percent.

I decide these numbers are way too high. I cross them out and start again. Five percent for the drive each way, 30 percent for the village: 40 percent. Still too high. Five percent total for the drive, 25 percent for the village: 30 percent. Out of curiosity, I calculate the odds of being unlucky at Russian roulette—a little less than 17 percent—and then decide the whole exercise is a waste of time, that either something will happen or it won't.

But my fatalism wavers. I stare at the two pieces of paper in front of me, the word in blue ink on the Post-it note, my calculations on the page. I turn in the chair and look at Stanley. Even though he is asleep, I am surprised that he cannot feel my stare, that some unconscious alarm doesn't trigger him awake. I slowly press against the chair back until it creaks. I wait for his eyes to snap open, for him to bolt up in the bed and meet my gaze.

I believe that if Stanley wakes up right now, I will tell him we're not going to do it. I believe I will show him the numbers in my notebook, explain that we might die over what is written on the Post-it note, tell him that it was a crazy idea, that I am frightened. But Stanley doesn't wake up, and I lack the courage to make him.

At some point, I began to take relics with me when going into war zones. It started unconsciously—a seashell here, a girlfriend's silver earring there—but my collection steadily grew until it filled a small plastic bag tucked into a corner of my rucksack. I think at first I carried these things because they reminded me of the world outside of war, small and lightweight links to my normal life; it was comforting to fiddle with an old Budweiser bottle cap or a Lion Brand matchbox or a familiar stone bead when I was bored or lost, when I was waiting for something to happen or something to end in a dangerous place.

Gradually, though, I saw that my relics were becoming talismans. I developed the habit of carrying some of them in the left front pocket of my trousers, occasionally replacing them with others from my plastic bag. I knew this was a bad sign, for it meant that I was inventing good luck to keep me safe, that my sense of immunity was gone.

Late one night in mid-January 1987, I lay on a deck chair beside the pool of the Galle Face Hotel in Colombo, the principal city of Sri Lanka, smoking cigarettes and staring up at the fronds of palm trees, thrashing and black against the sky. In my left front pocket was an American bicentennial quarter, the key to an apartment I no longer lived in, and a tiny anteater figurine made from yellow rubber. Behind my head was a stone seawall against which the Indian Ocean—turbulent and at high tide—rhythmically crashed.

The Galle Face, built at the height of the British empire, was a pile of mahogany and rattan, slow-turning fans and ocean breezes, but in 1987 the civil war in Sri Lanka was entering its fourth year and the tourists had long since abandoned "The Pearl of Asia." Now the Galle Face and the other luxury hotels along the Colombo waterfront were virtually shuttered, their lobbies filled with forlorn maids and bellhops and reservation clerks. On afternoons, my brother and I would sit by the Galle Face pool, the only charges for the five uni-formed attendants there.

The first time I climbed the seawall and prepared to dive into the ocean the attendants beseeched me to stop. It was dangerous to swim there, they said, there were reefs and sharks, strong currents that could sweep me out into the shipping lanes. I looked out at the sea. The waves were high, cresting at eight or ten feet, and it was true that no one was in the water. I told the attendants I would be fine and dove in. On that first day, I went out only a short distance, maybe fifty yards, treading water and riding the swells, and when I turned, I saw the five of them in a row behind the seawall, staring at me. I waved and they all waved back.

It became a daily ritual, and each day I went out farther, out to where I could begin to feel the current pulling me away, and where I had to struggle a little harder to get back. And each day the attendants and I exchanged our reassuring waves across the water.

I could not explain to them that I went into the ocean because there I felt in control over what happened to me. At least in the ocean I knew the dangers I faced, and the effort to stay calm, to override the fear of riptides and sharks and deep water, was an act of free will and a mea-sure of power. How could I possibly explain this to the attendants! For them, caught in a country at war, their futures and their children's futures becoming bleaker by the day, such a needless tempting of fate could be viewed only as an absurd extravagance. Better that they regarded me as an unusual athlete or a friendly fool.

Earlier that night, I had set out across the city in a restless search for diversion and had ended up at the former Hyatt hotel. With its vast vacant atrium and ascending tiers of empty rooms, the hotel had the feel of a great mausoleum that no one visited, its gloom deepened by a spirit of desperate optimism: piped Indian pop music—frenetic and reedy—drifted on the still air, and at various intervals in the hollow building, teams of cleaning women rubbed its marble and gold to a high polish, as if preparing for a party.

There were four customers in the lounge, three Asian businessmen at a table and a white man sitting alone at the bar. He was in his mid-thirties, with short blond hair, and he perked up at the sight of me, as if he had been awaiting my arrival. I sat a few stools away, ordered a beer, and within seconds he was at my elbow, his hand extended.

"New in?" he asked. "Where are you posted!"

His name was James, a thirty-year-old Briton, a mercenary pilot for the Sri Lankan government. It was an open secret that for more than a year the government had employed several dozen mercenaries—or "contract officers"—to run their air war against the Tamil Tiger guerrillas, and that it was now in the process of hiring more; James, in Colombo on a five-day R&R, had assumed I was one of the new arrivals. Although a bit disappointed to learn otherwise, he chose to make the best of it; it was not like he was going to find anyone else to talk to that night.

He told me that he flew a helicopter gunship and that his particular beat was the Jaffna lagoon on the northern tip of the island. It placed him at the center of one of the war's most crucial battlegrounds. The Tigers had held the narrow Jaffna peninsula for over three years and had repelled every army offensive against it, but they had one huge vulnerability: all their supplies, from food to bullets to medicine, had to come in by sea. A vital route was across the ten-mile expanse of the Jaffna lagoon. In the past year, James and his fellow contract officers had fumed the lagoon's waters into a shooting gallery.

"Anything that tries to go over," he said, "we kill it."

My meeting James was serendipitous, for ever since arriving in Sri Lanka, my brother and I had tried to devise some way to get to Jaffna. With the army controlling the peninsula neck, we had been told that the only possibility was aboard a Tiger supply boat trying to run the lagoon, but we'd also been told that such a venture would be extremely risky now that the mercenary gunships were killing anyone they saw. After several beers that evening in the old Hyatt, James came up with a plan.

"Here's how we can work it," he said, putting his hand on my shoulder. "We'll set up a prearranged time for you to go over and come back, and I'll just stay out of that zone. It would have to be a very small window, of course, but as long as you keep to schedule there shouldn't be any problem."

There was something both touching and ironic about this offer. Watching James's earnest face as he awaited my reaction, I knew that even more than wanting to help me he wanted to protect me. But I also thought of all the things that could go wrong and throw us off schedule—a flat tire, a flooded boat engine, a long-winded interview in Jaffna—how the smallest misstep could set into motion a course of events whereby this lonely man in the cavern of a hotel bar would, through no fault of his own, slip down from the clouds to become our destroyer. Well there's never a shortage of irony in war. As it was, all I could do was thank James for his offer and tell him I would consider it.

But walking back to the Galle Face that night, I had become aware of an odd discomfort in my chest. It was not an entirely new sensation, but on this night I felt it acutely, as one might feel the onset of a flu before it strikes. While lying in the lounge chair beside the darkened pool, staring up at the thrashing palm trees, I realized that I believed I might soon die.

At first, I was tempted to attribute this feeling to my conversation with James, my apprehensions about running the lagoon, but I knew it ran far deeper and had been with me for some time. It was why I had begun to carry talismans, perhaps even why I dove off the seawall to play with fate in the ocean's currents. It had to do with punishment.

I finally understood that I was not merely an observer of war and never had been. I had always been a participant—by my very presence I had been a participant—and war will always find a way to punish those who come to know it. I had watched people die. I had walked through killing fields and felt human bones break beneath my feet. I had picked up the skulls of murdered children and rearranged them with an eye to photographic composition. I had cajoled or intimidated or charmed scores of people into revealing their most intimate horrors, and then I had thanked them perfunctorily and walked away. If I was to be punished—and there were charms in my pocket to forestall this, there was an ocean behind my head to hasten this—it would be because I deserved it. God knows I deserved to be punished for the things I'd seen.

As it turned out, my brother and I did not attempt the Jaffna lagoon. Instead, we journeyed east, to the marshes and rice paddies along the windward coast, to the Tigers fighting there, to Athuma.

At 7:45 a.m., minutes before we are to set out for the village, I tell Ryan and Stanley that I am going to the town square for cigarettes and slip away from the house. The day has broken cool and the air is clear. By noon, the dust will rise to lie over the town like a shroud, but for now it is still wet with dew, and in the distance the snowcapped Caucasus mountains shine like glass.

In the square, the kiosk women are just setting up for the day, throwing open the wood shutters of their booths or laying out their wares on the sidewalk, blankets wrapped tightly over their shoulders. I buy three packs of Marlboros and push them into my coat pocket.

At one end of the square is a high school and, next to it, a small park, its entrance dominated by peeling portraits of men I do not recognize. I have passed the place often in the past few days, and on this morning I wander inside.

It is a very modest park and suffering from neglect—the paving stones of its path are shattered, and nothing has been pruned or trimmed in a very long time—but at its center I come to a massive, marble monument, a small eternal flame burning at the base. It is a memorial to the town's dead from World War II, and in the black stone are chiseled scores of names.

Standing before the flame and the list of war dead, I suddenly find that I am praying. I haven't prayed in twenty-five years and am not really sure anymore how it is done, if I'm supposed to preface it in some way or direct it to some god in particular. In any event, it is a selfish prayer; for the soul of my dead mother, for the safety of my companions and myself on this journey.

I hear laughter behind my back, and I turn to see two schoolgirls sitting on a nearby bench, watching me and giggling. I am embarrassed that they know what I am doing, that even though I haven't bowed my head or closed my eyes, they know I am praying. I stoop down to pick up a pebble from the path, then leave, finishing the prayer in my mind as I walk. In the left front pocket of my trousers is a fossilized shark's tooth from Florida, the keys to my apartment in New York, and a tiny 1973 two-kopeck coin I found in the gutter of a Moscow street. At the entrance to the park, I slide the pebble into my pocket, one more charm to keep me safe.

In my absence, the ambulance has arrived at the house, and my companions stand in the street, waiting for me. The relief worker, Alex, is a tall, rail-thin Hungarian in his early thirties, an Oxford divinity student, of all things, on leave to perform rescue work in Chechnya. There is something in his quirky, rather dandyish manner—his vaguely British accent and soft stutter, the long woolen scarf he habitually wears—that seems both charming and brave in its incongruity with this place. On this morning, he appears to be in high spirits—cleanshaven and jaunty—and he bounds over the dirt road to shake my hand.

"Nice weather for it," he says, glancing up at the blue sky, "but I suspect we'll find mud in the mountains." He turns to me, still smiling his crooked smile. "In any event, perhaps we should take a closer look at this note from the liaison. Wouldn't want to walk into a trap of some sort, would we?"

Alex says this without any hint of real concern, and I take the Post-it note from my back pocket. He studies the single word for a moment, his fingers distractedly playing with the frame of his hoary-rimmed glasses, then hands it to Aslan.

Aslan reminds me of other young men I have known in other wars,

the native "taxer" hired by Western visitors—journalists, relief
workers—to get them in and out of dangerous places. He is in his mid-
twenties, with dark hair, sunglasses, and a black imitation-leather jacket.
Others have dressed differently, of course, have been Asian or African or
Latin, but what unites them all is a cocky bemusement at our ignorance
and bad ideas. Aslan glances quickly at the note and shrugs.

"I don't know what it means. It's in code."

"Nothing for it, then," Alex says, merrily. "We'll just have to go and
find out."

And so we set off, the boxes of medical supplies—gauze bandages,
glucose solution, antiseptic wash—jouncing and sliding in the ambulance bay. We follow the path of my imagination: over the plain, into
the foothills, and then there is the dirt track, the river, and we are in
the mountains. The day is bright, a blinding light reflecting off the
snowcapped peaks to the south, but the small valleys below us are
cloaked in morning shadow and fog. We are still on neutral ground,
but that doesn't mean much here, and out of habit I watch the valleys,
look for a flash of refracted light in a dark recess, a sudden swirl in a
fog cloud, for some sign that a trolling gunship is rising out of the
depths to meet us. But there is no flash or swirl, and the only sounds
are those of the wind and the grinding of the ambulance engine. We
pass no one on the track—no cars, no homes—and we do not talk. It
is as if each of us is making this journey utterly alone, each in his own
private ambulance on a ridgeline at the top of the world.

About an hour after crossing the river, Alex, sitting in the front passenger seat, suddenly points down the hillside. We are skirting a
mountain, somewhere near the unmarked frontier between neutral
ground and war, and in the pasture below is a haphazard cluster of
large, rectangular stones.

"They look like ruins," Alex says excitedly. "Old ruins."

As Aslan continues to steer along the track, the rest of us peer out
the windows. It is a strange sight, this jumble of square-edged rocks in
the middle of nowhere, but not strange enough to dispel our stupor of
silence.

It was a very hot day. The air was still, and thick with the smell of paddy water and sweat, and when Athuma was led into the hut, the sun was behind her so that for a moment she was only a silhouette against hard light. That is how I remember it, how it looks when I return to it.

The day had started off very differently. In fact, it started the way I, as a child, had imagined war would be but war had never been: grand, cinematic. The night before, a messenger had come with our instructions, and at noon Jon Lee and I had walked into the marketplace of the government-held town and two Tiger guerrillas had suddenly appeared beside us on their motorcycles, motioning us to get on. There had been a wild, careening ride, down side streets and narrow alleys, dodging army roadblocks and personnel carriers, until finally we burst free from the town and were in the countryside, speeding past farmhouses and rice paddies and palm trees, and my life had never felt so much like an adventure.

The sensation lasted for a time, through the dash across the lagoon in the motorized canoe, through the half-hour drive on the other side, crammed in the back of a battered Jeep with a half-dozen Tigers. It ended at an old farmhouse hidden in a grove of trees. It ended the moment I saw Kumarappa.

He was twenty-seven years old, the Tiger commander for the region, with a pistol on his hip, a potbelly, and dark, dead eyes. His young followers—weighted down by weapons of every kind, ampoules of cyanide hanging on leather thongs around their necks—gathered close to his side, as if posing for a group photo, as if mere proximity to him bestowed status. And because they were only boys, and because they had been living in the bush, the Tigers could not hide their excitement at our presence; they whispered animatedly to one another, smiled shyly in our direction. But not their leader. Kumarappa stared without expression, his eyes unblinking, as if we were not really there at all.

The Sri Lankan army was closing in on Kumarappa's group. In the last few days, they had launched a series of lightning assaults in the area, coming ever nearer to the base camp. Just that morning, helicopter gunships had swept in over the lagoon and killed several people caught out in the open. It was now only a matter of time—probably a very short time—before the army moved on the old farmhouse amid the rice paddies, and if his boy followers hadn't figured that out yet, it seemed that Kumarappa had; it was dying time, and Kumarappa was already there.

He motioned for us to follow him to the main hut, a long dark room with reed walls and a thatched roof. Four wicker chairs were arranged around a low table, and upon this table a young Tiger placed three bottles of warm orange soda.

Hunched in his chair, his weapon-laden boys gathered behind him, Kumarappa began to talk of death, of the cyanide ampoules he and his Tigers would bite into when the final moment came.

"It's a good death. Yeah, it's a good death. Our soldiers do that. It's a very brave death . . . I'm not afraid to die, you know?"

He talked of spies, of the spies who were all around him, in the villages, in the rice fields, even coming into the area from other places. They were trained by British intelligence or the Israeli Mossad, maybe even the CIA, and Kumarappa was always uncovering them, getting them to confess, tying them to lampposts and blowing off their heads as examples to others who would betray.

"Sometimes we put them on the lamppost," he said, cradling his bottle of soda. "Sometimes, you know, we have the explosive wire—just around the body, and then we detonate it. This is our maximum punishment. We do it sometimes. Two or three times we've done it."

And as he spoke, I felt Kumarappa was studying me. I don't know if this was true or merely my imagination, but every time his empty, dead eyes fumed in my direction, I became more certain that I was the subtext of his rambling conversation, that in me Kumarappa was deciding if he had found his latest spy.

Once this conviction took hold, it became paralyzing. Even as I tried to meet Kumarappa's stare—and it is impossible to stare for as long as a madman can—I knew that the fear was registering on my face, that I looked, in fact, very much like someone with a guilty secret.

I felt caught in a deepening trap, fear giving way to a panic I wasn't sure I could suppress. At last, I simply dropped out of the conversation, let Jon Lee take over all the questioning, while I busily scribbled in my notepad, peered up at the thatched ceiling as if in deep concentration, anything to avoid Kumarappa's gaze.

"We can show you one spy that we have caught," I heard Kumarappa say after a time. "Would you like to see a spy?"

It was impossible to not look at him then, and when I did, I saw that he was watching me, the hint of an indulgent smile on his lips. It was the first time he had smiled, and it was the first time in my life I was sure I was about to die.

I don't know how long this belief lasted—at most a few seconds—but then I looked down the length of the hut, down the passage that had suddenly formed between the gathered Tigers, and at the far end I saw the silhouette of a woman in the light, a silhouette being led toward us. That is when the belief leît me, when I saw I was to live, and this filled me with such relief and gratitude that I felt transported, as if on this broken-down farm in the marshlands a hideous miracle had just occurred.

They sat her across from me, in the empty wicker chair beside Kumarappa. Her name was Athuma. She was thirty-six years old, the wife of a peasant farmer, the mother of seven children. Among the many events that had, no doubt, filled her short life, only the following were now important:

The Sri Lankan army had taken her husband and tortured him until he was a cripple. They had taken her two youngest children and given them to the sister of a Sergeant Dissayanake. And then the army had told Athuma that she could change the situation, that everything would work out, that there would be money for food and the children would be resumed if only she gave Sergeant Dissayanake information about Kumarappa and his boy soldiers in the bush. And so, apparently, Athuma had.

But Athuma had not been a good spy—people who are coerced into it rarely are—and very quickly, before she was able to report anything of importance, the Tigers had found her and brought her to

Kumarappa. That was two days ago. After two days of torture—revealed in the swelling on her face, her shuffling, lopsided gait as she walked toward us—Athuma had confessed to everything. There was now just a little more torturing to be done, and then it would be over.

"She knows very well the final decision," Kumarappa said. "She knows we are going to kill her."

And then Athuma began to beg for her life. It began as a soft whisper but gradually rose to a high-pitched chant, a disjointed blend of Tamil and English, and this pleading was not directed at Kumarappa but at us.

"Save me, save me, save me."

It continued for a long time, became a keen on the edge of hysteria. Kumarappa turned in his chair to watch Athuma, appeared both bored and amused as she leaned over the table, looking desperately between Jon Lee and me.

"Save me, save me."

And we tried. Slowly, gingerly, we felt around for some hidden corner in Kumarappa's heart. We went over the circumstances that had led Athuma into being a spy, the fact that she had not told the army anything damaging. We asked what would happen to her children, both the stolen ones and those here with their invalid father, if she were to die.

But Kumarappa, his hands folded over his little potbelly, remained unmoved by any of this. Instead, a suspicious light came into his eyes, and this time there was no ambiguity, no mistaking what it meant; he was asking himself why these two foreign men were trying to rescue this spy.

As if Kumarappa's paranoia were infectious, the mood throughout the room changed. The Tigers who were gathered behind him— friendly, unsophisticated boys a moment before—turned suddenly sullen and dark, their faces set hard against us.

"Save me, save me."

Athuma leaned out from her chair toward me, compelled me to look directly into her eyes—hers were dark brown with flecks of yellow—and I remember opening my mouth to try one more time, but even while looking into her eyes, I felt the stare of Kumarappa and his boy killers, and I couldn't speak. I turned to Jon Lee, and in the gaze that passed between us was an agreement, an understanding that it was over, that we had tried and could not try anymore.

Athuma understood as well. As quietly as it had begun, her plea ended, and I will always remember the sound of her sitting back in the chair, the creak of the wicker, for it was the moment when all hope left her. I could bring myself to look in her direction only one more time. She was staring down at the table, her matted hair framing her bruised face, and she no longer seemed frightened, only sad and terribly tired. A few minutes later, they took her away, and she again became what she had been at first: a silhouette, limping and hobbled, this time receding, passing out into the light of day.

I was in New Delhi, eleven days later, when I learned of the assault on the farmhouse. The army had come in on gunships at dawn and encircled the area, then methodically worked their way through to the grove of trees, killing everyone they found. The Sri Lankan government was claiming 23 dead Tigers, including Kumarappa, while local residents were claiming nearly 200 dead, mostly civilians; the truth was probably somewhere in between. Indian television ran a video of the aftermath and there was a slow pan of a dozen torn bodies in a row beside the ruins of the main hut. I looked for Kumarappa among the corpses but couldn't find him, only a couple of the boys I had talked to.

Jon Lee had flown on to Europe for a reunion with his wife, and in a week I was to join him in London before we moved on to our next war zone. I had told him I was going to stay in New Delhi for a few days to relax—maybe go down to Agra to see the Taj Mahal—but what I really wanted was to be alone. I didn't know how the incident with Athuma had affected him—we had barely discussed it before parting—but I believed that he was less bothered by it than I was; my brother was older, tougher, more experienced at war; he surely knew how to handle such things.

For me, it had brought a sense of shame deeper than I had ever thought possible. On an intellectual level, I understood I was not responsible for what I had felt in the hut—for either the fear or the relief—but no matter how many times I replayed that afternoon in my mind, told myself it was irrational, I could not be rid of the belief that Athuma and I had somehow traded places, that I hadn't really done all I could have to save her because if she had lived I would not have.

My first two days in New Delhi I didn't leave the hotel room. I ordered food and beer from room service and had it left outside the door, told the maids there was nothing for them to clean or straighten. I watched television, smoked cigarettes, paced, stared out the window at the people passing in the street. I relived being in the Tiger camp and conjured up different scenarios, different endings. I played back the tape of that afternoon, listened to all the places where I should have said something but didn't. Then on the third day came news of the attack on the farmhouse, and I felt better. Now I could distract myself by envisioning how the Tigers died.

I knew Kumarappa hadn't eaten his cyanide; in war, the glory of martyrdom is reserved for children and rubes, those who don't know any better. I envisioned him trying to make a break for it, leaving his boys behind to die, flailing through the rice paddies with his pistol, perhaps getting far enough away to start believing he had made it that he was safe, before being cut down, and I hoped that his end had not been quick, that Kumarappa had died for a while.

I thought of one boy in particular, Shankar, a sweet-faced twelve-year-old with a beautiful smile and a Chinese sniper rifle, a boy so small he had sat on the lap of another Tiger when we interviewed him. I knew Shankar hadn't eaten his cyanide either. I envisioned him panicked as the soldiers closed on the farmhouse, lying wounded in the grass when the shooting stopped. I envisioned him crying for his mother and for mercy as a soldier approached, and I hoped the soldier had not been swayed, that he had put his gun to Shankar's head and pulled the trigger. What an awful thing, to hope for slow death, for quick murder, but it was these hopes, this hate, that enabled me to finally leave the hotel room and rejoin the life I had watched from my window.

It seemed that the world had changed in my brief absence; of course, it was I who had. Beginning the day I left the New Delhi hotel and continuing over the subsequent years, there was about me a new manner, a kind of taut gentleness. At one time, my pride had not allowed me to walk away from a fight. After Sri Lanka, I never showed anger, defused tense situations with an almost obsequious politeness. At one time, I had enjoyed going into the woods with a .22 rifle and shooting at birds and squirrels. Now I didn't want to kill anything, and even the feel of a gun in my hand was repellent. For a long time, I didn't want to go back to a war zone. When I finally did, it was only to "safe" battlefields—Belfast, Gaza—places where I was unlikely to look into the face of another Athuma.

There were other changes as well, a quirky, eclectic array. I discovered that I now had to live on the top floor of buildings, with large windows to view my surroundings. I was not comfortable in crowds or dark places. I no longer dreamed when I slept. I overreacted to sharp sounds. I felt nervous when helicopters flew overhead.

I understood that the incident with Athuma was not the cause of these changes but rather the culmination, the last link in all that had come before. I had been traveling a path ever since Beirut perhaps ever since I first heard Chiang Kai-Shek's rantings in the central square of Taipei—and at the old farmhouse in Sri Lanka the path had finally given way beneath me. I understood that it had always been only a matter of time before I met an Athuma.

What did not change was my reticence to talk about these things, about Athuma or anything else that had happened. Instead, I felt a keen desire to not do so, to partition off those memories as something that had no relevance to my new life. For some time, I seldom told new acquaintances I had written books, even more seldom the subject matter. To old friends who were curious about my apparent drift—why I wasn't working on another book, why I had moved to a seedy apartment in Baltimore, where I knew no one, or, later, why I spent two years doing clerical temp work in Boston—I offered the blandest of explanations, if any at all. Only to those closest to me could I talk about the farmhouse—and this only after four or five years had passed, only after I had extracted from them a promise of absolute secrecy. What also did not change were the returnings to that day, the sudden, always unexpected moments when I found myself back in the hut, Athuma coming toward me.

It was not until a number of years after Sri Lanka that I realized there was another force guiding my changed approach to the world. It was an unsettling force, one that I had briefly glimpsed in the New Delhi hotel and imagined to be temporary. Along with whatever other emotion had taken root—sadness, shame—now there was also rage, a well of directionless hate. If I had become a gentler person, it was at least in part because I was fearful of the alternative. I didn't get angry, I didn't fight, because I didn't trust what I would do. I wouldn't get near a gun because I was afraid I might use it. And in seeing this, the odd little set of neuroses I had developed did not seem so eclectic after all; guarding against the rage meant being vigilant and quiet, always in control, forever watching the horizon for signs of danger.

I found safe, discrete targets for my anger. Chief among them were those who advocated war or professed to understand it. In London, I watched leftist students, in sandals and patchouli, demonstrate in support of the Tamil Tigers. In the build-up to Operation Desert Storm, I watched Young Republicans at the University of Iowa conduct a mock trial and execution of Saddam Hussein, listened to them cheer and whoop when "Hussein" was made to kneel on the stage to be "shot" in the head. I listened to pundits and academics opine about why a war was or wasn't a religious conflict, an economic or constitutional one. I did not need to confront leftists, rightists, college professors, or yahoos holding forth in a bar; it was enough to loathe them in silence, and I nurtured this loathing as if it were something precious.

It was in the autumn of 1994, nearly eight years after Sri Lanka, that my brother and I talked about Athuma for the first time. We were sitting on the porch of our sister's home in Connecticut late at night. A week earlier, our mother, who lived in Spain, had arrived to visit me and my sister—the only two of her five children who lived in the continental United States. She had fallen ill suddenly, too suddenly for my brother, living in Latin America, or my two other sisters in Hawaii to reach Connecticut before she died. Now, the day after our mother's death, Jon Lee wanted to be told everything that had happened, the precise chronology of events in her rapid decline. Her passing had been a painful one, difficult to witness, but for several hours on our sister's porch I calmly, numbly, told Jon Lee all he wanted to know.

"I don't know why we couldn't save her," I kept saying. "It happened so fast, but I don't know why we couldn't save her."

After a time, though, my numbness wore off, replaced with the naked grief that tends to ebb and flow on such occasions, and amid this my sorrow expanded to encompass the other woman we hadn't been able to save, Athuma.

"Did we really do everything we could? Did we really?"

"Yes, we did," Jon Lee insisted. "We did everything we could, and it wasn't enough. We tried, and we couldn't try anymore." He said the right words, but in his eyes I saw that Jon Lee didn't believe them either, that he had remained haunted over the years as well.

And despite what is said, it is not always easier to grieve together. Sometimes it is easier to imagine yourself alone, to believe that others— stronger, tougher than yourself—have figured a way out and laid a trail that you might follow. Seeing the sorrows of my brother—the new one for our mother, the old one for Athuma—was not an easy thing. Along with tenderness, I also felt an anxious despondency: no one was strong or tough enough to emerge unscathed; there was no trail out.

A few months later, I decided I would return to Sri Lanka. I got the idea from watching television programs about American veterans who were returning to their old battlefields, to Okinawa, to Vietnam. I watched these programs closely, studied the faces of the veterans—especially those who, earlier in the programs, in their pre-journey interviews, had let their masks slip, had lost their composure in a moment of bad remembrance—because I wanted to see whether they finally found some measure of reconciliation, of peace, in the happy playfulness of the children in villages they had once fought over. The results seemed mixed at best, but the journeys also appeared to be the only thing these old soldiers could do, and I decided to copy them: I would go to Sri Lanka and find Athuma's children, those who were still alive. I would tell them what had happened, how I had tried. I would apologize.

Instead, someone called to ask if I would go to Chechnya, to follow

the trail of a middle-aged American man and his three companions
who had disappeared there, and a different image came to mind: this
man and his companions somewhere in the Caucasus mountains, cap-
tive, despairing, but alive, waiting for death or someone to save them.

And so, perhaps having not truly learned anything yet, I went to
Chechnya.

When a person believes he is about to die at the hands of another,
he does not look at all the way one might expect. He does not scream
or cry.

Rather, he becomes very quiet and lethargic, and his eyes fill with a
kind of shattered sadness, as if all he wants to do is sleep. It is only like
this with a certain kind of dying, I imagine, the kind where you have
been given time to see what is coming, where you have tried to nego-
tiate and reason and have failed.

In the front room of the farmhouse in the village, I see signs of this
exhaustion in all my companions: Alex hunched forward on the
couch, gazing miserably at the bare concrete floor; Aslan leaning
against the wall, his arms wrapped about his middle, staring down at
his shoes; Stanley's eyes fixed on the far white wall, distant and puzzled; even Ryan seems chastened, his habitual grin gone, his eyelids
heavy. I am reminded of looking into the face of Athuma that last time.

We had been stopped as soon as we reached the outskirts of the
village, hustled out of the ambulance and led into the stone farmhouse that was the rebels' command post. They were startled to see
us—the village was closed to civilians, the track in "restricted"—but
at first we were treated more with curiosity than with suspicion; we
drank tea and shared cigarettes, the rebels talked animatedly about the
war and why they were fighting. It was when the commander arrived
that everything changed.

He was in his forties, wearing a black leather jacket and strange,
ankle-high boots. He shook each of our hands without smiling, then
sat on the edge of the broken-down couch and leaned onto his knees,
and in the long silence that ensued he seemed lost in thought, methodically massaging his fingers, staring down at the floor. At last, he sighed
and looked up at me.

"You are not supposed to be here. No one is allowed here. How do I know you're not spies?"

The note from the liaison was gone. I had given it to one of the rebels who first stopped us, the one who seemed most senior, and he now made a great show of looking for it, rummaging through the various pockets of his fatigues and turning up nothing.

"I must have given it back to you," he said to me. "You must have it."

He was lying, but I didn't know to what end. Was he protecting us or doing the opposite? It was impossible to know, and there was no time to ponder or watch for clues.

In the absence of the note, the commander began his slow, calm interrogation of us. He asked why we had come, who had sent us, and studied our identity papers as if they were weighty evidence. To his questions we gave the most innocent of answers—that Alex had come to deliver relief supplies, that I had come to chronicle the mission—but nothing swayed the commander. Instead, it seemed that everything we said, every insistence of our simple intentions, served only to convict us more, lead us that much closer to a bad end. Everyone in the room knew what was happening—the rebels who a short time before had given us tea and cigarettes now looked away, refused to make eye contact—and it was the interminable slowness of our descent, our grinding inability to find an ally or the words that might save us, that finally led us into a crushing apathy, to this place where our strongest remaining desire is simply for the process to end.

And then I find the words that cut through. Or maybe it is not words at all but the way I look unblinkingly, guiltlessly, into the commander's eyes. Or maybe it isn't any of this but only a capricious shift in the executioner's heart—suddenly we find the interrogation is over and we are free. Still dazed by the speed and mystery of our deliverance, we are led to the ambulance, and the rebels gather around to shake our hands, to slap us on the back, to wish us a safe journey, as if we are close friends they are sad to see leave.

While driving back through the mountains, I remember the man I had gone to the village to find. I never asked the rebels about him, and for the first time I grasp the colossal scale of my hubris. What had I expected? That I would stumble upon the American and his companions standing at the roadside? That I could go to the village, meet the men who had almost certainly murdered the lost group, and have them confide in me? What had I been thingking?

During the slow quiet drive away from the village, I am reminded again of what it is about war that has always tormented me, that I have never been able to reconcile. Although it has been proved in front of my eyes a dozen times, I have never truly accepted that what separates the living from the dead is largely a matter of coincidence, of good luck or bad, that in war men and women and children die simply because they do, and that there is no plan or reason to any of it. If a faith has guided me, it has been one of arrogance, the belief that I have power, that I can save, that vigilance will see me through.

Athuma was dead before I saw her, she was dead sitting across from me, and she was dead when I left. There was nothing I could have done to make it turn out differently. There was nothing I could have done to save the American man in the village, and there was nothing I could have done to save myself or my companions—no note, no talismans, no words. But this impotence is almost too much to bear. It is easier somehow to endure the self-tortures—of rage, of shame, of hope—that come with the belief that there is a pattern, that we can shape it.

Perhaps this is because of the greater powerlessness that lies beyond, the inability to ever go back. Returning to Sri Lanka and seeing Athuma's children would not have changed anything. Finding the American man in the village would not have canceled out Athuma in the farmhouse. If the goal is to reconcile, to "get over" what has happened, the self-torture will never end; grace can come only in knowing that the wounds never heal, that they have become a part of you and are to be carried. That you can't atone, that you must stop trying.

About an hour after leaving the village, while skirting a hillside, we come upon a Toyota Land Cruiser stuck in the mud up to the floorboards, its three occupants sitting dejectedly in the grass. It is the only other vehicle we have seen all day, and, following the etiquette of the mountains, Aslan stops the ambulance and starts to fashion a towline from a coil of rope. The rest of us step out to stretch our legs. By coincidence, we have stopped above the same small glade where Alex pointed out the unusual sprawl of stones that morning, and for several minutes, the four of us stand silently on the edge of the bluff, staring down the hillside at them.

I look to the far side of the road and notice that we are directly below the crest of a flat-topped mountain, a mesa. Most of the slope is dirt, but at the crest is a uniform, six-foot seam of rock, and I see that the square boulders in the pasture below are not old ruins but simply sections of the escarpment that have fallen away. I turn to point this out to my companions, but it is too late; Alex has begun running toward the rocks. I watch him go—an awkward girlish run, his scarf snapping in the breeze—and I am seized with a dread that, at first, I cannot identify. I clamber down into the mud, to where Aslan is busy with the towline.

"Is this area mined?"

Aslan looks up and seems to sniff the air, as if I've asked him if it might rain. He shrugs.

I climb back to the edge of the bluff and see that Alex has reached his destination. He is standing atop one of the immense stones, his hands on his hips, and although he surely knows now that his ancient ruins are only fallen boulders, he seems quite pleased with himself, a preening explorer.

I shout down to Alex, tell him to be careful, that there might be mines. Even across the long expanse of pasture, I can see the tension come into his body, and I know the weight that has dropped into his chest, the ringing emptiness that has replaced his thoughts. I watch him gingerly pick his way back up the hill, his shoulders stooped like an old man. I try to remember the way he was just moments ago—happily running through the meadow grass, exultant upon his rock—and I am held by the sadness of how he has changed, of how we all change out here.

from Kigali's Wounds, Through A Doctor's Eyes

by John Sundin, M.D.

Surgeon John Sundin worked at the Red Cross Hospital in Kigali, Rwanda during the Spring of 1994.

May 13

I'm living and working at a Red Cross field hospital that was set up a month ago in a converted Catholic convent. It is situated on a hill, looking out over the green hills of Rwanda. Rwanda is known as the Switzerland of Africa, but the comparison stops at the landscape. The country is ravaged by a savage war between the government—Hutu—and the "rebels"—Tutsi. Two tribes, two politics—very complicated. It's war, nevertheless, fought not with planes, bombs, tanks, or missiles but rather with rifles and mortars, and with a fair share of less sophisticated weapons: machetes, clubs, and spears.

Today started at a leisurely pace. There are seven people on the medical team, and we have about two hundred patients staying on the floor and in tents. I am the surgeon, and work with two nurses in our two operating rooms, which were classrooms a month ago. Our cases today included the closure of the scalp over the machete-exposed temporal lobe of a boy. Another: finishing touches on a leg blown off last week by a mine. A woman who, four days ago, was nine months pregnant—until someone clubbed her badly and she delivered a dead baby too quickly. She needed her torn vagina sewn up. A leg that I thought would have to be amputated looked okay, so I will look again in a few days. And this was a good day! I've done maybe twenty amputations of legs, hands, and an eye over the last week.

Sometimes the taste of flesh and pus stays on my palate after the day's work. It's hard to sit down and eat meat, but I do because at night the international team—French, Swiss, Dutch, Danish, Finnish, and me (the American)—sits around a table. We eat what we have, and drink what we can, and smoke like there's no tomorrow. Then to sleep to the sounds of gunfire and awake to start again.

May 15

I'm dragging. To the operating room. Cover a machete cut to the skull four inches long with exposed brain. Nasty. He will probably die. After lunch I return to my room—sleep is what I need. Three weeks here seem like a year. I check my temperature; I have a fever of 101. That's a good sign—it's not stress alone that's making me feel so bad but some tangible pathogen. Water and aspirin and vitamin C. Fever now 102. Fitful sleep, this side of delirium. Stretchers, thousands of stretchers. Like Chaplin's *Modern Times*—an assembly line of stretchers and wounds, wounds, wounds. There's no other doctor here, so I'll have to treat myself. Dangerous. What's wrong with me? The flu? Dengue fever? Encephalitis? Malaria? Nothing is worse than to be sick far from home. My friends nurse me. Aspirin, Fanta, soup. Doctors are the worst patients.

Night falls and my fever rises. Yes, it could be malaria. Kigali is a thousand meters high, but there are still mosquitoes and malaria. We have two drugs here that can treat malaria: Fansidar and Lariam. Neither is to be taken willy-nilly A complication of Fansidar is called Stevens-Johnson syndrome, also known as

Watch-every-square-inch-of-your-skin-drop-off syndrome. I saw a photo of it in a medical text. The odds? 1 in 10,000, 1 in 100,000. The odds of being eaten by a lion in New Haven are astronomically low, but if you are the one eaten by an escaped Barnum & Bailey lion then those reassuring odds are only statistics. Lariam—my own stock from Yale—can cause acute psychosis. I'll sleep on it. If my temperature is still up in the morning then I'll do something.

Sleep. Sweet sleep. Sweaty sleep. Mosquito nightmares. The sun again. The thermometer again. Higher, not lower: 103 and pushing 104. Brain-frying time. My head aches to the hair roots. Must treat myself. Fansidar or Lariam? Skin loss or psychosis? What a choice. Convoluted synapses. Feverish thinking. I decide on the Fansidar—all I have to lose is my skin. Better my skin than my mind.

Now the nurse from hell arrives. She's Dutch. Maybe fifty something, and looks like she was sired from stick insects. She's good—don't get me wrong. A veteran of Mogadishu, Kabul, etc. However, I suspect sometimes that she thinks we are in Amsterdam, not Kigali. Limits have to be set.

Anyway, this nurse knocks on my door, enters, and sits on my bed. I know there's trouble brewing. A new patient, twenty something, with a shrapnel wound in his left flank. Blood in his urine. Trouble. The left flank is where the kidney and the big aorta live. I'm dizzy even thinking about getting vertical, but there's no other surgeon. I operate and he may die anyway. I don't operate and he dies for sure. I operate and I am sick for three more days. I don't operate and rest, and can operate in a few days. Too late for him in a few days. Others may come in tomorrow. Must rest. Must get better. Must choose. Crazy place. No lawyers, only limits.

She pushes as she always does: "Well, he will die if we don't operate." I know she's right, but "No, I won't operate today" rolls off my tongue.

Charges: breach of Hippocratic oath. Plea: temporarily crazy place. Sentence: loss of all skin.

May 16

Recovered from my fever and my Fansidar dose with my skin gill intact. The flank wound died as expected. The team was eating together at the time of the news, and we all discussed our limits. The insect nurse is pushing to do more and more and more. Get blood donors! Fight to save every double amputee! It's her nature. The rest of the nurses (French, Swiss, Danish, Finnish) are more willing to accept the limits: very little backup, a sea of wounded, and limited supplies, including blood. Sure we could do a liver resection if we had to, but with no blood, oxygen, or ventilators, the patient is as good as dead anyway. I sense she faults me for not having operated yesterday—but sometimes, c' est la vie, c'est la mort.

May 21

Yesterday a man came in with his personality on the stretcher after getting shrapnel to the head. We have a zombie now. A woman buried alive in a mass grave dug herself out after twelve hours. She's pretty freaked out. I would be.

May 25

Bunkered in today. Mortar hit Red Cross compound next door, killing two and wounding five. Hospital staff leaves and wounded pour in. Fifty more today. Putting them everywhere on the Found now. No more tents. Sixty out of one hundred staff have left. Twenty cases to operate on but tomorrow will be another day of shelling. Phillip, our four-pack-a-day Swiss director, reassured us today that we were not a political target, only in a bad geographic place. Politically correct, geographically incorrect.

May 27

The situation is evolving—now very, very tense. Today, for the first time, I feared for my life. Shelling all day, bunkered in. Patients lying on stretchers for three days, waiting for surgery and dying. Patients are dropped off at the gate screaming. Before the military hospital was closed down, we were getting 90 percent Tutsi patients, and the Hutus went to the military hospital. Now everyone comes to us. We are becoming the nexus for these warring, century-old tribal hatreds.

Extremists still exist. The Hutu militia showed up at the hospital today with Kalashnikovs and clubs with spikes. These are the folks who kill Tutsi for sport—and they're in the hospital! They want to know why we treat Tutsi before Hutu. We can't even tell who is Tutsi and who is Hutu. They want to know what happened to one of their men who was brought in yesterday. He's dead. He was a fat man with a small hole up over his liver. There were five others ahead of him with their bellies sliced open. Twenty others with mangled limbs. Now they accuse us of killing this man. They want his body. They take our walkie-talkies. The local staff is in a panic. These are crazed armed killers, the same bunch who killed 150 patients in a Medecins Sans Frontieres hospital in Butare. Two staff leave through the back door saying, "It's finished, it's finished." I am finally really scared. We all are.

The militia take two Red Cross workers, Andre and Ischelle, to find the body, which is already buried in our own mass grave in the compound. They see the body has no surgery marks. They want his shoes. They say he had a million Rwandese francs in them. Not there now. They have murder in their eyes.

The U.N. arrives, only by coincidence. They want some bandages. The militia leaves with the body. They say they will be back. Foreboding. We have no security anymore. Our local staff has left. The military can't be trusted. They're about to be overrun.

I hid in a comer today, fully expecting to be murdered. They wanted the medical team that's "not treating their people." That's me: I'm the surgeon, the only one. This is really no joke. The locals see it, too. "They don't play games," a local says about the militia. The mortars have been a nuisance—a low probability of being hit—but now we are marked by killers who live down the road.

At Yale, we used to have weekly morbidity and mortality meetings where the surgeons tore one another apart like pit bulls for as little as a wound infection. Tame compared with the jury in this crazy place.

We are no longer safe, and the medical team knows it. Mortars are one thing, but killers are another. Tomorrow at sunrise we will give our decision: We cannot spend another day in the hospital with Kalashs at our heads. We get U.N. protection or we request evacuation as a group. We just can't do any more. Sacrificing our lives isn't in the job description. The chaos is peaking. Order is dissolving.

I'm too tired to be dramatic, but believe me, the situation is very, very, very tense. Please don't tell my mother.

June 11

It's happening: I'm burning out. I really noticed it yesterday while amputating a rotten leg at the mid-thigh—my back and hands sore, my gag reflex twitching. We had fifteen cases between 9 and 1—arms and legs to cut off or dress, a nose and two eyes blown away, a five-year-old leg connected by a thread of flesh. In the beginning we had a schedule. I saw wounds healing and grafts taking. I used to know the patients. Now there are so many wounded that it's assembly-line first aid.

There's another man on the ward with a very bad leg. He refused amputation a few days ago. He missed his chance. He's got the "gas" now—gas gangrene up to his flank. He'll rot from the leg up, like the others. He'll start to smell and the flies will come to feast and the nurses will say do something and I'll say no. I'll send him to our "hospice" tent and then I'll put him out of his misery.

I've lost my sense of humor. I'm beginning to feel a certain distance. People are beginning to look like insects. Bad sign. The end is not in sight on the military or political front. The end is not in sight for the wounded. But my end is in sight. I'm going to leave at the end of June. Three weeks seem like a very long time. Will I make it? Suddenly the edge has lost its romance.

Judgment Day

by Alan Zarembo

Rwanda's Hutu majority killed some 800,000 of their Tutsi neighbors during a roughly three-month period in 1994. Alan Zarembo wrote about the afternath for Harper's.

In Rwanda, 92,392 genocide suspects await trial

The inmates politely applaud and thousands of eyes follow the two Rwandan government ministers as they move toward a smooth wooden table furnished with two microphones and a plastic vase of fake flowers. It is late October 1996, and for the last few weeks the ministers have been on a tour of Rwanda's prisons, trying to convince tens of thousands of inmates to confess to genocide. Today has brought them to the prison in Kibuye, perched on Lake Kivu's stunning blue in western Rwanda, three hours from the capital, Kigali. Dragging a microphone toward him, one of the ministers launches into a lesson about the Holocaust, but his tales of blue eyes and blond hair six decades ago don't change the blank expressions in the sea of black faces before him, so he jumps to the hundred-day stretch in 1994 when the Republic of Rwanda's Hutu majority conducted a campaign of wholesale slaughter against the Tutsi minority. Ordinary citizens did much of the killing with the same tools they used to clear fields and butcher livestock. In all, roughly 800,000 people died, their corpses collecting three times as quickly as did dead Jews in Nazi Europe.

Although this is the first time the inmates have heard the government's plan for their fate, many seem distracted by simpler concerns. They lean on one another, forearms on knees, palms on foreheads, cheeks on shoulders—the world's biggest game of Twister. Hundreds wrap their shirts into turbans as cover from the alternating drizzle and equatorial sun. A baby screams until a prisoner pushes her shriveled left breast into its mouth. The kitchen at one end of the yard resembles a steel mill, pumping black smoke from its eight chimneys as dinner for 2,797 is prepared below. The cooks, wearing soft pink uniforms coated with soot, shout orders over the cacophony of rakes shoving hot coals, long wooden clubs beating maize flour into a rubbery paste, shovels scraping the sides of giant pots, and machetes splintering logs in quick, precise hacks.

The inmates can be trusted with machetes for the same reason that most peasants outside the prison gates can: although it was the main instrument of death during the genocide, the machete quickly reverted to its traditional status as a farm tool. Many in Rwanda would prefer to forget the machete's history, to let the genocide itself slip into the murk of oblivion, but the new Tutsi-controlled government, which ousted the former Hutu leaders in July 1994, cannot allow this to happen, and so it has jammed 92,000 suspects into prisons throughout the country to rate each crime on a sliding scale of brutality. Most of the prisoners are rank-and-file Hutu peasants who were directed to kill their Tutsi neighbors by radio propaganda and given specific targets by local Hutu leaders. So the ministers are offering them a deal: admit to your sins and squeal on your accomplices and superiors in exchange for a sentence short of life in this brick-and-plastic slum. The ministers are political evangelists, trying to convince the throng below that the only way to heal Rwanda is to follow them, as if these microphones, these history lessons, and these neatly wrapped stacks of the new genocide plea-bargain law could methodically undo the insanity the country has inherited.

What the ministers never tell the prisoners, what is never transmitted through the thick black cable that snakes through the crowd to three loudspeakers set on a pickup-truck roof, is that they are worried. Not because their bodyguards have propped their AK-47s against the rusty red prison gate to pass around a cigarette and are only half watching the thousands of suspected murderers but because of a much more ominous fact: the genocide was a nearly perfect crime. Proving that it happened is easy; even proving that certain people were involved is not hard; but pinpointing exactly who did what may be, without confessions and betrayals, impossible.

Now the new Tutsi-controlled government wants to save Rwanda with the same forces that perpetuated the slaughter, to sort out guilt and innocence with the same authority that allowed the old Hutu bosses to oversee the massacres of 1994. For the genocide was produced not by a culture of chaos but by one of controlled docility, in which pleasing one's superiors is reason enough for existence.

When has a killer gone too far? There were those who competed to murder 200 Tutsis first, the man who crushed 900 people in a church with a bulldozer, and the teachers who killed their students. Where does a man who butchered five people, the same number as did the Manson family, rank on the Rwandan killing scale?

Take the case of innocent Nsengiyumva, a farmer in his mid-twenties, whose only extraordinary trait is that he confesses to his crime and does not recant—at least not during the first week after soldiers lock him in a military jail. Innocent rarely leaves the dark cell he shares with about twenty other men, and he hesitates when a soldier lets him out to talk with me. His splayed feet and narrow shoulders seem as unlikely as his name; as he speaks, he hugs his torso.

The number of Tutsis he slaughtered could have been many more than the two children he admits to. He can't remember if the victims were boys or girls, only that they each must have been about six, siblings.

For two weeks—or was it two months? he can't decide—he was part of the local mob. He enjoyed hunting Tutsis but was sorry to murder. He was ordered to do it, but not by anyone in particular.

Killing was a job. The local Hutu official had a list of victims, and each morning the peasants gathered with their weapons—machetes for most, a homemade wooden club spiked with nails for Innocent. For the first week he only watched, he says, "like a child watching something his father is doing." The killers drank at the bars they passed, went home for lunch, and resumed in the afternoons. His turn came when the crowd spotted the two children. They didn't try to escape, he says, and didn't scream until he sunk the nails into the side of one of their heads.

I ask the obvious question. "How could you kill children?"

"If you were there . . . Things were strange. I can't find any way to explain it to you. Can you imagine the radio saying, `Go kill these people'? The message got to the local authorities. They mobilized the soldiers and the militias, and they were going to the villages getting civilians to kill people. We accepted. They said we were fighting for the country."

"What would have happened if you'd refused to kill?"

He looks bewildered, tugging at the sleeves of his mangy red blazer. "Nobody refused."

A man named Innocent murdered two six-year-old children—a piece of absurd horror that leads to another. In deciding his fate, prosecutors must determine whether Innocent's malice was "excessive," whether, under the new plea-bargain law the ministers have been peddling, he qualifies as a "Category 1" killer, and therefore for the death penalty. The designation is reserved for the genocide's leaders and their lieutenants—priests, local authorities, and militia members—"sexual torturers," as well as "notorious murderers who by virtue of the zeal or excessive malice with which they committed atrocities, distinguished themselves in their areas of residence or where they passed."

There are more than 90,000 Innocents. And so it is that a mountain of Day-Glo folders, freshly shipped from prisons and still bound with twine, are piled on a chair in the waiting room outside the office of Emmanuel Rukangira, Kigali's prosecutor. He spends much of his time sorting the files into stacks—stacks that decide life and death. Ranking brutality may seem surreal to outsiders, but to Rwandans, raised in a pecking-order culture, it makes perfect sense. Rukangira explains how one man became notorious for burying people alive, a method that automatically places him in Category 1.

"Is it worse to bury one person alive or kill ten people with a machete?" I ask Rukangira.

He smiles, as if he's thought about this before. "With a machete, you can do it with one hack. To bury somebody alive, it takes him a long time to die. Sometimes they didn't bury him completely. They left him there alive and came back in a couple days with a stick to finish. Others killed pregnant women and cut the babies out of their wombs. That is a cruel way to kill. Category 1."

Only about 2,000 Hutu suspected mass murderers will make the honor roll. The rest are Category 2, the common killers who will serve seven to eleven years if they confess before charges are brought, twelve to fifteen if they confess after, and life in prison if convicted without confessing. Category 3, those who maimed but did not kill, can get off with one third the penalties mandated in the standard criminal law. Category 4 includes those who looted the homes of the dead, crimes so relatively minor that Rwandans have been told to work out compensation plans among themselves.

But it is too soon to classify thousands of inmates. Before prosecutors can gauge malice, investigators must make files, and for files to be made each Hutu prisoner must first be identified. This is not easy. When the new Tutsi-led government seized power, thousands of suspects were denounced by neighbors, arrested by Tutsi soldiers, and locked up without records. Files were made later, often based solely on information the prisoners provided themselves. In some prisons, foreign aid has allowed the government to correct that sophistry with another: inmates are now photographed in the hope that their accusers can provide their real names.

In Mbogo, forty miles north of Kigali, new arrestees line up at the door to investigator Ephrem Sikubwabo's office, a concrete cubicle that reeks of sweat and fresh paint. Spiders have strung their webs across the metal bars on the windows; crumpled sheets of carbon paper spill out of a cardboard box onto the floor. Twenty-seven-year-old Sikubwabo sits behind a desk, listening to a transistor radio while he hammers out interrogation transcripts on a manual typewriter. In an assembly line of denial, inmates enter one by one, sit, clench the sides of the wooden chair, and proclaim their innocence.

As long as they remain silent, the genocide will remain a collective act.

When the Tutsi rebels first took power, it was common for Hutus to admit to—even boast of—their role in killing Tutsis. But behind prison walls the indoctrination has turned tactical. Now not only do most dispute their crimes but many deny that the genocide ever happened. Portraying themselves as victims of the Tutsis, the prisoners have taken on an unusual role for suspected killers: the spokesmen for due process.

"He who has done a bad thing must be punished," declares a chubby-checked inmate of the Cyangugu Central Prison. "But I don't under stand why we must wait two or three years to be judged."

To reach him, I have had to follow two barefoot prisoners lugging an oil barrel full of beans down a corridor carpeted with an interlocking weave of outstretched prisoners, past men scrubbing plastic plates in the gray water that ripples through the gutters, and into a room dank with sweat and breath. Every prison has a hierarchy, and it soon becomes clear that I have been led to Cyangugu's City Hall—and that the inmate with the chubby cheeks, Theodore Munyangabe, No. 1,550 on the Category 1 list, is Boss.

Munyangabe's ward resembles a two-story chicken coop. A vent in the roof casts a strip of sunlight across the top roost, a plywood shelf where he sleeps in a row of twenty men. Twenty more sleep on the bottom shelf. As I watch a prisoner on the upper deck wash his feet in a bucket, another inmate shimmies out of the one-foot crawl space beneath the bottom shelf, where yet another twenty sleep. Convincing a fellow inmate to sell his shelf space can cost more than $100, nearly half of what most Rwandans earn in a year, so the poor fan out to sleep on the rafters, the cement floors, the corrugated tin roofs, and the cardboard sheets that cover the pit latrines. They are used to the stench of shit.

"In every society there are some people who are better off than others," Munyangabe says with a shrug. He employs a teenage prisoner to wash his clothes and deliver his meals, and pays the boy in biscuits handed out by the Red Cross; another inmate cuts his hair. Testimony from these low level prisoners would probably be enough evidence to convict men like Munyangabe, but I wonder whether Rwanda's new leaders will ever be able to convince them to rat out their bosses. Clearly, Munyangabe is doing his best to keep their lips sealed.

I ask him about the plea-bargain law. "If I am a murderer, the court must prove it. It is not [my job] to prove to the court that I am a murderer. If I had done something bad, I would tell it. It isn't easy to confess something you haven't done." I ask him if there was a genocide. "I can't be quite sure, but I think there are people who have done bad things."

Until he was arrested in March of 1995, Munyangabe, forty-two, was a deputy governor in Cyangugu Prefecture, tucked between Zaire and Burundi at the south end of Lake Kivu. His slight lisp, round face, and powder-blue shorts give him a boyish quality as he leans on a rafter and scoops maize paste into his mouth. "They say I have killed men. I don't know who. And I don't know who says so."

Munyangabe may never have touched a machete or fired a rifle, but in Rwanda guilt is inversely proportional to how low you are on the killing chain. Human-rights investigators believe that he led a massacre of hundreds at a church, then accompanied the governor to a nearby stadium where Tutsi men were herded into groups to be killed. Nearly a year later, Munyangabe caught word of his impending arrest and went to meet Jane Rasmussen, a United Nations human-rights monitor. They sat on the office porch for more than two hours; she took notes of their conversation. Yes, he drove grenades to the Cyimbogo church, where hundreds of Tutsis had taken refuge, but it was his driver who tossed the grenades inside. He thought about saving Tutsis instead of driving them to roadblocks manned by militiamen, but as a member of the government he really had no choice.

"He was not lying and shameful but pleased to present the story of himself as a good man trapped in a bad situation, who'd done the best he could," Rasmussen remembered. "I was thinking, why was he telling me all this? Did he feel a need to confess? Did he want legal advice? This is the creepiest part: I think he really didn't understand anything he had done was wrong, legally or morally. It's the perfect example of how people's sense of right and wrong got turned around in the genocide."

Back in the Cyangugu prison the rain starts. Inmates string up tarps and rush to catch the runoff in buckets. A muscular man in red bikini underwear foams with soap lather, a crucifix swinging from his neck, as I head toward the prison's exit. The only guard left on duty padlocks the main gate and, after bidding me goodbye, heads home for the night.

The prison stands on a hilltop like a medieval fortress. I can hear the din of thousands of voices from behind the thirty-foot-high brick walls as my translator and I descend into the valley. Along the way he says, "You people are lucky—you muzungus [white people]. When there is something wrong you say it. You say, `Fuck you.' But us, we play diplomacy. We are not open. We don't show everything."

"What do you mean?" I ask.

"I can smile at you, drink with you, and eat with you—and have something bad against you. This evening I can come and kill you, even though we were together today. Between Hutu and Tutsi there is always doubt."

He is a Hutu in his mid-twenties. I will call him Pierre. During the genocide he hid a Tutsi carpenter in his house. One day he returned home to find a mob in his front yard; they were cousins and neighbors, some of the same people we had just seen in the prison. "They said, `There was a Tutsi in your house,' and I said, 'Not.' And they said, `Yes there was, and we killed him. Here he is.'" At their feet was the body, his skull dented, a gash across his neck. Pierre went inside and closed the door.

He says that most of the killers enjoyed their jobs, each day working a different side of town, each night swilling beer and dining on the freshly butchered cows of dead Tutsis. I ask him how such celebration was possible.

"When somebody is your enemy, killing them is nice."

"Did you kill?"

"No."

"Why not?"

"I don't know why I wasn't interested. People were getting rich from it. Those who were killing were boys and bandits. I had no reason to get more things. My father can feed me." Then he offers that he refused to feast on the fresh beef. "The same machete that killed a man killed a cow. l am eating the cow, so I am eating the man."

"Would you ever testify against the killers you saw?"

"Even if they arrest me and say, `Tell us what you know,' I would not say anything."

"Why not?"

"It's not my job."

Anyone who saw mutilated bodies flicker across a television screen in the spring of 1994 might dismiss the genocide as yet another African tribal war unleashed in yet another lawless African state. Hutus make up 85 percent of the population; Tutsis, most of the rest. But the problem is that there is little consensus about whether Hutus and Tutsis can be called tribes at all. Before colonialism, Rwanda was a highly organized feudal kingdom. The overlords were Tutsis, but not all Tutsis were privileged. The two groups meet none of the standard conditions that define tribes; for centuries they have lived on the same hillsides, spoken the same language, shared the same burial customs, and intermarried.

The Belgians, masters of Rwanda and neighboring Burundi for four decades, tried to quantify the differences between Hutus and Tutsis. Belgian ethnologists claimed that the average Tutsi nose was

55.8 millimeters long and 38.1 millimeters wide, compared with Hutu dimensions of 52.4 and 43.2. Other dubious distinctions were based on property: those who owned fewer than ten cows were said to be Hutus; the rest, Tutsis. The colonial government issued each group identity cards and forced Hutus to work for free while Tutsis supervised. The first massacres in Rwanda erupted in 1959, when Hutus slaughtered Tutsis in order to consolidate power before the country's pending independence in 1962. Roving the hillsides in squads, they chased tens of thousands of Tutsis into exile, the same Tutsis who would multiply in asylum, creating a generation of expatriates who would return to take power after the 1994 genocide.

Far from being another lawless African country, independent Rwanda became and remains a model of order. The country is divided into 12 prefectures, 154 communes, 1,600 sectors, and tens of thousands of cellules—a top-down network of officialdom rooted in a precolonial kingdom, codified by colonizers, and preserved after independence. Once Hutus had vanquished the Tutsi elite, it used the pre-existing social structure to exercise complete control over the populace. Residents had to ask permission to leave their hillsides. Everybody became a de facto member of the only political party, Hutu President-for-Life Juvenal Habyarimana's Mouvement Revolutionnaire National pour le Developpement (MRND). When opposition parties were legalized in 1991, MRND tacked "et la Democratie" to its name, but nothing about Rwanda was very democratic. It was a nation of followers, a culture that foreign-aid donors believed contributed to progress: more than 60 percent of Rwandans were Catholics, a higher proportion than anywhere else on the continent; there was very little street crime; and peasants spent two days a month planting trees, terracing fields, and paving roads in a national service program called umuganda, which amounted to forced labor. The crews were called Interhamwe: those who work together.

Foreigners refused to see the bigger national project in the pipeline. They could have looked for clues in Burundi, where over the last three decades the Tutsi minority had kept their grip on power by periodically massacring Hutus, as many as 300,000 in 1972. Both countries have the same ethnic mix, but lacking the revolution that brought Hutus to power in Rwanda, Hutus in Burundi had grown so obedient to their Tutsi overlords that they dug their own graves and reported to police stations for their scheduled—and sometimes rescheduled—executions. Some twenty-two years later in Rwanda, it was Tutsis who would die, and this time it would be the civic duty of Hutus to kill them. The ideology of Tutsi extermination would flow down the hierarchy of command into virtually every home, the churches would fill with bodies, the terraced fields would become mass graves, Hutu soldiers would speed across the country on some of the best roads in Africa, pink identity cards would help determine who would live and who would die, and Interhamwe would refer to a new kind of work crew: not tree planters but militias made up of peasants and unemployed young men recruited from the ranks of ordinary Hutus on every hillside, the gangs that became the most notoriously brutal killers.

The seeds of genocide were planted in late 1990, shortly after the Rwandan Patriotic Front, a rebel army led by English speaking Tutsi refugees, invaded from Uganda. Three years of fighting ended in a stalemate, forcing the MRND to sign a power-sharing agreement with the Tutsi RPF rebels. But the Hutu leaders delayed implementing the agreement, and extremists within the government began to enact a plan to exterminate not only all Tutsis but Hutu sympathizers as well.[*] On April 6, 1994, President Habyarimana's plane was shot down—most likely by his own extremist Hutu allies—killing him and providing the pretext for the massacres.

---

[*] Extremists pushed an ideology known as Hutu Power via propaganda such as Kangura, a magazine that in 1990 published "The Hutu 10 Commandments," which warned Hutus not to intermarry, fraternize, or go into business with Tutsis. Commandment 8 states simply, "The Hutu should stop having mercy on the Tutsi." Commandment 10 proclaims that "the Hutu Ideology must be taught to every Hutu at every level. . . . Any Hutu who persecutes his brother Hutu for having read, spread, and taught this ideology is a traitor."

Enlisting civilians to kill was a deliberate attempt by the ruling Hutus to create a society that Tutsis could never govern. And it may have worked. Although in 1994 the RPF defeated the Hutu army, stopped the genocide, and took power,[*] the only beneficiaries of their revolution so far have been the army officers who claimed hillside villas and the roughly 800,000 Tutsi refugees who returned from three decades in exile to replace the dead. The RPF set up a coalition government that blames tribal distinctions on colonialism and avoids using the words "Hutu" and "Tutsi," but few believe the pretense of kinship. Hutus in the government are figureheads; intermarriage has all but ceased; and Hutu extremists still kill Tutsi survivors and foreigners as part of ongoing attempts to destabilize the Tutsi-led government. Many of the estimated 6 million Hutus view their new bosses as a foreign army of occupation. Imagine the Jews picking up arms in 1945, taking over Germany, and then having to run the country.

But even this comparison falls short. At the height of the Holocaust in 1944, the Nazis executed about 400,000 over a three-month period, the same length of time it took Hutus to kill twice that many. If Nazis ran killing factories that most Germans never had to confront directly, Rwandans murdered intimately, spattering their clothes with the blood of their neighbors. A U.N. survey of more than 3,000 children after the war showed that 69.5 percent had watched murders or maimings, 78.5 percent had heard screams, and 16 percent had hidden under corpses. Nobody knows how many people actually took part in the slaughter, but without gas chambers and crematoria, the number of executioners had to be far greater than in Germany.

Therein lies the dilemma. Can an ethnic minority control a country simply because of the evils perpetuated by the majority, no matter how awful? Is justice, or revenge, a solid enough foundation for a nation-state?

---

[*] Ironically, the downfall of the Hutu regime may have been due to its dedication of men and resources to the genocide rather than to fighting the highly disciplined RPF, which forced the Hutu army and militias into exile in Zaire.

"There is no Republic of Genocide," one foreign diplomat tells me. I ask him what he means. "Genocide is the basis for the existence of this government. Arresting people is the only way it has to assert its authority."

The first time I visited a Rwandan prison was October 1994, three months after the Tutsi rebels took power and not long after I arrived in Rwanda. I had lived in Africa as a college student and had written a thesis about why Uganda had sponsored the 1990 RPF invasion; back in the United States I couldn't understand why some nice people half a world away were butchering their neighbors. So about the time that Americans were watching O. J. Simpson's Bronco ride, I quit my newspaper job, traded my rusting station wagon for a plane ticket, and convinced the warden to open the single padlock on the gate at the "1930," the Kigali central prison. The name refers to the number displayed above the door, which is the year the Belgians built the compound.

Back then, the prisons held about 6,000 inmates. By January of this year, my third in Rwanda, 92,392 people were stuffed into fifteen prisons and 183 local jails, some so packed that inmates must take turns sitting down. And just when the prisons seemed full, the army, as if conducting an experiment on claustrophobia, shoved in more people—an average of 600 a week last year. By official admission, some of those jailed are innocent, turned in by people who wanted their houses, cows, or fields—some sense of compensation for their dead relatives short of finding the real killers.

One Monday last October, in a Kibuye jail, a 15-by-12-foot cell held about seventy-seven inmates. They competed for air and light through three small windows. That night soldiers squeezed in forty-five more, bringing the density to about six people per square yard. The guards heard shouts and banging on the door, but refused to open it until the next morning. By then, sixteen were dead.

Such incidents are all too common, but the new government is faced with three grim and equally absurd options: ignore an atrocity, answer it in kind, or slowly sift through a mountain of individual brutalities, grading each one using methods that are at best terribly slow and at worst entirely arbitrary. One afternoon, resuming from a prison with Gerald Gahima, the deputy justice minister, I told him how I once entered a reporter's lottery to watch the hanging of Westley Allen Dodd, who had killed three children in southwest Washington. Gahima responded, "Anybody who kills three babies deserves to die. He deserves more than death. But what do you do when everybody has killed three babies?"

The young judges stroll into the classroom in the town of Gitarama. None carries a briefcase or legal pad. Only three out of the fifty-odd men and a few women wear spectacles, though more probably need them. As they enter, a clerk tears open a brown envelope and passes out copies of the new plea-bargain law, printed in French, English, and the country's indigenous language, Kinyarwanda. The clerk paces down the aisles like a high school proctor, distributing notebooks and blue Bic pens. A throat clears when one judge in white patent-leather shoes saunters in fifteen minutes late.

If the judges seem unseasoned, it is because most have no legal experience at all. More than 80 percent of the former judicial officials fled or were killed during the genocide; many participated in it. There are few left to help judge the 92,000 inmates who give Rwanda the distinction of imprisoning a higher percentage of its population than any other country in the world. In 1996, 46 Manhattan judges heard 259 murder cases prepared by 600 prosecutors. As of January of this year, Rwanda had 201 judges, 132 prosecutors, and 157 investigators. Even if each of Rwanda's twelve genocide courts could try one case per day, the trials would continue for twenty-nine years. The government says it is too poor to hire defense attorneys, and the country's 33 private lawyers have expressed little interest in representing genocide suspects. Last year the justice minister was fired, though never prosecuted, for allegedly embezzling $100,000 and trying to clear her uncle of genocide charges.

The majority of the new judges are Tutsis with few memories of Rwanda. They either were born in exile or fled the country as children in 1959, returning to their homeland after the 1994 genocide had

ended. Some of the judges are Hutus, and some are Tutsi genocide survivors like Sylvestre Bizimana, a towering thirty-one-year-old with a
whispery monotone and a pewter Marlboro belt buckle. Before the
war, his family ran variety shops in two towns. Three brothers, his
father, and dozens of relatives were killed. "After the war, nothing was
left," he says. "I wanted to serve my country."

Elsewhere, judges whose families were massacred may recuse
themselves from hearing massacre cases. In Rwanda that is not an
option, so Bizimana answered a radio advertisement. Applicants for
judgeships had to be at least twenty-five, have a secondary school
diploma, and be free from criminal convictions. Hundreds showed
up for the hour-long test. Part One was an essay question worth
twenty points: "In a democratic state, it is essential that a government not interfere in the decisions of judicial tribunals. Discuss."
Part Two was a set of twenty questions, worth one point each. Here
are some of them:

1. What is the capital of Canada?

2. The Hippocratic Oath is sworn by members of which
profession?

8. Jean-Paul Sartre is author of:
a) *The Second Sex*
b) *The Outsider*
c) *Being and Nothingness*

13. The chemical symbol for sodium is
a) Na
b) Cl
c) So

14. Humans first landed on the moon in:
a) 1969

b) 1970

c) 1972

15. The president of the Supreme Court of Rwanda is

16. Croatia was formerly part of
a) the Soviet Union
b) Czechoslovakia
c) Yugoslavia

17. The cornea is found
a) in the eye
b) in the heart
c) on the foot

19. The author of *The Republic* is
a) Plato
b) Aristotle
c) Euripides

20). "Extradition" means:
a) to convict someone twice for the same offense
b) to convict someone in his or her absence
c) to remove a person to a country where he or she is accused of a serious offense

The top scorers won a four-month course on Rwandan law and an $88-a-month job. Today is their final classroom lesson before they take the bench to judge genocide defendants. The lesson is on the new plea-bargain law. "I didn't write the law. I've only been asked to teach it," an appeals-court prosecutor says before instructing the judges to open their copies to page 10. His disclaimer is understandable. The law has spurred a divisive political debate. Punishments must be stiff enough to satisfy genocide survivors' craving for justice but light enough that prisoners have an incentive to confess. Many survivors believe that execution is the only suitable punishment for the killers, even for children who followed the example of their parents. Other opponents say that the courts will become so clogged that eventually innocents will make up confessions; otherwise they could easily spend more than fifteen years—the maximum sentence for admitted Category 2 killers—awaiting trial.

Larger fears loom over Kigali authorities. What will the world think if they start executing the guilty en masse? Will the sentences incite Hutu prisoners—and, more importantly, fugitive militants—to further violence? Can the government safely free the innocent after their trials and the guilty after they serve their sentences! The Ugandan-raised health minister, Colonel Joseph Karemera, tells me, "We can't release prisoners until we brainwash the population to accept them."

Clutching a pen and notebook between his handcuffed palms, Deogratias Bizimana hops off the tailgate of a pickup truck at gunpoint. Rwandan cameramen shove boom microphones in his face as he enters the courtroom in the eastern town of Kibungo on December 27. The audience of several hundred claps vigorously as the prosecutor reads the charges, a catalogue of evil that qualifies Deo for Category 1: leading gangs of killers, carrying a grenade, theft, doing nothing to help people in danger. Children gather on the window ledges outside, clinging to one another as they peer in at the thirty-seven-year-old suspect standing at the bench in his baggy prison shorts and rubber flip-flops. He is the first genocide suspect to be tried in Rwanda.

Before him, three stone-faced judges sit at a table draped with the Rwandan flag, dressed in black robes piped with saffron cuffs, hearing the first criminal case of their lives. All three grew up in Zaire, where one was a teacher, another studied banking, and the third got a business degree.

The trial lasts about four hours, with more than a quarter of the time taken up by a debate between Deo and the judges over whether he will be allowed to speak French. The judges decide that since most of the crowd understands only Kinyarwanda, he must speak it too, even though French is one of Rwanda's three national languages. A Rwandan radio journalist leans over to me to joke, "He must have used the machete in French."

Deo has no defense attorney and was given only Christmas Day to review his file. Although the families of the dead have lined up to stake claim to the defendants' belongings, the closest Deo comes to confronting his accusers—whose statements are read by prosecutors, not presented in person—is when a man in the audience rises to show the machete scars on his neck and scalp, then holds up his right hand to display the stubs of three missing fingers. Deo tries to defend himself with logic, refuting an accusation that he once stood up in a crowded tavern and beckoned Hutus to kill all Tutsis, including those present.

"If the witness was a Tutsi in the bar, and he is still alive, how did he come to know that statement?" Deo asks amid laughter from the crowd, as if he had said that the goat ate his homework. The prosecutor retorts: "[Deo] seems to be saying that the only witnesses are those he killed."

That may be true, and the irony of it all strikes me. If the old regime had succeeded in killing all the Tutsis, there would be no trials, no memories, no political dilemmas. Genocide, according to international law, is defined as "acts committed with the intent to destroy, in whole or in part, a national, ethnic, racial, or religious group"; the closer you come to destroying the whole, the fewer witnesses are left behind, and the harder genocide is to prove. A week later, such paradoxes don't prevent the young judges from sentencing Deo to death. As the pickup pulls away to take him back to prison, he vows to appeal, a process that could delay his execution by a few months at best.

Was justice served? Hours after the sentencing, back in Deo's village, his Tutsi neighbors tell me yes. His Hutu neighbors say maybe not. One woman who listened to the proceedings on the radio stops short of calling him innocent but says that some details presented in court were wrong. She nervously looks around for the Tutsi spies she fears may be hiding in her bushes before saying that investigators never questioned her and that many Hutus are too afraid even to attend court, let alone present evidence to contradict the prosecution.

If this was the first trial—presumably among the strongest cases—I wonder what trial number 4,156, or number 33,372, will be like.

Rwandan officials make no apology for imprecise justice. They say that meeting Western standards would mean freeing large numbers of killers for lack of witnesses or due to legal loopholes, which would be disastrous for a government that derives its legitimacy from the wrongs of the old regime. The alternative may be executing some innocents, but officials say that it is hypocritical for the world to criticize Rwandan justice when, as of February 1997, the U.N. international tribunal set up in Arusha, Tanzania, to punish the masterminds of the Rwandan genocide has yet to convict anyone.[*]

Hamstrung by mismanagement and bureaucracy, the Arusha tribunal is the scorn of Rwanda, in part for not using the death penalty. The chief prosecutor until September 1996—Richard Goldstone—also headed the Yugoslavian tribunal, and in nearly two years he spent just seven days in Rwanda. Most genocide planners continue to live comfortably in exile. The tribunal did indict Colonel Theoneste Bagosora, a top army officer believed to be among the Hutu inner circle. He was originally arrested in Cameroon, not for killing Rwandans but for the murders of ten Belgian U.N. peacekeepers in Kigali.

---

[*] Indeed, the tribunal workers seem too busy conducting bizarre experiments in cultural relevancy to concern themselves with justice. In September 1996, a week before the first trial started in Arusha, only to be delayed for months, tribunal member Gregory Gordon was onstage playing Hamlet in a production cosponsored by the United States Information Agency. The program noted that Gordon, "when not engaged in theatrical activities, is helping to prosecute war criminals for the International Criminal Tribunal for Rwanda." Other tribunal employees played the King, Queen, Horatio, and Laertes; the USIA flew in a drama consultant from Chicago. Comparing the Danish prince's existential crisis to the genocide, the director, who also played Horatio, billed the play as a form of national therapy, telling one reporter, "What the play is actually about is to speak the truth about what happened here, about ambition and corruption gone awry." On opening night in Kigali there were no more than three Rwandans in the audience.

The executions of the Belgians were a calculated attempt on the part of Hutu extremists to make the world turn away so that the genocide could continue unimpeded. It worked. The Genocide Convention, signed by dozens of nations after World War II, proved futile when the United States, wary of another Somalia, dodged its international obligation—leading other countries to do the same—by refusing to use the term "genocide" in public until the 1994 massacres were nearly over. The U.N. force was reduced to a skeletal crew as soon as it evacuated all foreigners, leaving Rwandans—including those who worked for the U.N., foreign governments, and aid organizations—behind to die.

One of those left behind was Bonaventure Niyibizi, the top Rwandan working for the United States Agency for International Development in Kigali. He smiles wanly as he tells in an unbroken voice the story of his mother's three-day execution: the killers sliced her Achilles tendons the first day, hacked off her legs and head the next, and finally returned to toss her body in the river. He attributes his own survival to sheer luck.

A year after the genocide, Niyibizi was invited to the U.S. State Department auditorium in Washington to accept an award, which he guessed—wrongly—was "foreign employee of the year." When he was called to the podium, the head of USAID, Brian Atwood, handed him a wood-and-bronze plaque, and the audience applauded. The inscription read: "A unit citation to USAID/Kigali for working together in a situation of great peril to make and implement decisions resulting in the safe evacuation of the entire American mission staff." It was USAID's congratulations to its Rwandan employees for saving their American co-workers. A copy of the citation was sent to each one, even to the fifteen who had been killed.

Back in Kigali, Niyibizi mounted the plaque next to his door. "I am keeping it in my office," he tells me, "not because I am proud of it, not because I deserve it, but to remember how we have no value."

Hope for a lasting peace is fragile and requires a national consensus on the fair administration of justice. But Rwanda's 800,000 victims and 92,000 prisoners form an elaborate puzzle of accusation in which each piece stubbornly refuses to fit its obvious match. On a hilltop in Mbogo, I meet Odette Mukandekezi, a Hutu woman who denounced Athanase Mujyambere, a prisoner in the "1930," for killing her Tutsi husband. She thinks she is thirty-two. A deep scar emerges from her left ear, juts across her forehead, and curves down into her right eyelid. A gray cardigan is draped over her shoulders, hiding the fact that her left forearm is gone, and as she speaks, she rubs her right thumb over the stubs of her index and middle fingers, severed at the knuckles with a machete by a neighbor who attacked her in April 1993 for being "a friend of Tutsis." That year, the government was sponsoring small-scale massacres in what amounted to a practice run for the genocide. One year after being brutalized, she watched Mujyambere order a mob to exterminate hundreds of Tutsis gathered in a church.

"I remember Mujyambere saying to the others, `These are snakes, let us kill them,'" she tells me. "I can't tell you who did what, only that when he said to kill, they started with machetes and guns. There were lots of people. I cannot even remember their names. Mujyambere was the chief, in charge of making sure nobody was missed."

I return to the "1930" to confront Mujyambere with her accusation and ask whether he thinks it is fair that prosecutors have put him in Category 1. More than 8,000 suspected murderers are packed into a space built for 2,000. Like most Rwandan prisons, the "1930" is run by the inmates. In the United States this would be a recipe for chaos, but the opposite is true in Rwanda. There are few escape attempts, and violence is rare. The orderliness of Rwandan society has been replicated in the prisons and color-coded. Inmates with money and stature have had the pink prison uniform fabric fashioned into double-breasted suits and trench-coats. The poor hang bundles of their ragged clothes from the rafters like carcasses in a butcher's freezer. Those at the top of the hierarchy wear royal blue baseball caps, each labeled "capita" and numbered 1 to 12—these are the captains of each of the twelve wards. Other colors denote health workers and Red Cross assistants. Yellow berets perched on their heads, the inmates in charge of security look like Boy Scouts, but slightly sadistic ones; they herd their fellow prisoners by swatting them with long sticks.

Several yellow berets greet me inside the "1930" gate. As if part of a performance artist's critique on authority, one carries a toy pistol, holster, and walkie-talkie, all made of tinfoil; another has fashioned a badge out of a Michael Jackson photograph and pinned it to the front of his hat. They fetch Mujyambere while I take a tour, stepping over potholes, passing a neatly dressed man peering into a small mirror while he trims his chin whiskers. Four men draw a diagram of a gasoline engine. Nearby a man irons uniforms while a teacher quotes Mao, comparing China's cultural revolution to the 1959 uprising of Hutus in Rwanda. Within the compound are Bible-study classes and computer courses using keyboards drawn on cardboard. The less industrious prisoners sit in plastic hovels smoking cigarettes and playing cards.

Suddenly a stooped man with specks of white hair on the sides of his shiny head and curly tufts growing out of his ears is delivered to me. Scrawny legs poke out of his pink Bermuda shorts. He wears a fuzzy blazer over his uniform, ornamented with a strand of rosary beads and a medallion of the Virgin Mary. "Mujyambere," a yellow beret announces.

He speaks only Kinyarwanda, no French. He says that he is sixty-one, and that he opposed his son's decision to join the Hutu army during the genocide because "he could have been killed." Mujyambere says that he was not especially close to the authorities on his hillside, as he had retired from the government years ago. When I ask him what he was doing during the spring of 1994, he says that he stayed on his farm.

"I didn't see anybody dying. I didn't see anything. No bodies. Nothing. In our sector, the Tutsis fled. The military chased them to kill them. It was only the young people. The old people didn't join in the killings."

"Why are you here?"

"They say I have killed some people, but I didn't."

He claims that Mukandekezi, her children, and another neighbor denounced him in September of 1994 so that they could steal his five cows. I ask for more details. He says that she is a Hutu and that her husband, who may have been a Tutsi, died in the war. He doesn't know the circumstances. He makes no mention of the missing forearm.

In a church in Kanzenze, twenty miles from the capital, loose dirt and cobwebs coat hundreds of garbage bags filled with skeletons collected from the pews and the countryside. The polyurethane stretches over skulls and rib cages; a few tibias pierce through. Gaspard Musonera, a Tutsi whose smooth face and slight build make him look younger than his thirty-two years, says that somewhere in the bags are pieces of his parents, three brothers, and one sister. He survived because he fled north to join the rebels. A year after taking power, the Tutsis appointed him mayor.

Some Hutu prisoners have pledged their loyalty to their new mayor, who says, "When I ask them why they killed, they say, 'Because the government told us to. And since you are the authority now, we would do it for you, too.'"

You too might obey orders to kill even if you believed killing was morally wrong—for example, to save your own life. That is not what happened in Rwanda. The genocide happened so swiftly, with so little internal resistance, that there was no time for a national moral dilemma. Some killers proved themselves equally capable of good and evil, hiding Tutsis by night, butchering them by day. The genocide had less to do with whether ordinary Hutus believed killing their Tutsi neighbors was a good idea than with upholding the standards of good citizenship, which in the spring and early summer of 1994 was to kill Tutsis in broad daylight. Ironically, such civic devotion may be the only chance for healing Rwanda. The idea is less absurd, and more hopeful, than is the fatalistic myth of Rwandans as a people forever condemned to follow feral impulses.

"The culture of obedience was a reaction to oppression. You have to respect a dictator," says Colonel Karemera, wild-eyed and grinning. "We are lucky to have this culture. It can make people do bad things, but it can also make them walk ten kilometers to make bricks to build homes. They respect whoever is ruling them."

Last May, Hutu militants based in Zaire crossed the border to attack a jail in Cyangugu, freeing about eighty genocide suspects. Over the next few days, more than twenty resumed and checked themselves back in. When I ask them why they would give up freedom to spend years waiting for trial in a victor's court, their responses sound almost rehearsed and have little to do with repentance.

"We must obey the law," they say.

The answer seems ridiculous given the scale of killing in Rwanda, but it makes a certain sense. It is the reason why few genocide survivors have sought revenge, why pedestrians stand at attention at rush-hour traffic stops when the Rwandan flag is raised and lowered, why the once bloodied churches fill up again every Sunday, why Rwandans still come by the thousands when the government radio announces umuganda workdays, why genocide suspects are allowed to use machetes, why some prison fences are made of eucalyptus branches, and why inmates applaud for the government ministers who imprisoned them.

The "law" that the resumed prisoners are talking about is not a permanent set of ethics written in the Rwandan criminal code or the Bible but the directives of whoever is currently in power. And in that sense, Rwandans are among the most law-abiding citizens in the world. The genocide was not an eruption of tribalism but the rote conduct of a society raised on reverence for even the most wicked leaders. Killing was the law, and Rwandans followed it.

Anaconda
by John Sack

Operation Anaconda occurred in Afghanistan during the Spring of 2002. It was American troops' bloodiest battle since Somalia.

I. Company C (March 2 to March 3)

Imagine this. Imagine you're a country doctor up in the Adirondacks, and your first patient today is your brother. "I have this cough," he reports, and the X ray reveals he has lung cancer, clearly terminal. Bad enough, but your second patient today is your sister, and the Pap smear shows terminal cervical cancer. And knock, knock, knock on your door come your beloved brothers, sisters, close cousins, come all morning, afternoon, evening, come in the throes of some dreadful disease—imagine it, I ask you. Imagination aside, no doctor in the Adirondacks (or anywhere else in America) has had the unbearable heartache such a cortege would occasion, but in the American infantry lots of medics have had it. In combat, when they hear a cry of "Medic!" "Corpsman!" or "Doc!"—a hysterical cry that like "Help!" "Man overboard!" or "Fire!" pounces on everyone's senses like a

Doberman pinscher, generating adrenaline, dilating carotid arteries, pounding on everyone's heart like the kettledrums in *Day of Wrath*, by Berlioz—when they hear a cry of "Medic!" "Corpsman!" or "Doc!" it comes from one of their buddies, someone they've lived with, trained with, partied with, someone they love as they love their blood brothers.

Near the Adirondacks stands the 10th Mountain Division. In one platoon of one company of one battalion of one brigade, the one and only medic is a twenty-one-year-old from Ellenville, New York, near the Catskills: Specialist Eddie Rivera. One day in September, two airplanes hit the World Trade Center, and Rivera watches the TV incredulously, his fingers against his forehead, *my head's still here, my head's still here, no, I'm not dreaming this,* as the two towers collapse, as two towers of ashes supplant them, as ash-plastered people run from the great catastrophe. "An attack on America," the TV announcer calls it, and Rivera at once phones the girl he fell deeply in love with in medic (not medical) school and tells her, "I may have to go somewhere."

Unpromising. That's what Rivera was until three years ago. His parents both Puerto Rican, his skin olive-colored, his hair curly black, his brows black, too, his mustache a thin black streak that at one end broke up into shapeless bristles, he usually was a no-show at Ellenville High. At six every day, his mother went to work making knives, and Rivera (an hour later) called up his friends and said, "I ain' goin' to school today. You shouldn' either, come over here." If the truant officer didn't come, too, Rivera and a half dozen friends would party, drink Bacardi, listen to rappers, and on TV play video games as their cheerless peers sat in accounting, studying double entries. The parties sometimes continued past three, past Rivera's mother's return, Rivera's mother saying, *"No tienes tiempo para esto"* "You don't have time for this!"

But one day Rivera was partied out and, still hungover, showed up at Ellenville High. "You're late," the accounting teacher said.

"So what? I'm *always* late."

"We're taking a test today."

"Oh, no." The test being handed him, the very first question stumped him. Rivera took out his textbook, raised his hand, and said, "What page is it on?"

The whole class laughed, but the teacher didn't. "You can't ask me! You can't look it up!" the teacher cried. "Ten points off!" and the class laughed again. Went *hahaha,* its teeth almost biting at Rivera.

Now, Rivera liked being laughed *with,* not *at.* He liked being class clown but not class knucklehead, and he stopped playing hooky, made up his classes, graduated, and joined the American Army.

At medic school in Texas he smelled a few aromas absent from basic in Georgia, aromas like Bath & Body Works. They came from the women soldiers—*women soldiers*—who barracked upstairs of him and did their exercises beside him, the panty lines pressing against their shorts. He soon went so steady with one, the sergeants discovered her field blanket in his rucksack and his RIVERA camouflage shirt upon *her.* The sergeants called them Mr. and Mrs. Rivera and said, "You two like being together? All right, go down together," meaning drop to the ground and do twenty push-ups together. A runner-up for Miss San Francisco, Krystal was black, round-faced, long-haired, a girl whose smile melted artillery pieces, and Rivera yearned to spend every day of his life with her. From medic school, Rivera went to the camp near the Adirondacks and Krystal (an army reservist) went to a college nearby, and it's she who on Tuesday, September 11, Rivera tells presciently, "I may have to go somewhere."

"I'll wait for you, I promise," Krystal says.

He and his whole platoon, company, battalion don't go to Afghanistan, not yet. A country to its immediate north is where they're deployed, a country known as Uzbekistan. As rich as it is in Asian relics, golden temples, marble mosaics, intricate filigrees, turquoise cupolas, towers, all the marvels of Xanadu, the soldiers immured in their secret camp are of necessity bored, bored, bored. All there's to do is play spades, crazy eights, and Scrabble and eat Combos from the PX. Never did they salute officers back in the Adirondacks, but they must crisply salute them here in Uzbekistan. So despondent is one lonely soldier that he shoots his brains out and ("Medic!") becomes Rivera's first case. "Breathe, breathe," incants Rivera. "You're all right, buddy, breathe," he conjures, his Ringer's solution dripping into the soldier's corpse.

Rivera becomes despondent, too. He walks around like an abandoned dog, his head hanging down. He broods that Krystal will slough him off, and either to precipitate this or forestall it, he phones her and says, "I know you miss me—" "I do. I miss hanging out with you. I miss cooking dinner for you. I miss kissing you, and I miss laying with you."

"But Krystal. I know you're crying. I know you're going through heartache. If you're unhappy, then I'm unhappy, too. I don't know when I'm coming home. Just leave me, Krystal. Do what you want to, and have a good time doing it."

"Stop talking crazy," says Krystal, and Rivera can see her right index finger shaking at him from the Adirondacks. "I want many things, you're right. But for them all, I want you."

And hanging up, Rivera thinks, *As soon as I'm home, I'll put a ring on her finger.* But home isn't where the sergeant says that Rivera's assigned. "We got another mission," the sergeant says as Rivera's hands curtain his eyes, *No, I don't want to believe it.* He flies by cargo plane to a camp in Afghanistan, then by Chinook (a long green helicopter, one rotor fore, one rotor aft) to what's about to be America's bloodiest battle since Somalia a decade ago. His "aid bag" between his shoulders, he flies by this giant helicopter to Operation Anaconda.

His aid bag. As big as an ottoman, inside it are scissors, needles, catheters, syringes, bags of Ringer's solution, vials of Nubain—a synthetic narcotic—vials of EpiPen, ketorolac, Rocephin, and Xylocaine, bandages, dressings, cravats, and a few hundred yards of Kerlix gauzes and Ace wraps. As if this weren't enough, on the previous evening the chief medic stuffed it with many more needles, catheters, et cetera, until the bag weighed forty pounds and Rivera, carrying it, his rucksack, his sleeping bag, his helmet, his bulletproof jacket—his aptly named Interceptor—and his shotgun, needed help to stand up. At two in the morning, sitting on a steel runway waiting for the Chinooks, he griped to his fellow soldiers, "Who do I look like? Hulk Hogan?" He flexed his miniature biceps and said, "Do I look like I work out at Gold's? Look at this monster aid bag. I feel there's a child inside it."

At five in the morning came the Chinooks, and with someone's heave-ho he stood up and got on. By now it's six and his helicopter still isn't at Anaconda's locale, seventy-five miles south of Kabul. The helicopter's at ten thousand feet, and Rivera stares out a rare window at snow-sided mountains and at—well, what? camels? gazelles? oryxes? yaks? at animals running down them and, in the valleys, at Afghan people outside their adobe homes. *A real nice place,* thinks Rivera. *It's sad what'll happen here. Hey Eddie,* he corrects himself as his eardrums detect the Chinooks coming down. *Snap out of it! You're not a tourist today!* In one corrugated valley, the helicopters land, the sergeants cry, *"Get out, get out!"* and after saying, "Help me up," Rivera jumps onto the red-colored, snow-covered mud.

It's chilly outside. The helicopters take off. The plan is, up in the mountains are hundreds of Qaedas who our Afghan allies should rout and who the Americans should subsequently ambush. But the first casualty of any war is the Plan. In seconds, a boy in Rivera's platoon cries, "I see somebody." He then cries, "He's wearing black," and Rivera, using binoculars, says, "Oh, I see somebody, too," a Qaeda, a scared civilian, an anthropomorphic oryx—*what?* running from left to right forty meters away. Shoot him, is that what these soldiers should do? No one has answered when the black-wearing apparition drops into a little hollow and *ffft! ffft!* starts shooting at the soldiers themselves. *Let's light his ass up,* Rivera thinks, but as soon as the whole platoon and (*"Hooah!"* the jubilant soldiers cry) two Apache helicopters, two cannon-shooting, rocket-shooting, missile-shooting helicopters, try to light it, *boom,* near the platoon there falls a rocket-propelled grenade. One, two, three kilometers away, high on a snow-sided mountain, unpurged by our Afghan allies, a Qaeda (a man who's invisible but by inference is Qaeda) has shouldered something like a bazooka, and the foot-long grenade inside it has fallen close to Rivera's wards. And within minutes from the same unassailable mountain there comes a mortar round, *boom*, and Rivera hears someone cry, "Doc! Doc! Doc!"

No, not this soon, Rivera thinks, but he runs toward the "Doc!" while the boy who's shouting it runs to Rivera. In all this platoon, there's no one who's less of a brother to Rivera than this Private Horn. Just after training, he joined the platoon in Afghanistan, and Rivera's only encounter with him was "Hey, I'm your medic. If anything's wrong with you, tell me." Today there's nothing terminal wrong with Horn. A piece of the mortar round grazed him, his shin started bleeding, his pants became bloody. Off comes Rivera's aid bag. Swiftly, Rivera cuts open the red-stained pants, looks at Horn's minor wound, and says, "You're all right." He swathes it in Kerlix and says, "How you feelin'?"

"I'm good."

"You're lucky."

"I'm ready to go."

"Then go," says Rivera with a big-brotherly slap on Horn's other leg, and Horn returns to the uninterrupted battle.

A battle it is. To the platoon, from the distant mountain, the bullets, grenades, and mortar rounds come. The dirt kicks up as if underneath is a new volcano announcing itself. A bullet bounces off a boy's rifle barrel, sending sparks like a children's sizzler, and the boy bitches, "My fuckin' weapon got hit!" A boy who's a Muslim but even more an American prays, "Hey, Man Upstairs? If it's my time to go, I want to go fightin'!" At what, they don't know, but the boys fire guns, machine guns, and, in time, mortars ("Adjust! Two hundred meters left! Adjust! Go back fifty meters!") in the mountain's direction. Also firing are the Apaches, but no one in this platoon is now shouting "Hooah." On everyone's face, Rivera's included, is an It's-game-time mien. Anaconda! We aren't playing soldier! We can get hurt, very hurt!

And three soldiers are. No soldiers in this platoon, but in one that landed synchronously a hundred meters away. As its medic it doesn't use Specialist Rivera but Specialist Miranda, but among the three soldiers stumbling down to Rivera is, you guessed it, Miranda. Once, near the Adirondacks, Rivera borrowed Miranda's cell phone and, in one month, talking to Krystal long distance, ran up a $2,000 bill, and he's been lavishing a third of his salary paying off Miranda. And now his creditor teeters as though he's drunk and says not "Doc!" but "Eddie! Oh, help me!"

"Oh, shit! What's wrong?"

"I don't know. My back."

"That scares me," Rivera says. His friend can't be moved from the incoming fire if his spinal cord's hit, but Rivera runs fingers on Miranda's bulletproof jacket—Miranda's Interceptor—and says, "There's nothing wrong with it. It's all right." But on Miranda's seat there's blood, and as Miranda screams, Rivera rips open his camouflage pants, pulls out a piece of a mortar round, a sharp piece as big (or small) as one of Miranda's teeth, says, "It ain't too bad. You're all right," and, giving the souvenir to Miranda, replaces it with sterile stuffing, with Kerlix. He then finds a scalloped hole in Miranda's right hand, some shrapnel having passed like a dumdum bullet in one side and out the other.

Then *boom!* A mortar round scores an ear of one of the two other casualties.

The two other casualties. Besides Miranda (who swathes his right hand himself), there's Sergeant Abbott and Sergeant McCleave. Abbott's the sergeant for the other platoon, where, at his instigation, everyone addresses everyone else as Brother. "Brother, can I have some polish?" "Brother, you need any cocoa?" McCleave has the cot right next to Rivera back at their base camp. Moving in, he said to Rivera, "Thank God! I'm sleepin' nex' to my medic!" and Rivera said playfully, "Well, I hope your feet don't stink." The mortars now chasing them, the two medics and the two sergeants run and stumble to a safe haven behind a small knoll, and Rivera starts ministering to Abbott and McCleave. Abbott's got a piece of a mortar round in his triceps, and Rivera treats it by the book, wrapping it in Kerlix while saying, "You're all right," but it's impenetrable what's wrong with McCleave. On his clothes is no blood, but in back of the knoll he sits as though wearing a sign saying HOMELESS. He stares as though waiting passively for a *clink* in his dented tin cup.

"Sergeant McCleave," says Rivera. "What's wrong with you?" "Who . . . are . . . you . . . ?" McCleave doesn't say it, just looks it.

"Sergeant McCleave! Please tell me! What's wrong with you?"

"Where . . . am . . . I . . .?"

"Sergeant McCleave!" Rivera screams, shaking him vigorously.

Some slobber comes to McCleave's lips, and he says audibly, "I . . . don't . . . know. . . . "

"Sergeant McCleave!" says Abbott, the shrapnel-suffering sergeant. "Tell the doc what's wrong with you! Or you'll die!"

Or you'll what? As slowly as worms, these words wend their way to McCleave's addled brain. "My hand . . . , my back . . ."

Rivera rips off McCleave's gloves and says, "Good." He looks at McCleave's Interceptor and says, "Good." He cuts McCleave's pants, and on both of McCleave's legs, both upper and lower, he sees dozens of holes from the same indiscriminate mortar round that hit Miranda and Abbott. Now, shrapnel is painful wherever it is. Unlike a bullet, it enters red-hot, and it starts burning the flesh, fat, muscle, nerves of the boy who haplessly caught it. McCleave's state of shock isn't in any way overwrought. He can't raise either leg, so Rivera props each leg on his knee like a two-by-four that he's sawing as, with his hands, he wraps on the Kerlix, lest his good buddy bleed to death and, at their camp, his cot right next to Rivera's become unoccupied.

By now Rivera's the only medic in either platoon, or so Rivera reasonably believes. But now from the other platoon, a hundred meters away, a hundred meters of bullets, grenades, and mortar rounds raising divots, there comes a cry of "Doc!" and Rivera, as intuitively as a champion sprinter at the cry of *Go*, commences a deadly hundred-meter dash. *I'm running,* he thinks philosophically—*running for my life for someone else's life.*

• • •

He's scared. He runs anyhow. He pants, being ninety-two hundred feet high. In front of him—*ffft!*—some bullets raise dust like the bubbling mud at Yellowstone. Do any grenades come in? Do any mortar rounds come? If so, Rivera doesn't register them. The finish line, no frangible tape, is a pile of rocks behind which there lies the boy who cried, "Doc!" and Rivera dives at him like someone stealing second. He also dives at two soldiers he hasn't expected: the battalion medic (a boy who's wounded) and the battalion *doctor*, a major amazed to be at such remove from a MASH. Rivera's hundred-meter sprint wasn't in vain. The medic and doctor both have lost their aid bags, and at these guardian rocks the Kerlix, et cetera, is all in Eddie's monster. *Thank God I stuffed it,* Rivera thinks.

The casualties (by now there are two) are one boy who's saying, "I can't see!" and one boy who's gasping, "I can't breathe!" and, with Rivera's aid bag, the doctor treats both. "How you doin'?" Rivera asks them—asks, asks, even shouts from a hundred meters to the two sergeants and Miranda, "How you doin'?"

"We're all right."

"Just lay low," Rivera shouts, aware that if one of them falls asleep, his breathing might stop and he'll die. While shouting, Rivera's thinking, *Oh, God, will these casualties ever end?* No, they won't, for in this other platoon another mortar round just fell and the radio operator cries, "Doc!" The boy, PFC McGovern, is Rivera's phenomenal friend, phenomenal since each of his legs seemed wired to a separate cerebellum. "McGovern! What's *wrong* with you? You got two left feet?" Rivera agonized on countless occasions as McGovern tripped over his cot, the MRE box (meals ready to eat), or even the crack in the floor, spread-eagling. "McGovern!" Rivera agonized. "Did you not see it? . . . I seen it! I thought I'd get over it!" But now (it's just about noon) no fault attaches itself to McGovern as he lies sprawled, both feet, both legs, both arms full of fiery shrapnel.

"It's burning!" McGovern cries to Rivera.

"What's burning worst?"

"My feet!"

Rivera takes off McGovern's left boot, left sock. McGovern's left foot is a shrapnel-studded caveman's club, and Rivera instinctively shields his eyes.

"What is it? What is it?"

"You're all right, man," Rivera says, his hand raised, his fingers apart, a gesture meaning *Easy. It's all right,* his head turning toward the battalion medic, his lips pantomiming, *Oh, fuck.* He wraps McGovern's foot in Kerlix, but the Kerlix becomes blood-red, and he unwraps it and rewraps it in Kerlix, then Ace. "I know this hurts," says Rivera. "But you gotta try to wiggle your toes."

"I can! But they hurt!"

"I know they hurt, buddy."

"Oh, God! I can't take it!"

"But you'll be all right." But McGovern screams, and Rivera takes out his Nubain, injecting a minimal milliliter. "The pain, this'll get rid of it," Rivera says, then starts on McGovern's other foot, his legs and arms.

"The enemy," cries an undaunted sergeant, "wants us to sing the 10th Mountain Division Song!" Around him the soldiers start it: "We are the 10th Mountain Infantry / With a glorious history . . ." *Booooom!* It's the Air Force, thank God, but all the American soldiers recoil as a cargo plane metamorphosed into a bomber drops one of its one-ton bombs on the mountain that all this affliction comes from, on the cloud-covered heads of the Qaedas. As anyone would, as soon as the Qaedas hear those horrific bombers approaching, they go with lock, stock, and barrel (rifles, launchers, and mortars) into their caves, go, if they technologically could, into the fourth dimension until the bombers depart. But during every lull, Rivera runs to his patients in both platoons, asking them, "How you doin'? Are you awake? Now, don' become sleepy on me! Don' fall asleep! You need some water? Here, have some water. Man, you're all right. Man, you're all right. You're gonna make it," at times thinking privately, *Is he all right? Is he gonna make it? I don't know.*

"Doc," all Rivera's patients ask, "when are the medevacs comin'?" The boys mean, When are the choppers coming to carry us out?

"They're comin'. They're comin'," says Rivera while thinking privately, *When are the medevacs comin'?* He radios battalion, "Polar Bear? When are the medevacs comin'? When are the QRFs"—the Quick Reaction Forces—"comin'? Where's our help? What's takin' time? We got to get these casualties out!" On this wide-ranging radio, the officers at battalion can't say, "They're tryin'! The medevacs, tryin'! The other companies, tryin'! But the LZ's too hot! The landing zone's inaccessible!"

Then *booooom!* The soldiers cringe, the bombers conclude, the Qaedas, unchastened, undismayed, come from their caves, their rifles, launchers, and mortars coming, too, and "Incoming!" the soldiers shout. To shield him, Rivera lies on top of McGovern, the boy with wounded feet, legs, arms, the boy benumbed by Nubain, he puts his head on McGovern's and hears him say, "Please please please." Then *boom*, a mortar round hits First Lieutenant Maroyka. Then *ffft*, a bullet hits Specialist Almey, a boy who played basketball with Rivera, shooting, shooting the ball like some repetitive plastic toy. Then boom, a mortar round hits Major Byrne, the doctor far from a MASH and, with Rivera, the last intact practitioner here. Then boom, another mortar round hits the battalion medic, this one from two feet away. Then *ffft*—

It's midafternoon and it's still going on. How many soldiers in two platoons of Company C of the 1st Battalion of the 87th Regiment of the 10th Mountain Division of the American Army were hit? Restrict yourself, the Army adjures me, to "Casualties were light," "were moderate," "were heavy."

Casualties were heavy.

I tell people, "you're all right," thinks Rivera. *But who'll tell me I'm all right?* It's moratorium time as the bombers inconvenience the Qaedas, and all right he's certainly not. Rivera's worn out. His day began at two this morning, and he hasn't eaten since then. He's hardly had water, either. His face is charcoal-colored due to close mortar rounds, and on his hands there's blood, other people's ectopic blood. On all three browns of his camouflage clothes is this same inappropriate red. If someone cries, "Doc!" Rivera expects to run up and treat him. But can he? *Whatever I have, I'm about to lose it,* Rivera thinks. *What am I even doing here?*

And then Rivera remembers the World Trade Center. Remembers the flaring fires like Zeus' lightning bolts. Remembers the businessmen *(My God! How desperate were they?)*—businessmen and business-women throwing themselves to the plaza, eighty floors below. The towers collapsing, the ashes supplanting them, the ash-plastered people running away. The people doing the rounds of the hospitals, asking, "Did you see this man?" "Did you see this woman?" And hearing repeatedly, "No, I've not." And never discovering them. And never burying them. It's not two platoons, it's not sixty people the mourners sought, thinks Rivera. It's three thousand people! As bad as Anaconda is, Rivera thinks, *We're better off. We'll never ask, "Did you see my mom?" "Did you see my dad?" "Did you see Krystal?"*

He thinks of the wife who must have asked, "Did you see Steve?" Steve was the paramedic at a Harlem station in New York City who, after medic school in Texas, Rivera did six weeks of training with. "Do you want to do an IV? . . . Do you want to do an EKG?" *Do you want to,* Steve always asked, and Rivera always said yes. Now, Rivera has heard that on Tuesday, September 11, the North Tower collapsed on Steve, the deed of the organization on the mountain in Rivera's plain sight. And now Rivera remembers why he's here. It's for the three thousand dead. It's for their bereaved, to let them know they're avenged. It's for the heroic paramedic at the Harlem station, Rivera apostrophizing him, "It's for you. We're gettin' 'em for you, Steve."

It's then that Rivera hears, "Doc!"

Rivera springs up. He starts running. In his own platoon a mortar round's burst, and he must retrace his bullet-pelleted hundred-meter dash. He succeeds. The source of the "Doc!" is Sergeant Wurtz, a boy he's played one-on-one basketball with, Rivera teasing him, "You cannot play me, Sergeant Wurtz. You'll lose." "We'll see." But now Wurtz is lying supine as if he's been grievously fouled, his combat boot off, his foot above him, his hand holding it as if, if he carelessly let go, it would fall off. He's rocking like a child's seesaw, screaming, but as Rivera wraps his Kerlix, another mortar round comes in, the Qaedas are zeroing onto them. On one pogo-stick leg, Wurtz hops, hops, in Rivera's embrace to a safe haven higher up, the Kerlix trailing behind him. "Oh, fuck," says Wurtz, gasping. "I thought I'd blown off my foot."

"It's all right."

"I don't know. It's burnin' like hell."

"Shrapnel's hot."

"Is my foot ever gonna get better?"

"Sure, it's gonna."

"Am I ever gonna get outta here?"

"Sure. You're gonna be playin' basketball next week. But," says Rivera, "you're still never gonna beat me."

The two take refuge behind some rocks. The day's last casualty is the radio operator for Rivera's platoon, Specialist Stanton, a bullet in his right foot, and Rivera helps him hop to the wounded ward on the invaluable rocks' safe side. The ward looks like Rubens's *Massacre of the Innocents*, minus any of Herod's assassins. "Doc," a number of innocents say. "I can't feel my arms," "I can't feel my legs."

"They'll be all right," says Rivera, concealing that this means damaged nerves.

It's now six o'clock. Night's coming on, the dark's coming on, and the temperature's dropping toward twenty. Rivera's polypropylene coat, polypropylene gloves, polyester sleeping bag—Rivera's "snivel gear"— isn't with him, Rivera like most soldiers having shed it this morning on exiting the Chinook. It's many kilometers away (if it were nearer, he'd give it to patients anyhow), and all Rivera has on is T-shirt, shorts, and four-colored camouflage clothes, just what he'd wear on an Adirondack dog day. He shivers. To listen to, his teeth could be a train on irregular rails, rattling. He lies down with two patients, keeping them warm and, at least slightly, himself warm, too. It's a three-soldier night.

• • •

"The night belongs to us," the American Army says. American soldiers have NODs, night optical devices, the world around them as bright as twilight although it's a worrisome bilious green, and the Qaedas don't have them, not yet. Tonight what the Qaedas can see are the flash, flash, lightning flash of America's bombs, but not America's infrared lights, lights in a druid circle, lights the American soldiers meticulously laid out. The lights encircle the LZ, landing zone, for the medevacs, if the medevacs actually come and if, by tomorrow, the casualties will be en route to Frankfurt or Washington, D. C. And lo! at eleven o'clock appear a couple of angelic medevacs that the Qaedas, unable to see, apparently hear. The Qaedas launch a Stinger missile, and, to avoid it, the medevacs disappear again, none of Rivera's patients aboard. "I can't believe this," says Rivera, though not to his anxious patients. "They," the Qaedas, "aren't gonna let us leave! At dawn they're gonna be shootin' again!"

He prays for the first time today. In his pocket, he clutches a little white cross. "Whoever dies wearing this," the cross's embossment says, "shall not suffer eternal fire," and, as one hand clutches it, the other crosses himself and Rivera prays, "Lord, if I can't make it out of here, please take care of my mom and dad and please take care of Krystal. Krystal," Rivera continues, hoping she'll hear him as God just did, "whatever we do, to do it together's better. If we were poor, were dressin' in rags, were sittin' in cardboard boxes, we would be happier together. I love you." It's then that the medevacs return, take on the prostrate patients like McCleave and McGovern, take off, and it's one hour later that the Chinooks return, their rotors (thinks Rivera) glistening in the full moon like the pearly gates. They take on the walking wounded like Miranda and Abbott, then all of Rivera's platoon, platoons, then with an exultant roar take off, Rivera whispering, "Thank you, Lord," and saying aloud, "We made it! We made it!"

An hour later, Rivera is in his quiet, lightless, motionless tent. He sits at the stove, letting the warmth like a bowl of hot soup saturate him, then has a bowl of hot soup indeed, in thirty hours his first nourishment. On his cot he just passes out, but rest for the weary isn't his.

"Get up! Get up!" a soldier surprises him at a god-awful reveille. A soldier from Company B, he's scarcely known to Rivera. "Get up!"

"Get outta here," Rivera mutters.

"Get up!" says half of Company B, assembled at Rivera's cot. "We were at the radio yesterday, listenin' to Company C! It was like the Superbowl!"

"What was?" Rivera mutters.

"You!" say the soldiers of Company B. "You saved the whole company! We don't know how you did it! We call you Superman!"

As soon as the telephone's up, Rivera calls Krystal. She says, "Hello?"

"Hey, baby."

"Oh my God! Are you all right?"

"I'm all right."

"You don't even know. Someone called from the 10th Mountain Division. He said they'd heard a medic was hit. How bad, they didn't know, but I was cryin' like crazy. I called your mom, and she was cryin', too. She called the Red Cross. But they knew nothin', so I watched the TV news, and I just knew you're in Anaconda. I was scared."

"Baby, I wasn't hit. But now I know: I don't want to live away from you. As soon as I'm back I want an apartment with you. I want to live with you, I want to marry you, and I want to have babies with you."

"Slow down," says Krystal, laughing through tears. "I'm not ready for babies yet."

"I don't care what you're ready for. As soon as I'm home I'm makin' babies."

"No you're not."

"Oh yes I am."

"Wait till I finish school," says Krystal, still laughing. "Then we'll start doin' other things. I'm so glad you're okay."

"Oh, baby, I still can't believe it. All day we're takin' fire. All day my buddies gettin' hurt. All day my buddies tellin' me, 'Help me, Doc.' And you know what? I helped them. I was scared, and I didn't know if I'd get out, but I helped them. All that stuff that I thought I'd forget, I remembered. I did what I was taught to do. I can't believe it," and Rivera, tears in his eyes, slams his fist on the telephone table. "But baby, because I helped them, they didn't die! All of 'em, they didn't die!"

II. COMPANY B (March 3 to March 10)

There but for the grace of God go I. No one, but no one, thought this in Company B as it listened in distant tents to the "Superbowl" and the vicissitudes of Rivera's buddies. Why, these were B's buddies, too! Were boys who B had partied with in America, had played dominoes with in Uzbekistan, had slumped on red canvas seats with on the plane to Afghanistan! All day, B sat entreating its lieutenants, "We gotta help 'em! We gotta join 'em!" One lieutenant had a friend who'd died at his desk at Cantor Fitzgerald, a desk in the airplane's flaming path in the north tower of the World Trade Center. On each of his hand grenades, the lieutenant (a former broker, too) had written his friend's five-syllable name—STERGIOPOULOS—with a Magic Marker, and B entreated him, "Please! Just get us a Chinook!"

"No, the LZ's too hot."

"Then land the Chinook five miles away! We'll walk in!"

"No . . ."

The next day, B got its Chinooks. Quite typically, B has three platoons, and in the avenging lieutenant's platoon is a boy who saw the events at the World Trade Center in real life and not on TV. He was on leave in Paterson, New Jersey, fifteen miles away, and was asleep when his brother awoke him. "Come upstairs."

In his boxers the boy went upstairs, looked out the window at New York City, and said, "Holy shit! What happened?"

"The building fell down."

"Holy shit!"

The boy's name is PFC Shkelqim Mahmuti. Born in America to Albanian parents, he's a Muslim like them. Even before the Towers fell down, a Muslim was often picked on in America. In grade school, in high school, his coevals laughed at Mahmuti, "Ha-ha! Pork is good for you! Fuck Mohammed!" Later, at United Parcel, the other drivers said

to Mahmuti, "What are you? Muslim? . . . Yes." "I'll be watching you."
All this discrimination would cease when he joined the American
Army, Mahmuti thought. It wouldn't.

His face was dark, his nose was sharp, his brows were a
Mesopotamian's: thick, black, unbroken. A *hood* is what these features
meant to many policemen in Paterson, and Mahmuti at age fifteen in
fact dealt marijuana, cocaine, crack, in New Jersey. He was often
arrested, and in April last year, telling himself, *I gotta change,* he needed
a half dozen waivers from three courts to join the American Army. He
took basic training in Georgia, took graduation leave in New Jersey,
saw the great tragedy in New York, and one week later joined the 10th
Mountain Division at its frantic camp near the Adirondacks, frantic
due to his sergeant's announcements of "Here's your packin' list!"
"Here's your malaria pill!" "Here's your orders!" "We're leavin'
tomorrow!" Were leaving to Asia, leaving to fight the—*Muslims.* One
fellow soldier asked him, "You know what side you're on?"

"Yeah. I know what side I'm on."

It wasn't the Muslim side, Mahmuti sincerely believed. He believed
he could aim, fire, and kill a Muslim even if, as he also believed, the
Muslim would go to paradise while all Mahmuti's fellow soldiers went
to Muslim hell. In his own pocket, the Koran said, "Lo! The worst of
beasts in Allah's sight are the Unbelievers," but also the Koran told
how Muslims killed Muslims without the Koran's complaint. Nor did
Mahmuti's parents demur at Mahmuti's killing another defender of
Allah. "Don't sweat it," Mahmuti's father phoned him. "To say this
isn't easy for me, but if you must kill him, kill him."

"It'll be him before me, Dad."

But one doesn't know, does one? till the Moment of Truth, the
unpredictable confrontation on Muslim turf.

To kill the Qaedas was what every soldier brooded about as, on the
first night of Anaconda, the casualties came in. Mahmuti's sergeant,
Sergeant Fuentes of San Antonio, prayed: "Take care of us, Lord. I've
got these young soldiers with me. Guide me so I can take care of 'em."
But the Lord isn't the only presence the soldiers count on. The next

day, the sergeant wears on his helmet a G. I. Joe, a doll his son mailed from Texas, and, while walking to the Chinooks, the whole platoon devoutly touches it. "He'll take care of us," say the soldiers, then the Chinooks take off, and the soldiers applaud and say, *"Yeah!"* . . . "One hour," the helicopter pilot says.

"Any way we can get there in thirty minutes?" asks Mahmuti.

At two in the afternoon, the Chinooks drop onto the same corrugated place that Rivera's did, and the sergeants cry similarly, "Get out!" With rapid heartbeats the soldiers do. But now the Qaedas on the grim mountain are (to trust the American Army) dead, dispatched by white lightning bombs, or (to mistrust the American Army) alive on snow-crusted trails into Pakistan, and the Chinooks take off, the platoon's exposed, and for the moment no one's shooting at it. Lest someone does, it starts digging what it calls Ranger graves, which are foxholes one foot deep. His digging done, Mahmuti lies in this shallow grave, the sun setting, the evening constellations setting, the Qaedas (if any) firing no bullets, grenades, or mortar rounds, but our Afghan allies firing tracers of red, orange, green, and blue at (if any) the Qaedas, and the American Air Force bombing them. At two in the morning, Mahmuti rises like Lazarus and, with his platoon, walks east until dawn, then west until noon. To quote no lesser enthusiast than Irving Berlin, *This Is the Army, Mr. Jones.*

At last the durable order comes to Mahmuti's platoon, Dig in on top of this small-sized hill.

A small-sized but oh-so-steep-sided hill, a hill for alpinists with rope. His helmet, Interceptor, rucksack, and rifle encumbering him, Mahmuti (with his platoon) climbs up, the gray shale crumbling underfoot, turning into gray dust. On top of the hill, surprise—the Qaedas rematerialize, the Qaedas start shooting at the startled platoon from God knows where. And *ffft! ffft!* from somewhere below the Americans come the Qaedas' bullets, then *boom! boom!* come the Qaedas' notorious mortar rounds. The first of them falls where the soldiers just were, Mahmuti thinking, *Holy shit! We could've been dead!* On the hilltop, most soldiers look for the Qaedas, shouting, "I don't see 'em," but some soldiers in this sudden baptism of fire just cower behind boulders, among them the soldier who in the Adirondacks asked Mahmuti, "You know what side you're on?"

Mahmuti is looking for the Qaedas. So is his Sergeant Fuentes. Borrowing someone's binoculars, the sergeant suddenly cries, "I see 'em!" Some with Russian rifles, some with Russian mortars, the Qaedas all are competent soldiers, staying apart. All are standing, walking, or running in the old corrugated valley below the Americans, reversing yesterday's hierarchy and, in consequence, reversing yesterday's odds, for now it's Americans sitting pretty and Qaedas sitting ducks. "You see 'em?" the sergeant asks a heavy-machine gunner near him.

"No, I don' see 'em."

"One's over here. Two's over there. And one's runnin' toward those trees."

"I still don' see 'em." The gunner fires blind and kkk! the cartridge sticks. "It's jammed!"

"Damn." The sergeant turns to another gunner. "Shoot this way!"

"Where's he at?" asks Mahmuti. He lies by the sergeant, excited.

"Son, hold these bines. I'll shoot tracers, that's where he's at." On one knee, the sharp-sighted sergeant fires at a Qaeda eight hundred meters away, and the second machine gunner fires that way. The sergeant fires at a Qaeda six hundred meters away, and (the gun functioning now) the first machine gunner fires that way. The sergeant then fires at a Qaeda five hundred meters away, the Qaeda who's running toward trees.

"I'm ready to cover your fire," says Mahmuti.

"All right, Mahmuti." It's five o'clock, and Bob (the big orange ball) is setting before them. In the valley, the Qaeda's shadow is longer than the Qaeda himself. The two rifles almost touching, the sergeant fires once and Mahmuti twice. The first bullet hits the Qaeda's chest, the second two hit his stomach, and he falls down undisguisedly dead.

"Holy shit!" says Mahmuti.

"We got him! We got the bastard!"

"That's good fuckin' shootin', Sarge."

"Good shootin', Mahmuti! I'm proud of ya!" The sergeant shakes hands with Mahmuti, shakes hands energetically, shakes hands as if Mahmuti, his son, has just won the Nobel Peace Prize. "Now let's get the other shit-heads!" And with rifles, machine guns, mortars, and, to gild this lily, a couple of B-52's the soldiers do what yesterday's soldiers, however willing, didn't: They kill the Qaedas.

A few days later, Mahmuti sees another Qaeda and, far from dispatching him, has a conciliatory conversation with him. The man, who Mahmuti meets in the valley in an adobe building full of Americans, is an American prisoner. He's shoeless. His hands wear plastic cuffs, and, in lieu of a proper blindfold, his head wears an empty sandbag like an empty grocery bag. By accident, Mahmuti in his combat boots steps on the Qaeda's bare foot and tells him, "My bad."

"Water."

"You're sayin' water?"

"Yes yes."

"You're speakin' English?"

"Yes yes." Mahmuti takes off the outlandish sandbag, and the Qaeda starts crying. *Man*, thinks Mahmuti, *I'm not gonna kill you*. But, thinks Mahmuti, *what if you weren't the prisoner and I was? My shirt says Mahmuti, my dog tags say Islam, my pocket carries the Koran. You'd call me a Muslim traitor. You'd say, "So you're against the jihad!" You wouldn't just kill me. You'd torture me*. Not reciprocating at all, Mahmuti gives the man water, socks, blankets, and asks him, "What's your name?"

"Mehmed Tadik."

At home, thinks Mahmuti, *I've got a Muslim friend named Tadik*. "You're a Muslim?"

"Yes yes."

"I am a Muslim, too."

He's mocking me, the Qaeda quite clearly thinks. His teeth start to grind as if they're chewing betel nuts. "You Shiite or Sunni?"

"Sunni. How about you?"

"I Sunni." But still the Qaeda looks skeptical, looks to Mahmuti as though, if he weren't handcuffed, he'd kill him.

Mahmuti assures him he's Muslim. He says the Arabic prayer *"Bismillah e Errahman e Erraheem"*—"In the name of Allah, the Beneficent, the Merciful." Again the Qaeda starts crying and, in English this time, Mahmuti asks him, "Are you Al Qaeda?"

"No no! I student Kabul University!"

"You're lying."

"No no! I no Al Qaeda! I peace!"

"Are you *harām*?"

"No no!" The word means sinful.

"You are *harām*. You aren't Muslim. We're pure, we Muslims. We don't go killing innocent people like in New York. That shit, we Muslims don't do."

"No no! I no kill! I student!"

Mahmuti walks away. He has little love for the Qaeda. But having met him, met Tadik, could Mahmuti do what five sunny days ago he did to another human being, another believer in Allah—could Mahmuti shoot him and say, "That's good fuckin' shootin'"? No way.

Regrets? That isn't what soldiers feel or Mahmuti feels. He thinks about the Qaeda he killed sometimes. He tells himself, *It either was him or me. I won't let Mom sit and cry because some fuckin' terrorist took me out. Just as Dad said: Who cares that he's Muslim? He's wrong.* At night Mahmuti prays to Allah, "Thank you for keeping *shaytān*, the devil, away from me. Thank you." But maybe Mahmuti has, well, not regrets, not remorse, but can I say qualms? Or why did Mahmuti protest to his sergeant one day, "We did the right thing."

"Damn right. We did the right thing."

"It wasn't for pleasure, God knows."

The seventh day out, Mahmuti and his platoon return to their camp, and Mahmuti calls up his father in Paterson. *"Unë mora nje,"* Mahmuti says in Albanian. "I took one."

"Shit!" says Mahmuti's father in English.

"Are you all right?"

"Yeah. No one got hurt. None of *us.*"

"Good good." His father pauses. "Good job." Mahmuti's sergeant calls up his wife in Texas. He doesn't tell her "I took one," but tells her, "A few things happened but I'm okay."

"In my heart," his wife says, crying, "you're a great warrior now. You've earned your feathers." His wife isn't being figurative. Despite his Hispanic name—Fuentes—the sharp-sighted sergeant is an American Indian, an Aztec, much as I thought that Cortés had exterminated them all. The sergeant grew up by an Aztec reservation in Texas, where, on his return, there'll be an immemorial ceremony for him, the great warrior getting a fifty-four-feathered bonnet, the feathers dyed red, white, blue, and (for the days gone by in Tenochtitlán) environment-emulating green. "You've earned your feathers," his wife says. "You know?"

"I know," the eagle-eyed sergeant says.

III. Company A (March 18 To March 29)
Why the continued resistance to Company B? It might be Osama bin Laden is hiding there, an American commander tells an Afghan official in *The New York Times*. To catch Osama, his subordinates, or any of his foot soldiers becomes the mission of Company A of the 4th Battalion of the 31st Regiment of the 10th Mountain Division. In one platoon, known as the Misfits, are two boys who, when the towers fell, still were in Georgia learning their *Right face, Left face,* were in the same exact barracks and, by extraordinary chance, in the same exact double bunk. Their names, ranks, to hell with their serial numbers, are Private Andrew Simmons of Newark, New York, near Rochester, and Private Andrew Starlin of Buda, Texas, near Austin. Two Private Andrew S.'s.

A baby-faced boy, Simmons has oval glasses, scholarly looking black rims. In high school he sang in the concert choir. The other boy, Starlin, is pink-nosed, pink-cheeked, round-faced. His innocent eyes say, *Me? I know nothing about it.* In junior high school he played in the band. Simmons and Starlin played football, too, Simmons guard and Starlin center. Last year Simmons graduated, Starlin got his GED, and, for money for college, the two joined the Army, doing their basic training together in Georgia.

The two didn't know it, but precious little of basic training would stand them in stead in Afghanistan. Saluting? Marching? Using their hands reciprocally, all in the service of *Right shoulder arms?* More folderol for *Port arms* and *Port arms salute?* What they would do in Afghanistan Simmons and Starlin didn't learn in Georgia: running into icicle-sided caves where maybe, maybe, would be Osama, firing their rifles automatically, firing their machine guns, and throwing their hand grenades like Bata pitching machines. From Georgia they went to Kuwait, another training place for the 10th Mountain Division. There they learned to eschew all Kuwaiti women. They learned to stand aside of Kuwaiti prayer rugs. Their shoe soles they learned to expose to no Kuwaiti.

To run into caves behaving deranged—no, Simmons and Starlin didn't learn that in Kuwait.

They flew by cargo plane to Afghanistan, then by Chinook to Anaconda's sometimes disastrous, sometimes felicitous locale. The sergeants yelling, *"Get out,"* the two soldiers did—the two soldiers do, and their first thought is *Oh my God!* Their shock isn't due to bullets, grenades, mortar rounds, or any other man-made devices but to God's mountains around them. Mountains like this, the Andrews (who scarcely have seen the Adirondacks, much less the Rockies) haven't known except in *National Geographic*. Steep, snow-sided, cragged, the mountains tower above them like heaven's immaculate parapets. A soldier with them from Alaska thinks of Louis Armstrong's "What a Wonderful World," and one from Michigan thinks of Dire Straits's "These mist-covered mountains/Are a home now for me" and the song's planetary conclusion, "We're fools to make war." A soldier from Arkansas thinks of the Bible, of God cutting stone on Mount Sinai, of how some stone-blind people look at creation and don't perceive there's a God. Or how some people, like Osama, their quarry today, Osama who pleads belief in God, look at these sacred mountains and say, "A good defensive position."

The soldiers are in the Qaedas' often-visited valley. To the east is the Qaedas' notorious mountain, and to the west is a humpbacked one the Americans call the Whale. It's there that Simmons and Starlin (and all the Misfits) deploy. Their helmets, Interceptors, rucksacks on, their rifles carried like quarterstaffs, the two tenderfoots (in army argot, crispy critters) start up the Whale's precipitous side. Like marbles, the pebbles skid downward and the two critters skid with them like Jack and Jill, first on their boots, then on their seats, then stoutly stand up and retrace their route, the top of the Whale two miles away whatever they do.

On top of the Whale with guns, grenade launchers, mortars are, in all likelihood, the Qaedas. To keep them down, Starlin's squad halts, and Starlin fires an antitank missile. His squad fires rifles, rifle grenades, machine guns as Simmons's squad approaches where the Qaedas should be. A white flare (a star cluster) signals cease fire, and Simmons's squad assaults the top of the Whale. Simmons's sergeant passes a cave that a Qaeda could at any moment storm out of, his Russian rifle smoking. "A cave! Get back!" cries Simmons's sergeant. "Frag out!" the sergeant continues, tossing a hand grenade—*boom!*— and the cave anorexically collapses. "It just caved in! Oh, fuck!" cries Simmons's sergeant, seeing, on a boulder above him, a Qaeda, a man in green camouflage and, on his shoulders, a yellow blanket—*bang*, and the sergeant shoots him. "I got one!" He sees another blanketed being— *bang!* "I got another!" He sees still another—*bang!* "I got three!"

Chaos is king. Dead, dead, dead at Simmons's feet are one yellow-blanketed donkey and two Qaedas, none of whom is Osama. Farther away is a Qaeda who Simmons, *bang bang bang!* keeps firing at but who escapes behind a boulder, and in the ground is a quite provocative hole that Simmons drops a hand grenade into, a hand grenade that falls, falls, like Alice in Wonderland and, in time, emits a chthonian *bing*. Such is the Great Osama Hunt for Andrew number one.

Still downhill is Starlin's squad. It sees another cave on the Whale's side. The Misfits conclude it's a man-made bunker: three walls of inter-locked rocks, the fourth wall the Whale, the roof perhaps plywood and, on top of that, more rocks. The question is, Where's the doorway that (at any moment) the Qaedas with Russian rifles might hurtle out of?

Starlin's squad searches for it. In the interlocked rocks it sees some interstices for the Qaedas' rifles, and Starlin tosses a hand grenade expectantly into one. He cries, "Frag out!" and runs up the Whale— *bang!*—and runs downhill to another interstice to toss another grenade in. Uphill, downhill, uphill, he's on a crazy gymnastics machine at an altitude twice that of Denver. He's winded. He breathes like a dog whose tongue's hanging out, huh huh, huh huh. At last Starlin finds the Qaedas' perilous doorway. Into it Starlin's sergeant throws another grenade—*bang,*—and tells him, "Go in!"

"I'll lead with lead!" The first *lead* rhymes with *deed*, the second rhymes with *dead*.

"Go for it!"

And through the doorway goes Starlin, shooting, apparently, at a Qaeda: a Qaeda's chest, a Qaeda's shirt, well, that's what the target appears to be. In comes Starlin's sergeant, shooting (shooting a shotgun) at the same man, and another sergeant shoots, too. Oh, Lord have mercy! Not falling down, the man keeps moving as Starlin and the two sergeants shoot. The smoke from Starlin's gun, the other gun, the shotgun, the crumbled rock, and, who knows? from the Qaeda is so thick it might be an hour past midnight. No one sees anything, but on Starlin's rifle, attached with duct tape, is a small flashlight, and Starlin cuts through the darkness with it. The little that's left of the target, which, it develops, is hanging by rope from the ceiling, might have been a T-shirt, blanket, sandbag, or Pillsbury flour bag but by no flight of anyone's fancy was ever a Qaeda. *Damn*, Starlin thinks.

"Holy shit! I can't believe it!" says Starlin. It's some days later, and Starlin sees something amazing. A bunker, a Qaeda bunker, is a true treasure house that Starlin, merely an American, might even envy. The tents aren't cheesecloth, the blankets aren't cotton, the sleeping bags could emanate from the U.S. Army Quartermaster Corps. In one corner is a propane stove—a cooking stove—and pots, pans, forks, spoons, teapots, teacups and saucers, and in another corner are scissors, needles, catheters, syringes, all the supplies that Rivera has plus Chap Stick and Vaseline. On the floor is no Persian carpet, but in some other bunkers (even on other bunkers' *walls*) are many, and, so help me God, in these other bunkers are Korans, boom boxes, audio recorders, audio players, video cameras, night optical devices, gymnasium bags from Adidas, sneakers, boxing gloves, punching bags, fingernail clippers, toenail clippers for Goliath, sewing machines, money—both Afghan afghanis and Pakistani rupees—a Russian sword that Starlin's sergeant appropriates, and a Casio watch with altimeter and compass that Starlin appropriates. "Holy shit!" says Starlin. "This mountain! I can't believe the Qaedas got everything up it!"

And more. In and around the bunkers are cartridges, mortar rounds, rockets, grenades that the Misfits detonate. But there're thousands, and for hours they're exploding, hitting the Whale, nearly hitting the Misfits. One rocket hits a red cedar, the tree catches fire, and the smoke floats to a Navajo soldier. He experiences déjà vu. Before coming to Afghanistan, he sat in a hogan in Arizona with a Navajo medicine man. In headband, turquoise necklace, crimson shirt, the man opened a leather pouch and on the hogan's earthen floor sprinkled red cedar shavings. He rattled a rattle, drummed a drumstick, sang a Navajo song the Navajo soldier understood, then set the shavings afire and, in Navajo, said, "Let mother nature help this boy. Let him come swiftly and safely home." In the smoke, the words rose into the soldier's nostrils, consciousness, self. And today in Afghanistan, the red cedar smoke and the words again envelop him. *It's mother nature's sign. I'll come swiftly and safely home,* the boy tells himself correctly.

To their sheltered camp come the Misfits. With time to reflect on it, Simmons is quite upset by his recollection of the two dead human beings, but Starlin thinks, *They screwed with us, so we screwed with them.* At night the Misfits use MRE boxes, other boxes, MRE plastic bags, even cargo-plane pallets to build a crackling campfire—*crack!* an MRE creamer exploding in blue-green sparks. A sergeant strums on his ukulele, singing a gospel song: "The Lord is my Light, / The Rock of my salvation / Of whom shall I be afraid? / Of whom shall I fear?" . . . "Know what I'd do if I found Osama?" a Misfit asks. "I'd cut him into little pieces. I hear they have a reward for him. I'd ask them, 'How much is each piece worth?'"

"No, you wouldn't. You'd do what you've been told to. You'd shoot him."

But really, did Simmons and Starlin ever come close? Did ever Osama live in the Whale? No one knows, although the Qaedas' paperwork showed that he scarcely needed to to account for the Qaedas' commitment. In the rubble the Misfits (and other boys in other ruins in Afghanistan) found these papers, dirty, dog-eared, charred papers in both of Afghanistan's languages and six other languages, too, and army intelligence translated them. They showed that the Qaedas came from Afghanistan and from Algeria, Arabia, Bangladesh, Bosnia, Canada, China, Egypt, Iraq, Jordan, Kuwait, Libya, Kyrgyzstan, Morocco, Pakistan, the Philippines, Russia, Somalia, Sudan, Syria, Tajikistan, Turkey, Turkmenistan, the United Kingdom, the United States, Uzbekistan, and Yemen. At their camps in Afghanistan, at 6:00 every morning, the Qaedas did exercises, averaging thirty push-ups, thirty sit-ups. All morning the Qaedas studied weapons, using, in English and Arabic, Dari, Pashto, Tajik, Urdu, and Uzbek translations, manuals from the American Army, Marines, and Special Forces and even articles from American hunting magazines. In the afternoon the Qaedas studied the Koran. They weren't taught *Right shoulder arms*, but to A, B, and C's common question of "Why were they such fierce enemies?" the Misfits found a troublesome answer. It simply is this: "We were good soldiers. And they were good soldiers, too."

Epilogue
In April the division comes home to the Adirondacks. Three boys have died, none of them in Afghanistan, remarkably. Two were killed by errant artillery rounds as they breakfasted in the Adirondacks, and one committed suicide in Uzbekistan. Another division, the 101st, from Kentucky, also fought in Anaconda. So did the Special Forces, and eight of its soldiers died. One fell from a Chinook as Mahmuti and his

platoon dug Ranger graves miles away, and six boys died while trying to rescue him. Another boy died in a Qaeda ambush.

Uninjured, undead, are all the Osama-stalking soldiers of Company A. They didn't catch him, but they neutralized his caves, bunkers, camps in Afghanistan, Osama becoming an impotent individual alive (or, who could disprove it? dead) in God knows where and God doesn't care. Of the Andrews, Simmons is single, but Starlin comes home to his second son, twenty ruddy inches long and one day old. His son says, "*Wah*," and Starlin says, "Wow," astonished at this little human being, a boy who, thanks to Starlin's army, surely won't die in an unprovoked holocaust, as a two-year-old did last September in the Center's south tower.

Also uninjured, undead, are the Qaeda killers of Company B. Mahmuti comes home to Paterson to a couple of younger cousins who ask him, "Did you kill anyone?" and he answers, "No." Fuentes, Mahmuti's eagle-eyed sergeant, comes home to the Aztec reservation near San Antonio, the warriors all racing barebacked horses and, in red-, white-, blue-, and green-beaded moccasins, dancing to the sun and the moon, the bells on their ankles tinkling.

Undead, thanks to Rivera, and still in Company C are Horn, Miranda, Abbott, McCleave, Almey, and Stanton, one hugging him and one patting him as Rivera receives the army commendation medal with a V for valor, but McGovern (two toes lost) and Wurtz still aren't back. Rivera comes home to Krystal's new many-mirrored apartment close by in Liverpool, New York. He buys her a half-carat diamond ring. One night, lying together, his fingers exploring her eyelids, eyebrows, hair, as if he's just discovered them on Jupiter, he tells her the ultimate truth of Operation Anaconda. "I love you, Krystal. But also," Rivera says, "I love those guys. So much that I might have died for 'em. Even those guys in cowboy hats and big-buckled belts, I *love* 'em. I don' listen to country music with 'em. I don' do the two-step with 'em. But when they cry, 'Doc!' I run like they're my own brothers. Because they are."

And crying, Krystal, a medic herself, says, "I understand."

Good Kills

by Peter Maass

*American soldiers who invaded Iraq in 2003 often had
trouble distinguishing Iraqi combatants from civilians. The
confusion had tragic consequences for both sides.*

As the war in Iraq is debated and turned into history, the
emphasis will be on the role of technology—precision
bombing, cruise missiles, decapitation strikes. That was what
was new. But there was another side to the war, and it was the
one that most of the fighting men and women in Iraq experienced,
even if it wasn't what Americans watching at home saw: raw military
might, humans killing humans. The Third Battalion, Fourth Marines
was one of the rawest expressions of that might. Based in Twentynine
Palms, Calif., it specializes in desert warfare, and its forces number
about 1,500 troops, equipped during the war in Iraq with about 30
Abrams tanks and 60 armored assault vehicles, backed up with whatever
artillery and aircraft were required for its missions, like 155-millimeter
howitzers and Cobra gunships and fighter jets. The battalion made the
ground shake, quite literally, as it rumbled north from Kuwait through

Iraq, beginning its march by seizing the Basra airport, continuing on past Nasiriya, into the desert and through a sandstorm that turned the sky red and became, at its worst moments, a hurricane of sand that rocked armored vehicles like plastic toys nudged by a child's finger. On the way to Baghdad, the battalion also fought fierce but limited battles in Afaq and Diwaniya, about 120 miles south of Baghdad, and in Al Kut, about 100 miles from the Iraqi capital.

On April 6, three days before the fall of Baghdad, the battalion arrived at the Diyala bridge, a major gateway into the southeastern sector of the city. The bridge crosses the Diyala River, which flows into the Tigris. Once across its 150-yard span, the Third Battalion would be only nine miles from the center of Baghdad. The bridge was heavily defended on the north side by both Republican Guard and irregular forces, and the battle to seize and cross it took two days. It was, in retrospect, a signal event in the war, a vivid example of the kind of brutal, up-close fighting that didn't get shown on cable TV.

The Third Battalion had a consistent strategy as it moved toward Baghdad: kill every fighter who refused to surrender. It was extremely effective. It allowed the battalion to move quickly. It minimized American casualties. But it was a strategy that came with a price, and that price was paid in blood on the far side of the Diyala bridge.

The unit's commander, Lt. Col. Bryan McCoy, had a calm bearing that never seemed to waver as he and his troops made their way through Iraq. His mood stayed the same, whether he was in battle or drinking his morning coffee or smoking a cigar; neither the tone nor the pace of his voice strayed from its steady-as-she-goes manner. Perhaps his calm came from experience. His father was an Army officer in Vietnam, serving two combat tours there. McCoy was born into the military and has lived in it for his entire life. This wasn't the first time he fought against Iraqi soldiers; he was a company commander during the Persian Gulf war in 1991.

When I spoke to him on the southern side of the Diyala bridge soon after the battalion arrived there on the morning of April 6, he was in a serene mood. "Things are going well," he said. "Really well."

When Colonel McCoy told you that things were going well, it meant his marines were killing Iraqi fighters. That's what was happening as we exchanged pleasantries at the bridge. His armored Humvee was parked 30 yards from the bridge. If one of the Republican Guard soldiers on the other side of the bridge had wanted to shout an insult across the river, he would have been heard—were it not for the fact that Colonel McCoy's battalion was at that moment lobbing so many bullets and mortars and artillery shells across the waterway that a shout could never have been heard, and in any event the Iraqis had no time for insults before dying. The only sound was the roar of death.

"Lordy," McCoy said. "Heck of a day. Good kills."

McCoy's immediate objective was to kill or drive away enough of the forces on the north side of the river to let him move his men and equipment across. He had no doubt that he would succeed. He was sitting in the front seat of his Humvee, with an encrypted radio phone to his left ear. He had the sort of done-it-again pride in his voice that you hear from a business executive who is kicking back at the clubhouse as he tells you he beat par again. Two Abrams tanks lumbered past us—vehicles that weigh 67 tons apiece do not move softly—and the earth shook, though not as much as it was shaking on the other side of the river, where American mortars were exploding, 150 yards away. The dark plumes of smoke that created a twilight effect at noon, the broken glass and crumpled metal on the road, the flak-jacketed marines crouching and firing their weapons—it was a day for connoisseurs of close combat, like the colonel.

"We're moving those tanks back a bit to take care of them over there," he explained, nodding to his right, where hit-and-run Iraqi fighters were shooting rocket-propelled grenades at his men, without success. Colonel McCoy's assessment was Marine blunt: "We're killing 'em."

He turned his attention to the radio phone, updating his regiment commander. His voice remained calm.

"Dark Side Six, Ripper Six," he said, using his call sign and his commander's. "We're killing them like it's going out of style. They keep reinforcing, these Republican Guards, and we're killing them as they show up. We're running out of ammo."

McCoy, whose marines refer to him as, simply, "the colonel," was not succumbing, in his plain talk of slaughter, to the military equivalent of exuberance, irrational or otherwise. For him, as for other officers who won the prize of front-line commands, this war was not about hearts and minds or even liberation. Those are amorphous concepts, not rock-hard missions. For Colonel McCoy and the other officers who inflicted heavy casualties on Iraqis and suffered few of their own, this war was about one thing: killing anyone who wished to take up a weapon in defense of Saddam Hussein's regime, even if they were running away. Colonel McCoy refers to it as establishing "violent supremacy."

"We're here until Saddam and his henchmen are dead," he told me at one point during his march on Baghdad. "It's over for us when the last guy who wants to fight for Saddam has flies crawling across his eyeballs. Then we go home. It's smashmouth tactics. Sherman said that war is cruelty. There's no sense in trying to refine it. The crueler it is, the sooner it's over."

When I suggested to Colonel McCoy one morning that Iraqi civilians might not appreciate the manner in which his marines tended to say hello to the locals with the barrels of their guns raised, he did not make any excuses.

"They don't have to like us," he said. "Liking has nothing to do with it. You'll never make them like you. I can't make them like me. All we can do is make them respect us and then make sure that they know we're here on their behalf. Making them like us—Yanks always want to be liked, but it doesn't always work out that way."

Though the fighting was lopsided, the marines did not get to the Diyala bridge unscathed. On April 3, three days before the battle for the bridge, the Third Battalion entered the town of Al Kut. It was an incursion intended to convey the point that, as Colonel McCoy described it, there were new "alpha males" in the country.

The attack began at dawn with an artillery barrage that had excited marines next to my vehicle. They yelled "Bam! Bam!" as each shell was fired into the air. Tanks led the way into town, and as I stayed a kilometer behind at a medic station, the sounds of battle commenced, mortars and machine-gun fire that were accompanied, as ever, by the visuals of war—smoke plumes that were an arsonist's dream.

A half-hour into the battle, a Humvee raced out of the city and stopped at the medic station. A marine, whose body was rag-doll floppy, was pulled out and put on a stretcher. A marine doctor and medics surrounded him. His clothes were stripped off and needles and monitors placed on and into his body, and the dialogue of battlefield medicine began among the team, all of whom had slung their M-16's over their backs as they tried to save their comrade's life.

"Left lower abdomen."

"He's in urgent surgical."

"Wriggle your toes for me."

"Ow, ow."

"He needs medevac, now."

"Iodine."

"My arms are numb."

"Keep talking, Evnin."

His name was Mark Evnin. He was a corporal, a sniper who was in one of the lead vehicles going into Al Kut. Iraqi fighters were waiting in ambush and had fired the first shots; one of them got him.

"Keep talking to us. Where are you from?"

"Remon," he mumbled.

"Where? Where are you from?"

"Verrrmon."

Evnin was not doing well. The battalion chaplain, Bob Grove, leaned over him, and because the chaplain knew Evnin was Jewish, he pulled out of his pocket a sheet with instructions for "emergency Jewish ministration." Grove read the Sh'ma, which begins, "Hear, O Israel, the Lord our God." Then he began reading the 23rd Psalm, at which point Evnin said, "Chaplain, I'm not going to die."

A Chinook landed 50 yards away. Evnin's stretcher was lifted from the asphalt and rushed to the chopper. Shortly after he was airborne, he went into shock and died.

Colonel McCoy was just a few feet from where Corporal Evnin was mortally wounded. "I saw him go down," he said afterward. "That fight lasted about nine seconds. We had about 15 human-wave guys attack the tanks. They were mowed down. They drew first blood. They got one of us, but we got all of them."

Corporal Evnin was the battalion's first K.I.A., but he was certainly not the only marine to die in Iraq. The men of the Third Battalion paid close attention to news of marine battle deaths. The day before they arrived at the Diyala bridge, a Marine tank was blown up by an explosives-laden truck that drove alongside it and was detonated by its driver. It was the realization of one of the marines' worst fears: suicide bombers.

McCoy remained focused; he told me that his mission, to kill Iraqi fighters, had not changed. "I'm not allowed to have the luxury of emotions to guide my decisions," he said. "It'll cloud my decisions, and I'll make a bad one if I submit to that. I have to look at everything very clinically." He reacted to the suicide bombing tactically: a new danger had emerged, and his troops would have to be on increased alert to the threat posed by civilian vehicles.

But the deaths of their comrades deeply affected the grunts, and when the battalion got to Diyala bridge, every man was primed to kill.

"There's an unspoken change in attitude," McCoy told me a few days before we reached the bridge. "Their blood is up."

The battle for the Diyala bridge lasted for two days. One of the bridge's main pylons had been badly damaged, and armored vehicles could not move over it. So after the first day of fighting on April 6, the battalion dug itself into the southern side for the night, giving itself time to plan an infantry assault over the span the next morning.

In the morning, the battalion released another round of heavy artillery barrages to soften up the opposition on the northern side of the river. In the fighting, two more marines were killed when an artillery shell hit their armored vehicle on the southern side of the bridge. Eventually, the battalion killed most of the Republican Guard fighters, or at least pushed them back from their dug-in positions on the northern side, and McCoy decided that it was time to try a crossing.

The men of the Third Battalion moved across the Diyala bridge "dismounted," that is, on foot. It was a tableau from Vietnam, or even World War II; grunts running and firing their weapons in front of them. This was, as McCoy described it, "blue-collar warfare."

When the marines crossed to the northern side, they found themselves in a semi-urban neighborhood of one-story shops and two-story houses, a few dozen palm trees and lots of dust. A narrow highway led away from the bridge, toward Baghdad. Immediately, they were met with incoming fire—occasional bullets and the odd rocket-propelled grenade, fired mostly from a palm grove on the eastern side of the road to Baghdad. Colonel McCoy set up his command position—basically, himself and his radioman—adjacent to a house by the bridge. Marines fanned out into the palm grove, while others moved north up the road, going house to house. Advance units set up sniper positions and machine-gun positions a few hundred yards farther up the road; beyond them, American mortars and bombs, fired by units near and behind Colonel McCoy's position, were loudly raining down.

One of Colonel McCoy's sergeants ran up to him and told him that Iraqi reinforcements had just arrived.

"A technical vehicle dropped off some [expletives] over there," he said, pointing up the road.

"Did you get it?" Colonel McCoy asked.

"Yeah."

"The [expletives]?"

"Some of them. Some ran away."

"Boys are doing good," the colonel said moments later. "Brute force is going to prevail today."

He listened to his radio.

"Suicide bombers headed for the bridge?" he said. "We'll drill them."

Then, one by one, about a half-dozen vehicles came up the road, separately, and the marines got ready to drill them.

Battle is confusion. If a military unit is well trained and well led, the confusion can be minimized, but it can never be eliminated. Split-second decisions—whether to fire or not fire, whether to go left or right, whether to seek cover behind a house or in a ditch, whether the enemy is 200 yards ahead or 400 yards ahead—these kinds of decisions are often made on the basis of fragmentary and contradictory information by men who are sleep-deprived or operating on adrenaline; by men who fear for their lives or for the lives of civilians around them or both; by men who rely on instincts they hope will keep them alive and not lead them into actions they will regret to their graves. When soldiers make their split-second decisions, they do not know the outcome.

The situation was further complicated on the north side of the Diyala bridge, because what was left of the Iraqi resistance had resorted to guerrilla tactics. The Iraqis still firing on the marines were not wearing uniforms. They would fire a few shots from a window, drop their weapons, run away as though they were civilians, then go to another location where they had hidden other weapons and fire those.

Amid the chaos of battle McCoy was, as usual, placid yet focused. Black smoke blew overhead and through the streets; hundreds of marines crept forward on their bellies or in low runs, darting, as fast as they could with their combat gear, from palm tree to palm tree or from house to house. On all sides, there was the sound of gunfire, an orchestra of sounds—the pop-pop of assault weapons, the boom-boom of heavy machine guns, the thump of mortars. Harmony was taking a day off. There would be a sudden burst of a few shots, then a crescendo in which, it seemed, every marine in the vicinity was firing his weapon at an enemy who was, for the most part, unseen; and then it would stop, briefly.

The bulk of the fire emanated from McCoy's forces, not the Iraqis. Some marines branched farther out to the east, beyond the palm grove. Others moved forward, straight down the road, trying to "go firm" on a front line there, to establish a defensive perimeter into which Iraqi fighters could not penetrate.

The plan was for marine snipers along the road to fire warning shots several hundred yards up the road at any approaching vehicles. As the half-dozen vehicles approached, some shots were fired at the ground in front of the cars; others were fired, with great precision, at their tires or their engine blocks. Marine snipers can snipe. The warning shots were intended either to simply disable a vehicle—wrecking the engine or the tires—or to send the message that the cars should stop or turn around, or that passengers should get out and head away from the marines.

But some of the vehicles weren't fully disabled by the snipers, and they continued to move forward. When that happened, the marines riddled the vehicles with bullets until they ground to a halt. There would be no car bombs taking out members of the Third Battalion.

The vehicles, it only later became clear, were full of Iraqi civilians. These Iraqis were apparently trying to escape the American bombs that were landing behind them, farther down the road, and to escape Baghdad itself; the road they were on is a key route out of the city. The civilians probably couldn't see the marines, who were wearing camouflage fatigues and had taken up ground and rooftop positions that were intended to be difficult for approaching fighters to spot. What the civilians probably saw in front of them was an open road; no American military vehicles had yet been able to cross the disabled bridge. In the chaos, the civilians were driving toward a battalion of marines who had just lost two of their own in battle that morning and had been told that suicide bombers were heading their way.

One by one, civilians were killed. Several hundred yards from the forward marine positions, a blue minivan was fired on; three people were killed. An old man, walking with a cane on the side of the road, was shot and killed. It is unclear what he was doing there; perhaps he was confused and scared and just trying to get away from the city. Several other vehicles were fired on; over a stretch of about 600 yards nearly a half dozen vehicles were stopped by gunfire. When the firing stopped, there were nearly a dozen corpses, all but two of which had no apparent military clothing or weapons.

Two journalists who were ahead of me, farther up the road, said that a company commander told his men to hold their fire until the snipers had taken a few shots, to try to disable the vehicles without killing the passengers. "Let the snipers deal with civilian vehicles," the commander had said. But as soon as the nearest sniper fired his first warning shots, other marines apparently opened fire with M-16's or machine guns.

Two more journalists were with another group of marines along the road that was also involved in the shooting. Both journalists said that a squad leader, after the shooting stopped, shouted: "My men showed no mercy. Outstanding."

The battle lasted until the afternoon, and the battalion camped for the night on the north side of the bridge. The next morning, April 8, I walked down the road. I counted at least six vehicles that had been shot at. Most of them contained corpses or had corpses near them. The blue van, a Kia, had more than 20 bullet holes in its windshield. Two bodies were slumped over in the front seats; they were men in street clothes and had no weapons that I could see. In the back seat, a woman in a black chador had fallen to the floor; she was dead, too. There was no visible cargo in the van—no suitcases, no bombs.

Two of the van's passengers had survived the shooting; one of them, Eman Alshamnery, had been shot in the toe. She had passed out and spent the night in the vehicle. When she woke in the morning she was taken by marines for treatment by their medical team.

Alshamnery told me that her home in Baghdad had been bombed and that she was trying to flee the city with her sister, who was the dead woman I had seen in the back seat of the van. Alshamnery said she had not heard a warning shot—which doesn't mean that one wasn't fired. In fact, it would have been difficult, particularly for civilians unaccustomed to the sounds of war, to know a warning shot when they heard it, or to know where it came from, or how to react appropriately.

Alshamnery, who spoke to me through a Marine interpreter, was sitting next to another woman, who gave her name as Bakis Obeid and said she had been in one of the other passenger vehicles that was hit. She said her son and husband had been killed.

There were other survivors. A few yards down the road from the Kia van, three men were digging a grave. One gravedigger gave his name as Sabah Hassan and said he was a chef at the Al Rashid hotel, which is in the center of Baghdad and, in more peaceful times, was where foreign journalists stayed. Hassan said he was fleeing the city and was in a sedan with three other men on the road when they came under fire, apparently from the marines. A passenger in his car was killed. I asked him what he felt.

"What can I say?" he replied. "I am afraid to say anything. I don't know what comes in the future. Please." He plunged his shovel back into the earth and continued his funereal chores.

Not far from the gravediggers, I came across the body of the old man with the cane. He had a massive wound in the back of his head. He died on his back, looking at the sky, and his body was covered with flies. His cane, made of aluminum, lay by his right hand.

Just a few yards away, a Toyota pickup truck was by the side of the road, with more than 30 bullet holes in its windshield. The driver, who was wearing a green military tunic, was dead, his head thrown back, slightly to the left. Nearby, the body of another man lay on the ground, on his stomach; attached to the back of his belt was a holster for a pistol. An AK-47 assault rifle was in the sand nearby. These were the only fighters, or apparent fighters, that I saw on the road or in adjacent buildings.

As I took notes, several marines came by and peeked inside the blue van.

"I wish I had been here," one of them said. In other words, he wished he had participated in the combat.

"The marines just opened up," another said. "Better safe than sorry."

A journalist came up and said the civilians should not have been shot. There was a silence, and after the journalist walked away, a third marine, Lance Cpl. Santiago Ventura, began talking, angrily.

"How can you tell who's who?" said Corporal Ventura. He spoke sharply, as though trying to contain his fury. "You get a soldier in a car with an AK-47 and civilians in the next car. How can you tell? You can't tell."

He paused. Then he continued, still upset at the suggestion that the killings were not correct.

"One of these vans took out our tank. Car bomb. When we tell them they have to stop, they have to stop," he said, referring to civilians. "We've got to be concerned about our safety. We dropped pamphlets over these people weeks and weeks ago and told them to leave the city. You can't blame marines for what happened. It's bull. What are you doing getting in a taxi in the middle of a war zone?

"Half of them look like civilians," he continued. He was referring to irregular forces. "I mean, I have sympathy, and this breaks my heart, but you can't tell who's who. We've done more than enough to help these people. I don't think I have ever read about a war in which innocent people didn't die. Innocent people die. There's nothing we can do."

Two days later, the Third Battalion arrived at the Palestine Hotel in the center of Baghdad, the first marines to reach the heart of the city. They had made it from the Kuwaiti border in 22 days. As the marines were taking up defensive positions around the hotel, I noticed a sniper I had become acquainted with during the past weeks. (Because he has children who do not know precisely what he does in the Marines, he had asked me not to name him.) He was squatting on the ground in Firdos Square, in front of the hotel, scanning nearby buildings through the scope on his rifle, looking for enemy snipers. About 150 yards away, at the other end of the square, one of the battalion's armored vehicles was in the process of wrapping a metal chain around the statue of Saddam Hussein, preparing to pull it down.

Although this was a moment of triumph, I was still thinking about the civilians killed at Diyala bridge, and I said to the sniper that I had heard that he was one of the men who had fired shots there. He nodded his head, and I didn't need to ask anything more, because he began to talk about it. It was clear the bridge was weighing on his mind, too. He said that during the battle, he fired a shot at the engine block of a vehicle and that it kept moving forward. For him, this had been evidence that the person behind the wheel was determined to push ahead, and to do harm.

I said that a civilian driver might not know what to do when a bullet hits his vehicle, and might press ahead out of fear or confusion.

"It's easy to be a Monday-morning quarterback on Monday morning," he replied. "But we did everything we could to avoid civilian casualties."

When I visited the kill box down the road from Diyala bridge the morning after the battle, I noticed that the destroyed cars were several hundred yards from the marine positions that fired on them. The marines could have waited a bit longer before firing, and if they had, perhaps the cars would have stopped, or perhaps the marines would have figured out that the cars contained confused civilians. The sniper knew this. He knew that something tragic had happened at the bridge. And so, as we spoke in Baghdad, he stopped defending the marines' actions and started talking about their intent. He and his fellow marines, he said, had not come to Iraq to drill bullets into women and old men who were just trying to find a safe place.

Collateral damage is far easier to bear for those who are responsible for it from afar—from the cockpit of a B-1 bomber, from the command center of a Navy destroyer, from the rear positions of artillery crews. These warriors do not see the faces of the mothers and fathers they have killed. They do not see the blood and hear the screams and live with those memories for the rest of their lives. The grunts suffer this. The Third Battalion accomplished its mission of bringing military calamity upon the regime of Saddam Hussein; the statue of Saddam fell just a few minutes after the sniper and I spoke. But the sniper, and many other marines of the Third Battalion, could not feel as joyous as the officers in the rear, the generals in Qatar and the politicians in Washington.

The civilians who were killed—a precise number is not and probably never will be available for the toll at Diyala bridge, or in the rest of Iraq—paid the ultimate price. But a price was paid, too, by the men who were responsible for killing them. For these men, this was not a clean war of smart bombs and surgical strikes. It was war as it has always been, war at close range, war as Sherman described it, bloody and cruel.

acknowledgments

Many people made this anthology.

At Thunder's Mouth Press and Avalon Publishing Group:
Thanks to Will Balliett, Sue Canavan, Kristen Couse, Maria Fernandez, Linda Kosarin, Dan O'Connor, Neil Ortenberg, Susan Reich, David Riedy, Michelle Rosenfield, Simon Sullivan, and Mike Walters for their support, dedication and hard work..

At The Writing Company:
Taylor Smith oversaw editorial and rights research.

At the Portland Public Library in Portland, Maine:
The librarians helped collect books from around the country.

Finally, I am grateful to the writers whose work appears in this book.

permissions

We gratefully acknowledge everyone who gave permission for written material to appear in this book. We have made every effort to trace and contact copyright holders. If an error or omission is brought to our notice we will be pleased to correct the situation in future editions of this book. For further information, please contact the publisher.

bibliography

The selections used in this anthology were taken from the editions listed below. In some cases, other editions may be easier to find. Hard-to-find or out-of-print titles often are available through inter-library loan services or through Internet booksellers.

Alexievich, Svetlana. *Zinky Boys: Soviet Voices from the Afghanistan War.* New York: W.W. Norton & Company, 1992.

Anderson, Scott. "Prisoner of War". Originally appeared in *Harper's,* January 1997.

Caputo, Philip. *Means of Escape.* New York: HarperCollins, 1991.

Finnegan, William. *A Complicated War: The Harrowing of Mozambique.* Berkeley: University of California Press, 1992.

Fisk, Robert. *Pity the Nation: The Abduction of Lebanon.* New York: Atheneum, 1990.

Hackworth, David H. with Tom Mathews. *Hazardous Duty.* New York: William Morrow and Company, Inc., 1996.

Hukanović, Rezak. *The Tenth Circle of Hell: A Memoir of Life in the Death Camps of Bosnia.* New York: Basic Books, 1996.

Kaplan, Robert. *Soldiers of God.* New York: Vintage Books, 2001.

Kelly, Michael. *Martyrs' Day: Chronicle of a Small War.* New York: Random House, 1993.

Maass, Peter. "Good Kills". Originally appeared in *The New York Times Magazine,* April 20, 2003.

Nordstrom, Carolyn. *A Different Kind of War Story.* Philadelphia: University of Pennsylvania Press, 1997.

Sack, John. "The Dogs of Bosnia". Originally appeared in *Esquire,* February 1997.

Sack, John. "Anaconda". Originally appeared in *Esquire,* August 2002.

Sundin, John. "Kigali's Wounds, Through a Doctor's Eyes". Originally appeared in *Harper's,* August 1994.

Zarembo, Alan. "Judgment Day". Originally appeared in *Harper's,* April 1997.